ADAPTABLE ENGLISH LANGUAGE TEACHING

In an age of rapid technological transformation and evolving teaching settings, the ELT community must adapt to the needs of emerging situations and a diverse range of learners. *Adaptable English Language Teaching* addresses this need by bringing together contributions from renowned scholars around the world with insights on all major areas of English language teaching with an emphasis on adaptability—of teaching method, context, skills, and priorities.

Organized around an innovative past-present-future structure, chapters offer methods, strategies, and perspectives that are adaptable to any difficult or under-resourced context. It delves into engaging through online applications, understanding emerging trends in computer-assisted language learning and teaching, and the implementation of virtual classrooms and multimodality in ELT.

Given its multifaceted focus, this book will provide ELT practitioners, trainers, trainees, and researchers with invaluable insights and research findings to effectively navigate and adapt to emerging circumstances.

Nima A. Nazari is Professor of Applied Linguistics and works as Centre Director at OnCampus London South Bank University, UK.

A. Mehdi Riazi is Professor of Applied Linguistics at the College of Humanities and Social Sciences of Hamad Bin Khalifa University (HBKU), Qatar.

ESL & Applied Linguistics Professional Series
Edited by Eli Hinkel

Creating Classrooms of Peace in English Language Teaching
Edited by Barbara M. Birch

Shaping Learners' Pronunciation
Teaching the Connected Speech of North American English
James Dean Brown and Dustin Crowther

Handbook of Practical Second Language Teaching and Learning
Edited by Eli Hinkel

English L2 Vocabulary Learning and Teaching
Concepts, Principles, and Pedagogy
Lawrence J. Zwier and Frank Boers

Praxis-oriented Pedagogy for Novice L2 Teachers
Developing Teacher Reasoning
Karen E. Johnson, Deryn P. Verity, and Sharon S. Childs

The Twenty Most Effective Language Teaching Techniques
I.S.P. Nation

Adaptable English Language Teaching
Advances and Frameworks for Responding to New Circumstances
Edited by Nima A. Nazari and A. Mehdi Riazi

For more information about this series, please visit: www.routledge.com/ESL-Applied-Linguistics-Professional-Series/book-series/LEAESLALP

ADAPTABLE ENGLISH LANGUAGE TEACHING

Advances and Frameworks for Responding to New Circumstances

Edited by Nima A. Nazari and A. Mehdi Riazi

NEW YORK AND LONDON

Designed cover image: derrrek / Getty Images

First published 2025
by Routledge
605 Third Avenue, New York, NY 10158

and by Routledge
4 Park Square, Milton Park, Abingdon, Oxon, OX14 4RN

Routledge is an imprint of the Taylor & Francis Group, an informa business

© 2025 selection and editorial matter, Nima A. Nazari and A. Mehdi Riazi; individual chapters, the contributors

The right of Nima A. Nazari and A. Mehdi Riazi to be identified as the authors of the editorial material, and of the authors for their individual chapters, has been asserted in accordance with sections 77 and 78 of the Copyright, Designs and Patents Act 1988.

All rights reserved. No part of this book may be reprinted or reproduced or utilised in any form or by any electronic, mechanical, or other means, now known or hereafter invented, including photocopying and recording, or in any information storage or retrieval system, without permission in writing from the publishers.

Trademark notice: Product or corporate names may be trademarks or registered trademarks, and are used only for identification and explanation without intent to infringe.

ISBN: 978-1-032-42206-0 (hbk)
ISBN: 978-1-032-41429-4 (pbk)
ISBN: 978-1-003-36170-1 (ebk)

DOI: 10.4324/9781003361701

Typeset in Galliard
by KnowledgeWorks Global Ltd.

CONTENTS

List of editors and contributors   *viii*

   Introduction   1
   A. Mehdi Riazi and Nima A. Nazari

SECTION I
ELT responses to new circumstances   **9**

 1 English language curriculum development in new
    circumstances   11
    John Macalister

 2 Sustainability in English language teacher education:
    Preparing teachers for an unknown future   25
    Melissa Reed, Yulia Kharchenko, and Agnes Bodis

 3 Understanding the needs of international EAP
    students: Adaptive progress   41
    Justine Light, Denise Lo, and Martin Guardado

 4 Silence as autonomy: Case studies of Australian
    and international students   56
    Dat Bao

SECTION II
ELT assessment, feedback, and managing classrooms in new circumstances — 77

5 New approaches to the assessment of English as an additional language — 79
Graham Seed, Angeliki Salamoura, and Nick Saville

6 Feedback to students in ELT — 96
Maddalena Taras

7 ELT classroom management in times of change — 114
Christopher Graham

SECTION III
Teaching English language skills and components in new circumstances — 131

8 Teaching listening in new circumstances — 133
Joseph Siegel

9 Teaching reading — 148
Peter Watkins

10 Challenges and opportunities in teaching speaking — 163
John Trent

11 L2 writing pedagogy: Responding to emerging needs and emergencies — 176
Ismaeil Fazel

12 Adaptable teaching of grammar, vocabulary, and pronunciation: Enhancing fluency and engagement through online apps — 195
Xinrong He and Barry Lee Reynolds

SECTION IV
The contribution of technology to ELT in new circumstances   211

13 Language teachers and teaching technologies: Valuing the teacher and teacher values in online learning   213
Jane Spiro

14 Computer-assisted language learning and teaching: Emerging trends, challenges, and solutions in ELT   228
Matt Kessler, Francesca Marino, and Sean Farrell

15 A multimodal analysis of roleplays between upper intermediate level learners: Lessons for teaching oral language competency in online contexts   245
Gerard O'Hanlon and Anne O'Keeffe

Conclusion   266
Nima A. Nazari and A. Mehdi Riazi

Index   *272*

EDITORS AND CONTRIBUTORS

Agnes Bodis is a Lecturer in Applied Linguistics and TESOL at Macquarie University, Sydney. Her research projects focus on language teacher training as well as multilingualism and linguistic inclusivity in internationalized higher education, including multilingual pedagogies. Agnes has extensive experience in language teaching, teacher training, language assessment and language curriculum design in many different teaching contexts in Australia and Europe and has published in international top-tier journals. Agnes is a member of the *Language on the Move* research team, where she blogs about her research.

Dat Bao is a senior lecturer in education at Monash University and editor-in-chief of the *Journal for Silence Studies in Education* (*JSSE*), founded in Australia. His areas of expertise include creative pedagogy, language and culture, communication, silence and speech, and curriculum development. He is the author of *Understanding silence and reticence* (Bloomsbury, 2014), *Poetry for Education* (Xlibris, 2017), *Creativity and innovations in ELT materials* (Multilingual Matters, 2018), *Transforming pedagogies through engagement with learners, teachers, and communities* (Springer, 2021), *Silence in English language pedagogy* (CUP, 2023). In 2019, Dat Bao received an Education Award for Excellence in Teaching at Monash University.

Sean Farrell is a doctoral candidate in the Linguistics and Applied Language Studies program at the University of South Florida. His research investigates issues pertaining to second language writing, with a focus on how the revision strategies of multilingual graduate students index academic socialization. He is also interested in how the affordances and constraints of digital technologies, such as online learning platforms and generative artificial intelligence, mediate language acquisition.

Ismaeil Fazel, PhD, is Lecturer at the Faculty of Education of the University of British Columbia in Vancouver and Professor of Liberal Arts at Yorkville University (BC Campus). His main research interests include pedagogy and assessment of English for academic, professional and publication purposes, and his scholarship has appeared in numerous refereed book chapters and reputable journals including *System*, the *Journal of English for Academic Purposes, and English for Specific Purposes Journal*. His most recent publication is a co-edited volume titled *Predatory Practices in Scholarly Publishing and Knowledge Sharing* (Habibie & Fazel, 2023) by Routledge (Taylor & Francis).

Christopher Graham is a freelance ELT consultant and author based in the UK. He has worked in the field since 1981 in over 30 countries for the British Council, ministries of education, and international publishers. He works extensively on Monitoring, Evaluation and Learning projects, and CPD design and delivery, particularly in the MENA region. He has a specific interest in teaching contexts in fragile and fractured societies. He is one of the founders of ELT Footprint, a 2020 British Council ELTons winner, and sits on the IATEFL conference committee.

Martin Guardado (PhD, University of British Columbia) is a Professor in the Department of Linguistics at the University of Alberta. His research interests include English for academic purposes, TESL and technology, Indigenous language revitalization, and heritage language socialization. His work has appeared in edited books and journals such as Computers and Composition, The Canadian Modern Language Review, and TESOL Quarterly. Four recent books have been published by De Gruyter Mouton and Palgrave McMillan as well as under a Creative Commons OER license (Open Education Alberta).

Xinrong He is currently a PhD student in the Faculty of Education at the University of Macau. With a keen interest in language education, she has accumulated a wealth of experience over the past five years, specializing in teaching English to diverse groups, ranging from young children to college students. Her passion lies in the field of English teaching and learning, i.e., the application of neuroscience techniques, such as eye-tracking, to the realm of vocabulary learning. By delving into the cognitive aspects of language acquisition, she actively engages in unraveling the complexities of language pedagogy. Her work is characterized by a desire to bridge the gap between theory and practical application.

Matt Kessler is an Assistant Professor of Applied Linguistics at the University of South Florida, where he teaches in the master's and doctoral programs in Applied Linguistics. His research examines issues pertaining to L2 writing, computer-assisted language learning, and genre-based teaching and learning. He is the author of *Digital multimodal composing: Connecting theory, research and practice in second language acquisition* (Multilingual Matters, 2024) and the co-editor of *Conducting genre-based research in applied linguistics: A methodological guide* (Routledge, 2024). He also serves as the co-editor of the Brief Reports section for *TESOL Quarterly*.

Yulia Kharchenko is an English language teacher and teacher educator. She lectures at Macquarie University, Sydney on a postgraduate Applied Linguistics and TESOL program and runs regular professional development sessions for teachers. Her interests include teacher agency, language policies in education, and multilingual pedagogy. She is a member of the Higher Education Research and Development Society of Australasia and the Applied Linguistics Association of Australia. She has published her research in practitioner-oriented ELT publications and serves on reviewer and editorial boards of several Australian and international journals.

Justine Light has worked in language teaching for more than 25 years, much of that time in English for academic purposes. She currently works at NorQuest College in Alberta, Canada as a Learning and Development Lead. She worked as a consultant on national and provincial initiatives including the Canadian Language Benchmarks Support Kit, and the Alberta Teachers of English as a Second Language Best Practices and Curriculum Framework documents. She spent a decade as a sessional instructor in the University of Alberta TESL program and has been nominated for and awarded numerous teaching awards.

Denise Lo is an English for academic purposes and Teaching English as a second language faculty member at Douglas College in British Columbia, Canada. She brings over 15 years of global experience to her current role from the University of Alberta, Canada, Yonsei University, Korea, and the University of Southern California, United States. Her experience extends to curriculum development projects, including the Le Mauril project with the Centre for Canadian Language Benchmarks and the Canadian Broadcasting Company. Additionally, she has shared her expertise in teacher education through the Norquest College TEAL program in Alberta, Canada. Denise has earned the University of Alberta Remote Teaching Award.

John Macalister is Emeritus Professor of Applied Linguistics at Victoria University of Wellington, New Zealand. Curriculum design and teacher education are among his areas of research and teaching expertise. He is co-author with I. S. P. Nation of *Language Curriculum Design* (2nd edition) and *Teaching ESL/EFL Reading and Writing* (2nd edition) and also co-editor of *Case Studies in Language Curriculum Design*.

Francesca Marino is a PhD candidate in the Linguistics and Applied Language Studies program at the University of South Florida. Prior to joining the program, she received her master's in Languages and Intercultural Communication in the Euro-Mediterranean Area from the University of Naples L'Orientale, Italy. Her research interests revolve around multimodality and digital media from both a pedagogical and discursive perspective. Specifically, they encompass digital multimodal composing and multimodal discourse analysis, particularly within online discourse. Francesca's work has appeared in journals such as *Discourse & Society*, *Discourse, Context and Media*, *ELT Journal*, and *Multimodal Communication*.

Dr Nima A. Nazari is an applied linguist with a specialisation in English language learning and teaching, holding a PhD from King's College London. With a career spanning over 25 years, he has been researching and teaching related subject areas at UK and overseas universities. He has also assumed leadership roles in Applied Linguistics and TESOL departments both in the UK and overseas. He has further contributed to the ELT community through service on the editorial panel of the *ELT Journal* and the advisory board of the *LLT Journal*. His diverse array of publications spans a number of areas of Applied Linguistics, with a focus on English language learning and teaching. He has also served as External Examiner for a large number of MA programmes and PhD viva voce examinations. He is currently a Centre Director at OnCampus London South Bank University.

Gerard O'Hanlon is a PhD researcher at Mary Immaculate College, University of Limerick, Ireland. His research aims to achieve insights into how English language learners employ pragmatic features of interaction via videoconferencing platforms such as Zoom. This process involves the recording and annotation of an audiovisual dataset for multimodal corpus analysis, focusing on aspects of the participants' spoken pragmatic interactions and related embodied features, such as gesture, gaze, or head movements. Gerard is also an English language teacher and teacher trainer with over two decades of experience.

Professor Anne O'Keeffe is Professor of Applied Linguistics at Mary Immaculate College, University of Limerick, Ireland. Her publications include Cambridge University Press titles *From Corpus to Classroom* (2007) *English Grammar Today* (2011) and Routledge titles *Introducing Pragmatics in Use 1st and 2nd edn* (2020) and *Routledge Handbook of Corpus Linguistics 1st and 2nd edn* (co-editor). With Geraldine Mark, he developed the Cambridge University Press *English Grammar Profile* resource. She is co-editor of two Routledge book series: *The Routledge Corpus Linguistics Guides* and *The Routledge Applied Corpus Linguistics*. She is also the founder and Director of the Inter-Varietal Applied Corpus Studies (IVACS) Network.

Melissa Reed is an experienced English language teacher and manager, who lectures on the postgraduate Applied Linguistics and TESOL courses at Macquarie University, Sydney. Her research interests include teacher education, professional development, teacher and learner agency, and sociocultural approaches to learning. Her recent doctoral research explores the professional development of English language teachers on social media. Her current project explores dialogic learning in higher education. She was a member of the steering committee for the English Australia Continuing Professional Development Framework Review.

Dr Barry Lee Reynolds is an accomplished academic and holds the position of Associate Professor of English Language Education at the University of Macau. Dr Reynolds has dedicated his scholarly pursuits to exploring diverse facets of language learning, spanning Vocabulary Acquisition, Written Corrective Feedback, Computer Assisted Language Learning, and Language Teacher Education, among others. His extensive portfolio boasts over 100 published academic journal articles, reflecting his expertise. He actively engages with the academic community, serving as an editor and reviewer for scholarly journals, and editing books and overseeing special issues for academic publications. He has taught the English language and trained language teachers in the USA, Taiwan, and Macau.

A. Mehdi Riazi is a professor of Applied Linguistics at the College of Humanities and Social Sciences of Hamad Bin Khalifa University (HBKU). Before joining HBKU in 2021, he worked at Macquarie University (2009–2021) and before that at Shiraz University (1995–2008). He is the author of *The Routledge Encyclopedia of Research Methods* (Routledge, 2016) and

Mixed Methods Research (Equinox, 2017). His most recent books include *Less Frequently Used Methodologies in Applied Linguistics* (John Benjamin 2024) and the co-edited volume titled *Studies and Essays on the Learning, Teaching and Assessing Second Language Writing*, which was published in 2020 by Cambridge Scholar Publishing. He is now co-authoring a book titled *How to Write Research Proposals* to be published by Equinox. He has also published widely in international journals and has presented at international conferences. He was also the chief investigator for three research projects with IELTS, Pearson, and ETS (TOEFL) on test validation

Nick Saville is Director of Thought Leadership at Cambridge University Press & Assessment (English) and Secretary-General of the Association of Language Testers in Europe (ALTE). He holds a PhD in language assessment specialising in test impact and has over 40 years' experience in language education. He is an advisor for the Council of Europe, including for the CEFR and its Companion Volume, and co-editor of the Studies in Language Testing series (CUP). His professional interests include English linguistics, plurilingualism, learning-oriented assessment (LOA), EdTech combined with educational uses of AI (EdAI), assessment literacy, and ethical frameworks in language assessment.

Dr Angeliki Salamoura has over 25 years of experience in the field of English education, as a teacher, researcher, research manager, and assessment and learning specialist. Currently, she is Head of Operational Research at Cambridge English and leads research into the quality and validity of learning and assessment products. Angeliki also has extensive expertise in Learning Oriented Assessment, integrated learning and assessment, education reform, impact, and the CEFR. In this context, she has led numerous learning and assessment projects in the K-12 and vocational sectors in Europe, Asia, and South America. She is one of the contributors to the PISA 2025 Foreign Language Assessment Framework.

Graham Seed is a Senior Research Manager at Cambridge University Press and Assessment, where he works on different projects relating to language learning and assessment. His current professional interests include multilingualism in assessment contexts, digital good practice for learning and assessment materials, and operationalisation of the CEFR. He holds an MA in Language Testing from Lancaster University, DELTA and CELTA, and previously taught EFL in Bosnia, Russia, and the UK. He is currently also the Secretariat Manager of ALTE (the Association of Language Testers in Europe).

Joseph Siegel is Professor in English with a focus on second language pedagogy at Stockholm University in Sweden, where he teaches TESOL methodology, linguistics, and applied linguistic research methods courses. He holds a PhD in Applied Linguistics from Aston University and an MA (TESL/TEFL) from the University of Birmingham. His recent research publications are on the topics of L2 notetaking, EMI lecture comprehension, EMI teacher education, listening pedagogy, and pragmatic instruction. His book on ELT pedagogy, *Teaching English in Secondary Schools* (Studentlitteratur), was released in 2022.

Jane Spiro is Professor of Language Learning and Teaching at Oxford Brookes University in the UK. She has run an MA for international language teachers, and teacher development programmes worldwide, including in Hungary, Switzerland, Poland, and Mexico. She has written a core MA coursebook, *Changing Methodologies in TESOL* (2013), resources for creative language teaching (*Creative Poetry Writing* and *Storybuilding*), a study of learning cultures (*Crossing Borders in University Learning and Teaching*), and multiple papers on creative and reflective teacher development. She is also a published poet and fiction writer, with a commitment to the creative development of teachers and learners.

Maddalena Taras researches all things assessment: developing original self-assessment process-models which support student inclusion and learning through assessment; evaluating and developing innovative theoretical frameworks for summative, formative, self-assessment and feedback, and how these relate to each other and to practices; developing and evaluating assessment theories and practices within and across sectors; identifying problematic theoretical claims for 'Assessment for Learning', providing solutions and relating them to classroom practices; evaluating linguistic and cultural influences on perceptions of assessment and resulting institutional discrepancies in assessment practices. She works in HE but her work on assessment is relevant to all educational and professional assessment contexts.

John Trent is Professor of Education and Associate Dean of the Graduate School at the Education University of Hong Kong, where he teaches language teaching methodology and research methods courses to postgraduate students and supervises doctoral students. His research interests include teacher identity, narrative analysis, and teacher education. His research output has appeared in a range of international journals, including the Journal of Teacher Education, TESOL Quarterly, Teaching and Teacher Education, Journal of Vocational Education and Training, Teacher Development, and Teachers and Teaching.

Dr Peter Watkins is a Principal Lecturer at the University of Portsmouth, UK. He has been a teacher and teacher educator for many years, working in a wide variety of contexts. His main research interests relate to teacher education and ELT materials writing and he has published widely in these areas. His Publications include *Teaching and Developing Reading Skills* (2017, Cambridge University Press), *The CELTA Course* (2nd ed. 2023, with Scott Thornbury and Sandy Millin, Cambridge University Press), and *Learning to Teach English* (2014, Delta Publishing).

INTRODUCTION

A. Mehdi Riazi and Nima A. Nazari

Background

We are living in a volatile and rapidly changing world. The COVID-19 pandemic reminded us of the unpredictable circumstances we are living in and how such events can affect all aspects of our lives. As seen during the COVID-19 pandemic, unforeseen circumstances can disrupt traditional teaching methods. As such, (English language) teachers should have contingency plans in place, such as remote teaching strategies and digital resources, to ensure that learning can continue even during crises.

Another unprecedented event was the introduction of generative artificial intelligence (Gen AI) and, in particular, a conversational and chat-based generative pre-trained (ChatGPT) at the end of 2022. The newly developed Gen AI tools are Large Language Models (LLMs) based on billions of conversational utterances capable of understanding and generating human language. Gen AI, with all its capabilities, will absolutely affect all aspects of our lives, including education and language teaching and learning.

In this volatile context, this edited volume attempts to take a role in envisaging future directions in English language teaching (ELT). The title addresses a crucial topic in education by focusing on ELT. The book is timely because we live in a constantly changing and evolving world. Collectively, the 15 chapters in this book will discuss the importance of adaptability in English language teaching and how ELT stakeholders can effectively respond to new circumstances.

The book's key message is that English language teachers must be prepared to adapt to the changes and unpredictable circumstances to ensure effective learning for their students. How this adaptability must be planned and implemented depends on several factors. One of these factors is adaptability in curriculum design and flexibility in pedagogical approaches. Such adaptability and flexibility entail the ability to employ diverse pedagogical approaches that can be tailored to different learning contexts. Whether our classes are in-person, online, or hybrid (including both in-person and online activities), we should be capable of adjusting our methods to suit the circumstances. Given the centrality of technology in today's education, integrating technology (in its broad meaning) is an essential aspect of adaptable teaching. For example, thinking of online teaching and learning, digital resources, including multimodal resources, learning management systems, and communication tools have become indispensable in ELT. Teachers should be proficient in utilizing these technologies to enhance students' learning.

Furthermore, responding to new circumstances involves being culturally aware and sensitive. Knowing that ELT teachers work with students from diverse linguistic, educational, and cultural backgrounds, they should adapt their curriculum and teaching methods to respect and incorporate different cultural perspectives, values, and communication styles. Responding to new changes also implies a shift towards student-centered approaches. That is, we should empower students to take an active role in their learning, allowing them to choose topics, set goals, and engage in self-directed learning when appropriate. Adaptable teaching means recognizing the individual circumstances and challenges students may face and providing support accordingly.

Related to cultural awareness and sensitivity are ELT teachers' assessment strategies. We need to use adaptable assessment methods since traditional exams and assessment systems may not be suitable in new situations. We might need to think about and explore alternative assessment strategies like project-based assessment, individual and group oral presentations, and even self-assessment to evaluate students' language proficiency progress and achievement. These and other suitable strategies can also be adapted to online teaching and learning.

The above points have implications for teachers to be lifelong learners, too. We need to stay up-to-date regarding latest developments in language teaching, pedagogy, and educational technology, engage in professional development, and network with colleagues to enhance our flexibility and adaptability. Along the same lines, collaboration with students and parents is essential when responding to new circumstances. Effective communication and teamwork can lead to innovative solutions and a better understanding of students' needs. In the next section, an outline of the book chapters will be briefly discussed so that readers come to grips with the content of each chapter and the book overall.

Outline of the book chapters

The 15 chapters in this book are divided into four sections. Each section focuses on a theme and includes several chapters. All chapters follow a similar, tripartite structure of The Past, The Present, and The Future to facilitate readers' reading. The purpose has been to present a trajectory of the development of the topic in discussion in each chapter by explaining its past and present trends and how its future can be envisioned.

The first section, including four chapters, addresses responses to new circumstances regarding curriculum and teachers' and students' needs. Chapter 1 by John Macalister focuses on English language curriculum development in unique circumstances. The message conveyed by Macalister is that we, as teachers, need to have a sound understanding of language curriculum design processes to deal with the constant change that characterizes our profession and our lives. Macalister believes we gain and develop our curriculum understanding through environmental scanning, needs analysis, and ongoing evaluation. These processes can help us to make informed and appropriate changes to what we teach, how we teach, and how we assess learners' learning and achievement. In a word, we need to ensure we are prepared to be adaptable.

The second chapter by Melissa Reed, Yulia Kharchenko, and Agnes Bodis is titled 'Sustainability in English language teacher education: Preparing teachers for an unknown future'. The authors have consciously chosen the term 'sustainability' to address how teachers' needs and well-being can be addressed to prepare them for future changes. They contend that the concept of sustainability encompasses the mindsets and skills of adaptability, critical reflection, collaboration, and autonomy, which will help student teachers become more flexible and prioritize their well-being throughout their careers. To achieve their goal, the authors discuss language teacher education through an ecological lens, with an understanding of contextual factors that affect teachers' lives. They provide practical examples of integrating sustainability into teacher education programmes.

The third chapter by Justine Light, Denise Lo, and Martin Guardado is titled 'Understanding the needs of international EAP students: Adaptive progress'. As it was cited earlier in introducing Macalister's chapter, we gain and develop our curriculum understanding through environmental scanning, needs analysis, and ongoing evaluation. Light, Lo, and Guardado discuss how an experienced EAP instructor transformed her practice based on analyzing EAP students' needs and adapting her curriculum and teaching. After providing a background to effectively identify international EAP students' needs, Light, Lo, and Guardado highlight a comprehensive range of approaches and tools currently used to support students' needs. They present and discuss how EAP instructors may respond to global upheavals.

The fourth chapter by Dat Bao presents and discusses multiple case studies of Australian and international students at an Australian University. Considering that students' characteristics and needs are different, leading to different learning styles, Bao argues that teaching needs to adapt to various conditions. As a case in point, Bao focuses on silent learning as an autonomous choice. Like the previous chapter, Bao presents and discusses a case study of international students, including 20 participants from Australia, China, Japan, and Korea at an Australian university. The chapter highlights less articulate but proactive students to reflect on how these students benefit from silent learning. The chapter draws on these students' experiences to develop scholarly insights to help teachers fine-tune their teaching strategies.

Section 2 of the book focuses on ELT assessment, feedback, and managing classrooms in new circumstances. This section includes three chapters. Chapter 5 by Graham Seed, Angeliki Salamoura, and Nick Saville focuses on new approaches to assessment in ELT. They draw on two recent distinct but complementary trends in English language assessment that emerged in the first two decades of the 21st century. These two trends are the increasing use of digital technology in testing and different views and conceptions about the construct of language proficiency and how it might be measured. The authors discuss different aspects of these two broad trends and conclude the chapter by providing an outlook on the future possibilities.

Chapter 6 by Maddalena Taras focuses on feedback to students in ELT. Taras starts with two crucial questions: whether feedback to ELT students differs from other subject areas and if feedback differs according to different language skills. To explore these questions, Taras evaluates the theoretical concepts of feedback and how these concepts are related to teaching, learning, and assessment. Taras contends that feedback needs to be understood within the assessment context and that clarifying this context is essential for students to develop their assessment literacy. Taras argues that involving students in peer- and self-assessment could efficiently induct students into assessment protocols and literacies.

Chapter 7, by Christopher Graham, addresses ELT classroom management in times of change. Graham suggests that classroom management is, above all, a tool of methodology and thus inextricably influenced by it. He looks at how classroom management is interacting with and being influenced by external developments in ELT, including the roles of increased social media use, the non-native speaker debate, and the resilience shown by the global community during and since the COVID-19 pandemic. In looking to the future of classroom management, Graham explores its interactions with emerging themes in ELT, including translanguaging, learner and teacher well-being, the integration of global and social justice issues, 21st-century skills, and educational reform.

Section 3 of the book has 'teaching English language skills and components in new circumstances' in its focus. Chapter 8 by Joseph Siegel discusses teaching listening in new circumstances. Siegel contends that, traditionally, listening has been the most neglected among the four main language skills—listening, speaking, reading, and writing. He conceives the ephemeral and receptive nature of listening as the grassroots for such neglect. This is while listening proficiency is essential for accessing meaning and providing input for language development. Siegel emphasizes the need for adaptability to the teaching of L2 listening. Siegel emphasizes how traditional teaching practices have evolved to accommodate and align with present-day L2 teaching, including synchronous and asynchronous online teaching, multimodal influences, and listening goals related to conversational and content-related (e.g., English medium instruction) input. He closes the chapter by outlining established models for teaching listening. He discusses how they can be adapted and applied within the constraints and opportunities of new and developing educational contexts.

Chapter 9 by Peter Watkins focuses on teaching reading. Considering reading as an integral part of the lives of many people used in different contexts for different purposes, Watkins discusses how reading has changed dramatically over the last quarter century—moving away from printed pages to reading from various screens. As such, Watkins discusses the nature of reading and how reading in the first and second languages is similar and different. He then criticizes how reading has been taught around the globe and looks at how the current models of teaching reading might be changed. He argues that this change is essential to prepare learners for the new challenges of reading in the 21st century.

Chapter 10 by John Trent discusses teaching speaking. Trent provides an overview of critical issues in the theory and practice of teaching speaking in second and foreign language contexts. Trent moves from elaborating on how speaking was taught in the past, focusing on accuracy and fluency, communication breakdowns, and dealing with errors, to how this skill is taught presently in light of online teaching necessitated by the COVID-19 pandemic. He then discusses the opportunities for teaching speaking in the future, including integrating in-class and out-of-class learning opportunities. He concludes the chapter by inviting teachers and learners in second and foreign language contexts to explore and take on new roles.

Chapter 11 by Ismaeil Fazel addresses L2 writing pedagogy in response to emerging needs and exigencies. Drawing on recent changes in language education, Fazel highlights the need for flexibility and adaptability to respond to evolving circumstances. He presents and discusses the evolutionary trajectory developments in second language writing research and practice and provides an overview of the major pedagogical paradigms that have shaped the foundations of L2 writing pedagogy. He ends the chapter by outlining recommendations for future directions in L2 writing research and practice.

The final chapter in Section 3, Chapter 12, by Xinrong He and Barry Lee Reynolds, discusses the adaptable teaching of grammar, vocabulary, and pronunciation using online applications. He and Reynolds argue that teachers must be open to adapting their teaching to the changing times by keeping in tune with the latest technological developments. They discuss the past trends of teaching and learning these three language components and explain the current trend in harnessing language learning strategy instruction to increase language learner autonomy. They also draw on the concept of engagement and how learners might engage in several out-of-class online platforms to enhance their learning. They end the chapter with a discussion on why it is essential for language learners to engage in informal language learning beyond the classroom and how English language teachers can encourage this engagement through future adaptation.

The last section of the book, Section 4, focuses on the contribution of technology to ELT in new circumstances. This section includes three chapters to cover this topic. Chapter 13 by Jane Spiro addresses learning technologies and teachers and the need to value the teacher and teacher values in a changing world. Building on language teachers' first encounter with computer-assisted language learning (CALL), Spiro raises consciousness about the fear that new technologies might take control of us. The fear includes replacing the teachers' roles, translation applications, and evaluation platforms. Considering the potential threats of new technologies, Spiro tracks the evolving perceptions of 22 language teachers during the COVID-19 pandemic when learning moved online entirely. Spiro discusses the challenges of teaching online as these teachers responded to the new situation, including retaining the humane aspects in a digital age. Spiro builds on these teachers' responses to the pandemic year to offer insights into how the 'human' teacher's contribution continues to have value alongside emerging and changing technologies.

Chapter 14 by Matt Kessler, Francesca Marino, and Sean Farrell focuses on computer-assisted language learning and teaching to understand emerging trends, challenges, and solutions in ELT. The authors first provide a background on the past trends in CALL and then showcase three emerging trends, including the use of multimodal activities, synchronous video computer-mediated communication, and mobile-assisted language learning. They discuss the theoretical underpinnings of these trends and provide examples of how these tools might be used in ELT classes. They conclude the chapter by discussing how practitioners and researchers might respond to new CALL-related challenges in the future.

Chapter 15 by Gerard O'Hanlon and Anne O'Keeffe discusses a multimodal analysis of roleplays between upper intermediate level learners and the potential lessons this can have for teaching oral language competency in online contexts. O'Hanlon and O'Keeffe examine a video-mediated dataset of online spoken B2-level learner interactions via *Zoom*. In this context, roleplays were used to elicit spoken request sequences. O'Hanlon and O'Keeffe explore these data using a multimodal corpus linguistics approach. They build on the results to show that English language learners employ a range of multimodal potentialities in their interactions despite the perceived restrictions of video-mediated interactions. The authors make the case that there is scope for further research using this multimodal corpus linguistics approach.

In conclusion, we argue that adaptable English language teaching and responding to new circumstances are fundamental aspects of effective education in the 21st century. Teachers must be prepared to embrace change, integrate technology, be culturally sensitive, and continuously update their skills to meet the evolving needs of their students and the educational landscape. Flexibility, creativity, and a commitment to lifelong learning are vital traits for educators to navigate these challenges successfully.

SECTION I
ELT responses to new circumstances

1
ENGLISH LANGUAGE CURRICULUM DEVELOPMENT IN NEW CIRCUMSTANCES

John Macalister

Introduction

I want to begin with a couple of memories from my time as a trainee teacher. One is learning to use the Banda machine, a form of spirit duplicator. This involved creating a master copy, handwritten as often as not, on carbon paper, then fitting it to the drum of the machine and turning the handle until sufficient copies were made, or the master copy lost its reproducibility. The end result was a spirit-infused, possibly still slightly damp, handout that learners would inevitably sniff. The other memory is of learning to photograph images and produce slides for use in class. This was a more specialised and time-consuming skill than using the Banda machine, but one that our teacher educators felt it important we acquire. Of course, these memories hark back to a distant time, and many readers might struggle to believe that this was once the height of technological sophistication. Today, it would probably be a rare teacher who did not do a quick online search to find a suitable image or other visual to insert into a presentation rather than laboriously producing their own, and Banda machines have long since been consigned to landfills. My purpose in recalling these memories, however, is simply to make the point that change and innovation in education are constant. The focus of this chapter is how language teachers can be prepared to deal with the ongoing change in their professional lives, whether expected or unexpected.

There is considerable literature on change and innovation in educational settings (e.g. Hyland & Wong, 2013). Two threads of that literature that are worth mentioning here are the source of change and teacher response to change. At its simplest, change can be thought of as emanating from either an external source, such as a principal or an education ministry, or the self. It is the externally driven, often top-down change that typically presents a challenge for achieving a successful outcome, and it is with this sort of change that this chapter is chiefly concerned.

Research does suggest that, over time, adoption of an innovation will resemble an S-curve, beginning with low and slow adoption, and that this reflects a categorisation of adopters into five groups from the innovators, which is a small group, through to the laggards, accounting for around one-sixth of the population (Rogers, 2003). But not all innovations will be adopted. There is also considerable literature on attempts to introduce change or to innovate that have failed. Markee (1997), for example, analysed a number of cases of curriculum innovation to identify principles that could be applied to increase the likelihood of success. Macalister and Phonekeo (2022) discussed more recent examples of the failure of and resistance to innovations in Malaysia, Japan, China, Papua New Guinea, Vietnam and elsewhere. There are many reasons for such failure, and it would certainly be a mistake to view English language teachers as solely responsible for this. While there will always be teachers who say 'I have been doing things this way for so many years; why should I change?' (Mohamed, 2008), attempts at change and innovation are just as likely, even more likely, to be set up for failure by being poorly introduced, under-resourced and not well-suited to the local context.

Yet failure is not inevitable. At this point it might be worth recalling the Goldilocks syndrome – the size of a change needs to be just right, not too big, not too small (Stoller, 1994). Teachers, in other words, need to believe that the change or innovation is both manageable and worthwhile. In addition to that, and the argument I am proposing in this chapter, teachers need to have an understanding of the factors that determine what happens in the classroom so that they are prepared to deal with the ongoing change in their professional lives. This is where having a model of language curriculum design comes into its own. However, before considering such a model, let us consider a little more deeply the question of teacher response to change, and especially why change or innovation can fail.

Background (the past trend)

Understanding resistance

Returning to technological innovation – and taking technological innovation as a proxy for change and innovation in general – I want to hark back to the time when computer-assisted language learning (CALL) was still new. Hubbard (2008, pp. 177–178), taking the position that there was a need for such courses, proposed seven possible reasons why teachers and teacher educators were not embracing the innovation. These he listed as:

- Inertia
- Ignorance
- Insufficient time
- Insufficient infrastructure
- Insufficient standards
- Lack of an established methodology
- Lack of experienced, knowledgeable educators

The first three are perhaps best viewed as teacher-internal factors and could be summarised as the 'I can't be bothered', the 'I don't know anything about it' and the 'I'm too busy' responses. The other four are teacher-external and could be invoked by those responding along the lines of 'I'm open to it, but'. It is also, of course, often the case that the development of infrastructure, standards, methodology and experience with a technology proceed after the introduction of innovation and that their absence can be a legitimate constraint on adoption.

What appears to be absent here, however, is a recognition that teachers and teacher educators might not be convinced of the merits of an innovation. In this regard, Salaberry (2001, p. 51) identified four important questions to ask in the face of a technological innovation, which can be summarised as:

- Will it help reach learning goals more effectively?
- What aspects of the new technology work for teaching?
- How can it be integrated into what currently happens?
- Is this an efficient use of time and resources?

If the responses to those types of questions are negative, the innovation should probably not be adopted. If the questions are not asked, an innovation that might not be worthwhile might be adopted. These questions, furthermore, are not restricted to technology. A great deal of learning time can be wasted by inappropriate games, for example. As mentioned earlier, to be adopted, a change or innovation needs to be perceived as both worthwhile and manageable.

Understanding language curriculum design

While there are many models of curriculum design, I am rather shamelessly but perhaps not unexpectedly going to draw on the one I know the best.

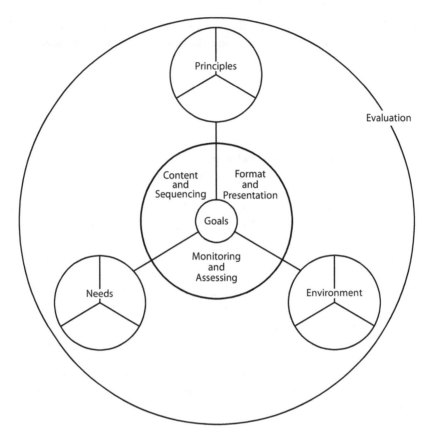

FIGURE 1.1 The language curriculum design model (Macalister & Nation, 2020)

This is shown in Figure 1.1 and is at the heart of Macalister and Nation (2020).

Sometimes known as the Mercedes model, it consists of five circles. At the very heart – the inner circle – is the classroom. The goals of the curriculum are intended to be achieved by decisions around content and sequencing, format and presentation and monitoring and assessing. Or, to put it in simpler terms, by decisions about what to teach, how to teach it and how we will know that learning is happening.

What happens in the classroom is not, however, determined in isolation. This is where information drawn from environment analysis, needs analysis and familiarity with research-based principles for effective teaching comes into play. For example, if there is a decision to incorporate extensive reading into the curriculum, this is likely to be determined by familiarity with the principles of comprehensible input and fluency (for more information,

English language curriculum development in new circumstances 15

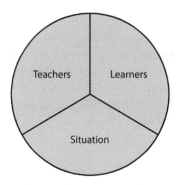

FIGURE 1.2 The division of the environment analysis circle

see Macalister & Nation, 2020, pp. 62–67), or more generally with the research that demonstrates the language learning benefits of extensive reading. It could also be a response to a top-down decree from a principal or ministry, in which case it would be a response to an environmental factor (Figure 1.2). Or, it could be a response to a different environmental factor, such as the fact that the target language is not used in the community and learners need opportunities to encounter and use it if successful language learning is to occur. Importantly, however, once the decision to incorporate extensive reading has been taken, there will need to be further decisions about the reading material – the content segment of the inner circle – in order for it to be at the right level for the learners. To do this, the teacher will need to know learners' vocabulary size and the lexical demands of the reading materials; this is the role of needs analysis. There will also need to be decisions around format and presentation – where will the reading take place, in class or in the learners' own time? Increasingly, too, there may be choices to be made between hard copy and online reading. Online extensive reading can certainly be implemented effectively, but it is not without its challenges (Bui & Macalister, 2021). Decisions here will be shaped by environment analysis – does the school have a library of graded readers? Do learners have equitable access to the internet? Finally, teachers will want to know if reading is actually happening. This is the monitoring and assessing segment of the inner circle, and the expectation with extensive reading is that the emphasis would be on monitoring rather than assessing.

The final circle encases the entire model of curriculum design. Evaluation ensures that a curriculum is dynamic and that it keeps improving. After trying extensive reading in the classroom, teachers might want to know the answers to questions such as: did the learners enjoy reading? How did it contribute to their language learning? What needs to change next time?

This explication of the language curriculum design model has, hopefully, demonstrated that its components are interconnected and that the model is dynamic. The components in this model are found to varying degrees, sometimes under different names, in other models of language curriculum design (as examples Graves, 2000; Lockwood, 2019; Mickan, 2013; Mihai & Purmensky, 2016; Murdoch, 1989) and as discussed in Macalister and Nation (2020, pp. 157–160).

Current trends

Rather than focusing here on the academic and theoretical literature, I want to understand current trends by discussing teacher responses to a recent unexpected, externally driven and sudden change in terms of the model introduced above and to understand responses in terms of the factors identified by Hubbard (2008) and Salaberry (2001).

The event I am referring to is, of course, the global pandemic triggered by the emergence of COVID-19 in 2020. As the severity of the health crisis was revealed, as the death toll soared into the hundreds of thousands and as health systems struggled to cope, governments around the world took action with varying degrees of speed and competence. In New Zealand, for example, where the official response was highly praised both nationally and internationally, the country went into lockdown. All educational institutions were closed, and learning switched from face-to-face to online. Networking platforms such as Zoom became the norm, and *pivot* became a buzzword.

At the simplest level, this shows how a change in a situational factor (part of the environment analysis outer circle, Figure 1.2) triggered a change in the format and presentation segment of the inner circle, the place where teaching and learning happen. But the environment analysis also revealed constraints that needed to be addressed for teaching and learning to take place in this new format, notably that an estimated 60,000 to 80,000 New Zealand homes where there were school-age children did not have a digital connection. The government worked with telecommunication companies to address this, just as it worked with schools and businesses to ensure as many learners as possible had access to devices (for more on the NZ response, see Education, 2021).

Apart from being led by a competent government, the NZ response to the pandemic was probably little different from that in many other countries, and how teachers responded to the shift to online teaching can be gauged by comparing two case studies from elsewhere. In the first, Oscar, a novice EFL teacher in Central America, appeared to embrace the 'pivot' successfully (Farrell & Stanclik, 2023). Establishing rapport between teacher and learners was an important principle for him, and he realised that his use of 'kinaesthetic activities' in the physical classroom would not work in the virtual classroom. In the online environment, creating rapport was more of a challenge, but his response was to use more small group work to give learners more opportunities to interact and, presumably, to bond with each other. In the second case study, however, Grace, an experienced ESL teacher in Hong Kong, also faced the loss of interaction in the physical space but responded by resorting to 'teacher-centred monologue' (Cheung, 2023). She did not use small groups and was not aware of the breakout room function on Zoom. For her, completing the course and preparing the learners for their exams guided her teaching.

These two case studies do demonstrate how the shift to online teaching differed because of the interaction between different elements of the language curriculum design model. Both teachers were, after all, in the same scenario – a change in the wider environment (the arrival of the pandemic) resulted in a format and presentation change (to online teaching). For Grace, that was the sum of it. She did not seem to be guided by any principles as such (remembering that principles provide research-based pointers to effective teaching) but by her beliefs about what was important (covering the material, passing the exam). This shows an interplay between teacher and situational factors (Figure 1.2). Interestingly, consideration of the learners does not seem to have figured in her thinking. Oscar's format and presentation decision (small groups), on the other hand, was influenced by the principles outer circle; although not named as a principle as such in Macalister and Nation (2020), rapport maps onto motivation and integrative motivation in their list of twenty important principles (2020, pp. 60–61, 75–77). His commitment to rapport also reflected his consideration of the learners, as was also clear in the case study from his decisions around content and sequencing. He used variation in and variety of content in order to keep learners engaged.

In Grace's response, many of the reasons suggested by Hubbard can be identified. She said she had insufficient time to take up any professional development available, she clearly did not know a great deal about the new technology, and her response was marked by a degree of inertia. All this was compounded by a lack of institutional support; according to Grace, her school was 'not enthusiastic' about the new developments. Oscar, by contrast, was far more positively inclined and appears to have been able to respond in the affirmative to the questions raised by Salaberry. It seems plausible to suggest that he found the need to shift online manageable, whereas Grace did not, and that he was able to use the technology in pedagogically worthwhile ways, something Grace did not attempt to do.

Looking to the future

It was not my deliberate intention, in discussing the two published case studies above, to make judgements about Grace and Oscar's teaching during the pandemic, although inevitably a whiff of judgement may have been detected. Accepting, then, that I found Oscar's response the more effective of the two, I want to suggest that he was demonstrating the dynamism of the language curriculum design model introduced earlier. In his response, multiple components can be identified as operating – environmental factors such as his openness to the new technology and awareness of the learners, and the value he attached to at least one principle, resulted in changes to what was taught and to how it was taught. This, of course, is based on my analysis. I am not suggesting he was consciously drawing on that or any model. In the remainder of this chapter, however, I want to touch on:

- What teachers can control and change
- What teachers need to know to make changes
- How teachers can be empowered to make changes

What teachers can control and change

The inner circle of the Mercedes model shown in Figure 1.1 is divided into three segments – content and sequencing, format and presentation and monitoring and assessing, and together these support the goals. By attending to the three segments, the goals can be achieved. It is in the inner circle that the teacher has the most ability to make change (for examples of such changes, see Macalister, 2016).

Ideally, goals would emerge from needs analysis – understanding what the learners can currently do and what they should be able to do at the end of the course. In this sense, needs analysis is acting like a GPS, mapping a route from Point A to Point B. Goals need to be realistic and so setting goals will also be informed by some information from environment analysis, notably the amount of time available for language learning. If learners' experience with the target language is solely restricted to the classroom, then goals will be less ambitious than if the target language is, or can be, used beyond the classroom. However, in many classrooms around the world, goals are centrally determined, and teachers may feel that they cannot be changed. In such cases, the three supporting segments of the inner circle must be considered.

Teachers who work in situations where goals are centrally determined may feel they have little control or ability to change what is to be taught, the content and sequencing. They may claim that they must follow a mandated coursebook in lockstep fashion, but this overlooks the decisions that teachers make about what to omit, or replace, or to add to or adapt existing material (Connolly, 2021; Grant, 1987). Teachers' ability to make these types of decisions has been often observed (Nguyen et al., 2018; Parent, 2011).

It is, however, in decisions about format and presentation – how something is taught – that teachers may have the greatest freedom. Oscar's decision to make greater use of small groups in online teaching and Grace's preference for teacher-centred monologue illustrate two different decisions in this regard. As a further illustration, when faced with an input text in a coursebook, teachers should be thinking of such questions as 'how am I going to make my learners interested in this', 'how am I going to give my learners a reason for wanting to find out what this text is about' or 'how am I going to make sure my learners can understand this text'. These, and similar questions, are about motivation.

The third and final segment of the inner circle is one that probably receives too little attention. How do teachers – and learners – know that learning is happening? In an ideal world, teachers would always be clear about the learning goal of an activity and what behaviours would indicate that the goal was being achieved. As an example, one take on the range of language learning activities that could be described as listen and do, or listen and draw or say and do (Lee, 1979) requires learners to complete a 3 × 3 grid according to teacher instructions (Macalister, 2016, pp. 61–62). A performance objective for this might read something like: the learners should be able to fill in a nine-block square following directions given by the teacher speaking at *normal speed* using *familiar items* with **100% accuracy** as measured by the correct items being in the correct blocks. Not only does this clearly explain the features of the activity (in italics), but it also describes what success will look like (in bold). The teacher can gauge whether learning is being demonstrated by observing how well learners perform. This can be done by moving around the room. It could be described as monitoring (as opposed to assessing) or as observation of learning. If learners do not perform at the desired level, then more work needs to be done to ensure learning occurs. If learners are successful, then the teacher knows they are ready to move on.

Of course, it would be unrealistic to expect or even to suggest that teachers have this type of detailed performance objective for all classroom activities. Learning to think in this way should, however, be part of what teacher education develops.

What teachers need to know to make changes

The changes that teachers make in the classroom – the inner circle – should be in response to information from the outer circles of environment analysis, needs analysis and principles (Figure 1.1). Thus, teachers need to know what these are and how to respond to them.

To begin with environment analysis, this means information about the learners, the teachers and the situation in which the language learning is occurring (Figure 1.2). The situation includes very localised information, such as the physical layout of the classroom, to the societal – what is the role of the target language in the world beyond the classroom, for example. It can also include governmental decisions about the curriculum, assessment and the time allocated to the target language. In the earlier discussion of extensive reading, various environmental factors were suggested. To take two of those that emanate from the situation segment, if a directive to implement extensive reading comes down from above (as has happened in, for example, Malaysia (Taib et al., 2022) and Hong Kong (Green, 2005) with mixed results), then teachers need to work with that. They need to make an attempt to respond appropriately. A different situational factor might be the lack of opportunities to use the target language outside the classroom. Assuming that teachers would see this as an impediment to learning, it is to be hoped that they would want to work against it. Incorporating extensive reading, whether as an in-class or out-of-class activity, or both, would be an appropriate curricular response (though certainly the best response, it need not be the only one (as nicely demonstrated by Samuel & Sithamparam, 2011)).

Moving to needs analysis, one way to think of this is to regard it as a tool to work out how to get learners' language from where it is now to where it needs to be. In this respect, and as mentioned earlier, it operates rather like a GPS. In the terminology of needs analysis, the teacher needs to know where learners are now (rather unfortunately referred to as 'lacks') and what they need to have learned (their 'necessities'). Surprisingly, this sort of information is often absent. Perhaps teachers make the assumption that they just know, possibly based on having taught a similar class before, or accept that the curriculum or coursebook is fixed, and so learners just need to fit in with that. Such attitudes are unfortunate and do not promote learning. These attitudes are even more unfortunate when you consider that there are practical, i.e. time-efficient and easy-to-mark, tools that can be used to get an indication of learners' lacks. Well-known examples are the Vocabulary Levels Test and the Vocabulary Size Test. Other possibilities are discussed in Macalister and Nation (2020, pp. 134–135).

Once teachers have some understanding of where learners' current language proficiency sits, they also need to have some understanding of the language demands of the texts and other input materials that the learners will be meeting during the course. There is little point in using texts that the learners will not be able to understand, and if there are required texts that are too difficult, then guidance or support will be needed. In the language of the Mercedes model, if the content is too hard (and cannot be changed), then the format and presentation have to be adapted to reduce the difficulty.

It can be difficult to clearly differentiate between environment and needs analysis, especially in relation to the learners themselves, and often the two are conducted simultaneously. Mihai and Purmensky (2016, Chapter 5) provide some excellent examples of tools that can be used at all levels, from beginner to advanced, to gather information about language needs, personal needs and sociocultural needs at the same time. Taken together, these provide rich information on which teachers can base inner circle decisions.

The final point – the key message – is that the world beyond the classroom is always changing, and as a result, what happens in the classroom needs to respond. That is the reminder that the evaluation circle encasing the Mercedes model is intended to convey. Here are examples of just a few of the possible reasons why change is necessary:

- A new year, a new class of learners; they will not be the same as last year's
- A new coursebook
- A new curriculum
- Changes in high-stakes final assessment
- Changes in language-in-education policy
- New technology
- New research suggesting more effective ways to teach and learn languages
- And, lest we forget, a global pandemic

How teachers can be empowered to make changes

The case I have been trying to make in this chapter is that teachers need to have an understanding of the factors that determine what happens in the classroom so that they are prepared to deal with ongoing change in their professional lives. My suggestion is that to achieve this, teachers need to have an awareness of a model of language curriculum design (which does not, let me emphasise, necessarily have to be the one I have been describing). The place for this to happen is during professional development, which can rather neatly be divided into pre-service and in-service teacher education.

It is not, however, a case of simply offering a course or a workshop on curriculum design. If the goal is to make teachers feel prepared to deal with change, the content and format decisions need to work towards that goal. It is widely accepted that teacher preparation programmes do not always succeed in preparing students for the reality of the classroom. This was certainly the experience of graduates from a New Zealand programme who found themselves novice teachers in diverse teaching contexts, very different from what they had previously experienced. To address this, Macalister and Musgrave (2015) developed 'graduate scenarios' as a way of preparing students for an unknown future. These were developed from experiences shared by former graduates and turned into problem-solving activities for current students. The core challenge was how to apply a principled approach to language teaching based on the four strands principle (Macalister & Nation, 2020, pp. 61–62; Nation, 2007). The four strands principle draws on research and theory about effective language learning and teaching. Its application here was designed to help students make sense of a situation that seemed at odds with what they had previously experienced or been prepared for; it was intended as a means to restore 'balance' in the face of 'dissonance'.

Such an approach could influence a course or a workshop on curriculum design. By creating scenarios based on examples of change from an external source, such as those listed above, or by examining case studies of examples of both success and failure, students can be encouraged to explore ways to respond in terms of the model of curriculum design. Thus, when they encounter external pressures to change in their careers, they will be better prepared to respond effectively than would otherwise be the case.

Teachers as agents of change

It should be clear that I believe that teachers have the agency to make changes in their classrooms in response to changes beyond those spaces. While the focus here has been on changes from external sources, not infrequently top-down, I do want to make the point that teachers can be – and often are – initiators of change without external pressure to do so. Evaluation as an activity is a recursive process in which all teachers should be engaging all the time. This is very much the realm of reflective practice (Farrell, 2015), but it can also be achieved through self-initiated professional development activities (Bailey et al., 1998) or ongoing needs and environment analysis leading to a cycle of continuous improvement to teaching materials (Davies, 2006). It is also, of course, related to the field of language teacher cognition (Borg, 2003), understanding the relationship between what teachers think, know and believe and what they do, but also importantly what influences cognition and how. After all, much professional development is intended to develop or change cognition.

For teachers to be agents of change, however, certain enabling factors need to be in place. The change or innovation needs to be seen as worthwhile (recalling the questions posed by Salaberry, 2001) but also manageable. Making the effort to implement a small change with a small effect may be manageable but not be seen as worthwhile. Conversely, a large-scale change that may be worthwhile might be daunting and might not be manageable. A change needs to be, as in the Goldilocks story, 'just right' (cf. Stoller, 1994). A tool for making change manageable is familiarity with a language curriculum design framework, a conceptual map for understanding how to respond. With that in place, teachers are less likely to be held back by the 'I can't be bothered', 'I don't know anything about it' and 'I'm too busy' responses. They will be more like Oscar in the case study discussed earlier, responding positively to unexpected external changes.

References

Bailey, K. M., Curtis, A., & Nunan, D. (1998). Undeniable insights: The collaborative use of three professional development practices. *TESOL Quarterly*, *32*(3), 546–556.

Borg, S. (2003). Teacher cognition in language teaching: A review of research on what language teachers think, know, believe, and do. *Language Teaching*, *36*(2), 81–109. https://doi.org/10.1017/S0261444803001903

Bui, T. N., & Macalister, J. (2021). Online extensive reading in an EFL context: Investigating reading fluency and perceptions. *Reading in a Foreign Language*, *33*(1), 1–29. https://scholarspace.manoa.hawaii.edu/server/api/core/bitstreams/b0c3435d-196f-4e2b-a334-f082f73350c4/content

Cheung, A. (2023). Language teaching during a pandemic: A case study of Zoom use by a secondary ESL teacher in Hong Kong. *RELC Journal*, *54*(1), 55–70. https://doi.org/10.1177/0033688220981784

Connolly, D. (2021). Practitioners respond to Freda Mishan's 'the global ELT coursebook: A case of Cinderella's slipper?'. *Language Teaching*, 1–4. https://doi.org/10.1017/S0261444821000185

Davies, A. (2006). What do learners really want from their EFL course? *ELT Journal*, *60*(1), 3–12.

Education, Ministry of. (2021). *Tackling the digital divide during COVID-19*. Retrieved 1 November, from https://www.digital.govt.nz/showcase/tackling-the-digital-divide-during-covid-19/

Farrell, T. S. C. (2015). *Promoting teacher reflection in second language education: A framework for TESOL professionals*. Routledge.

Farrell, T. S. C., & Stanclik, C. (2023). "COVID-19 is an opportunity to rediscover ourselves": Reflections of a novice EFL teacher in Central America. *RELC Journal*, *54*(1), 71–83. https://doi.org/10.1177/0033688220981778

Grant, N. (1987). *Making the most of your textbook*. Longman.

Graves, K. (2000). *Designing language courses: A guide for teachers*. Heinle & Heinle.

Green, C. (2005). Integrating extensive reading in the task-based curriculum. *ELT Journal*, *59*(4), 306–311.

Hubbard, P. (2008). CALL and the future of language teacher education. *CALICO Journal*, *25*(2), 175–188. https://calico-org.helicon.vuw.ac.nz/a-683-CALL%20and%20the%20Future%20of%20Language%20Teacher%20Education.html

Hyland, K., & Wong, L. L. C. (Eds.). (2013). *Innovation and change in English language education*. Routledge.

Lee, W. R. (1979). *Language teaching games and contests* (2nd ed.). Oxford University Press.

Lockwood, J. (2019). What do we mean by 'Workplace English?' A multilayered syllabus framework for course design and assessment. In K. Hyland, & L. L. C. Wong (Eds.), *Specialised English: New directions in ESP and EAP research and practice* (pp. 22–35). Routledge.

Macalister, J. (2016). Adapting and adopting materials. In M. Azarnoosh, M. Zeraatpishe, A. Faravani, & H. R. Kargozari (Eds.), *Issues in materials development* (pp. 57–64). Sense Publishers.

Macalister, J., & Musgrave, J. (2015). Dissonance and balance: The four strands framework and pre-service teacher education. In T. S. C. Farrell (Ed.), *International perspectives on English language teacher education: Innovations from the field* (pp. 74–89). Palgrave Macmillan.

Macalister, J., & Nation, I. S. P. (2020). *Language curriculum design* (2nd ed.). Taylor & Francis.

Macalister, J., & Phonekeo, S. (2002). Language teacher education, reading, and curriculum change in Southeast Asia: A Laotian perspective. *RELC Journal*, *0*(0), 00336882221094389. https://doi.org/10.1177/00336882221094389

Markee, N. (1997). *Managing curricular innovation*. Cambridge University Press.

Mickan, P. (2013). *Language curriculum design and socialisation*. Multilingual Matters.

Mihai, F. M., & Purmensky, K. (2016). *Course design for TESOL: A guide to integrating curriculum and teaching*. University of Michigan Press.

Mohamed, N. (2008). "I have been doing things this way for so many years; why should I change?" Exploring teachers' resistance to professional learning. *New Zealand Studies in Applied Linguistics*, *14*(1), 19–35.

Murdoch, G. S. (1989). A pragmatic basis for course design. *English Teaching Forum*, *27*(1), 15–18.

Nation, P. (2007). The four strands. *Innovation in Language Learning and Teaching*, *1*(1), 2–13. https://doi.org/10.2167/illt039.0

Nguyen, B. T. T., Crabbe, D., & Newton, J. (2018). Teacher transformation of oral textbook tasks in Vietnamese EFL high school classrooms. In V. Samuda, K. Van Den Branden, & M. Bygate (Eds.), *TBLT as a researched pedagogy* (pp. 52–70). John Benjamins.

Parent, K. (2011). The teacher as intermediary between national curriculum and classroom. In J. Macalister, & I. S. P. Nation (Eds.), *Case studies in language curriculum design: Concepts and approaches in action around the world* (pp. 186–194). Routledge/Taylor & Francis.

Rogers, E. M. (2003). *Diffusion of innovations* (5th ed.). Free Press.

Salaberry, M. R. (2001). The use of technology for second language learning and teaching: A retrospective. *The Modern Language Journal*, *85*(1), 39–56.

Samuel, M., & Sithamparam, S. (2011). Enhancing consumerist literacy practices in an urbanizing community. In J. Macalister, & I. S. P. Nation (Eds.), *Language curriculum design case studies: Concepts and approaches in action around the world* (pp. 178–185). Routledge.

Stoller, F. L. (1994). The diffusion of innovations in intensive ESL programs. *Applied Linguistics*, *15*(3), 300–327. https://doi.org/10.1093/applin/15.3.300

Taib, N., Nair, R., Gopalan, Y., & Sedhu, D. S. (2022). Towards an effective extensive reading programme for Malaysian schools. *The New English Teacher*, *16*(1), 29–58. http://www.assumptionjournal.au.edu/index.php/newEnglishTeacher/article/view/5420/3326

2
SUSTAINABILITY IN ENGLISH LANGUAGE TEACHER EDUCATION

Preparing teachers for an unknown future

Melissa Reed, Yulia Kharchenko, and Agnes Bodis

Introduction

There have been massive and profound changes in the way that we live, work and think in recent times. For instance, the COVID-19 pandemic proved to have a significant impact on education, in general, all over the world. The shift from face-to-face teaching to an online mode on a global scale prompted teachers already in service to seek out professional development in skills focused on information and communication technologies (Schleicher, 2020) but also to leave the profession (Neilsen et al., 2020). Today, the emergence of artificial intelligence is challenging education yet again, forcing us to promptly reconsider instruction and assessment practices in English language teaching (Hockly, 2023). Undoubtedly, future social and technological developments will transform teaching and learning further. These rapid changes should prompt us to re-evaluate past practices of language teacher education (LTE) to ensure that they serve the teachers of the future.

Preparing pre-service teachers for the complexities of English language teaching within a dynamic and complex system is of utmost importance. An ecological approach to teacher education helps us examine how changes in one or more aspects of the context, for instance, policy, institutional changes, curriculum and the teacher or student cohort, can impact learning and teaching. The ecological approach has its roots in Complexity Theory as applied in English language teaching (Burns & Knox, 2011; Larsen-Freeman, 1997; Larsen-Freeman & Cameron, 2008). Complexity Theory is, in its essence, a theory of change (Larsen-Freeman, 2019). It seeks to examine the way the interacting components of a complex system result in collective behaviour that interacts with its environment. In language education, Complexity Theory is a useful tool for examining the relational, adaptive and emergent relationships between the individual and their environment (Larsen-Freeman, 2019; Yuan & Yang, 2022). This approach has been argued to help humanise Teaching English to Speakers of Other Languages (TESOL) research by directing the focus on the individual and the situatedness of their experience (Pinner & Sampson, 2021) as affected by a range of variables. As teachers operate in ever-changing environments, constantly adapting to changes that may range from smaller or more familiar changes to bigger or unfamiliar ones, it is of utmost importance that teacher education enables the development of skills and a mindset to flexibly meet these challenges. This chapter will focus on the development of reflective practice and lifelong learning through the concept of *sustainability* as an alternative to more traditional practices of LTE. *Sustainability* in LTE means preparing graduates for an unknown future in which they will need to be adaptable and flexible in changing circumstances. To do this, we need to work with teachers on developing a mindset that enables critical reflection and autonomy. It is important that teachers feel empowered to take control of their own learning and identify areas of need as they progress throughout their careers. If we focus merely on teaching skills for today, our graduates may not be able to meet the challenges of tomorrow, which we, as teacher educators, cannot predict.

Although the concept of *sustainability* may apply to other educational areas, we discuss it through LTE and provide an example from our context in postgraduate TESOL courses in higher education. The next section will discuss past skills-based focus in LTE. Using a recent global health pandemic as an example, we review the reactive approach to an unforeseen crisis in education. We then review the most common changes and outcomes of this crisis that characterise LTE today. In the following section, we propose that a longer term approach to LTE can help prepare student teachers for a dynamic and changing future and introduce the concept of *sustainability* in LTE. We give examples from our own context to show how *sustainability* can be embedded into LTE and provide practical recommendations for teacher educators.

Past responses to rapid change—'fighting fires'

Past approaches to LTE tended to emphasise skills and pedagogical knowledge required by successful teachers. The view of LTE as mainly an acquisition of skills and competencies for successful teaching is problematic because 'effective teaching' means different things in various contexts (Farrell, 2019), and such understanding changes frequently (Collie & Martin, 2016). For that reason, teacher education and development that focuses mostly on skills can be retrospective – as new teaching and learning conditions arise or new technology appears, the profession is compelled to upskill. Such response to change can be described as 'fighting fires' – noticing the skill or knowledge gap that exists and attempting to rectify it. Although lifelong learning and professional development are undoubtedly important, language teachers today need to be not only knowledgeable but also adaptive and reflective educators who can function in complex educational systems (Johnson & Golombek, 2020; Parsons & Vaughn, 2016). The outbreak of COVID-19 in 2020 was a stark example of a rapidly changing situation that required English language teachers to be adaptable. For many, the onset of the pandemic marked the beginning of their online teaching experience, and numerous articles and special issues of journals now document local efforts in response to the so-called emergency remote teaching (Bissessar, 2021; Chen, 2021; Neilsen et al., 2020; Shin, 2020; Wong, 2020). Many noted a lack of preparedness among teachers to deliver instruction online. For example, a survey of 1,102 language teachers across the world found that the overwhelming majority (91%) had not taught online before the pandemic, and 83% of them did not receive sufficient training when classes moved online (Mavridi, 2022). It is not surprising, therefore, that the initial period of online teaching was characterised by teachers rushing to familiarise themselves with technology, attending skills-development workshops and exchanging ideas and resources within their communities. A plethora of advice was directed at them at the time, but as Rapanta et al. (2020) point out, it was mostly focused on tools and technologies, as well as 'tips and tricks' for teaching online, often without contextualising how these could be effectively applied.

The 'survival mode' of teacher professional development during the period of emergency remote teaching was soon recognised as neither coherent nor sustainable (Paesani, 2020). The tools-oriented approach to upskilling did not reflect best practices and was not based on a systematic analysis identifying the professional development needs of language teachers. In fact, it is argued that excessive focus on mastering the technology for online delivery caused the shortage of professional development specifically related to language teaching (Moser et al., 2021). In particular, it diminished the quality of language teaching resources and reduced exposure to best practices in lesson planning, instructional strategies and assessments. With time, numerous professional development measures helped teachers meet the demand to continue delivering lessons and courses online. Indeed, teachers around the world demonstrated remarkable determination to adapt to new teaching modalities and enhance their digital literacies (Mavridi, 2022).

Many now feel more confident about their teaching skills required for planned, regular online teaching and future employability.

The present state of play and the need for a new direction

Without a doubt, teachers' increased autonomy and incredible adaptability in ensuring continuity of teaching and learning is a welcome effect of the disruption described above. Despite the initial unpreparedness and a lack of direction in teacher education, language teachers demonstrated an exceptional amount of perseverance and autonomy in identifying their professional development needs. Once the pandemic upskilling 'fires' have been extinguished, and as teachers navigate online learning environments and technologies with increased confidence, more time and energy are available for creativity and reflection on their teaching practices (Rapanta et al., 2020). In LTE, the need to be cognisant of and prepared for the unpredictability of the future is increasingly discussed (Gravett & Petersen, 2022; MacIntyre et al., 2020). The overall goal in reimagining LTE is 'future-proofing' graduates and developing a tolerance for uncertainty by considering emerging practices in various teaching contexts. We argue that it is now resoundingly clear that language teachers need to be supported in developing adaptive expertise (Bransford et al., 2005), or the ability to modify and extend their knowledge and practices to new contexts (Paesani, 2020, p. 294). This expertise may be called upon during future sudden changes or gradual developments in education that we as teacher educators cannot predict.

There are other positive outcomes of the disruption to language education caused by the global pandemic. One is a sharper focus on teacher well-being, and another is the growing importance of the professional community. Undoubtedly, many language teachers have felt the negative impact of the pandemic on their well-being, emotions and motivation. Across the world, heightened workloads and a lack of training in online lesson delivery have been reported (Mavridi, 2022), leading to substantial amounts of stress (MacIntyre et al., 2020). Compared to general education, the domain of language teaching presents unique stressors that impact teacher well-being. These include energy-intensive teaching methodologies, intercultural demands, shifting identities and language anxiety (Mercer, 2021, p. 18). Well-being has been linked with teachers' reduced motivation (Collie et al., 2015) and, in turn, with diminishing students' academic success (Marks & Louis, 1997; Sutton & Wheatley, 2003). Therefore, pre- and in-service language teachers' preparedness for unforeseen situations of stress is increasingly being acknowledged as an integral part of their professional competence. A sharper focus on teacher well-being in future LTE programs is undoubtedly a welcome development emerging from the pandemic.

Increased collegial support is another feature of the initial phases of COVID-19 teaching that needs to be maintained and reinforced. Despite physical isolation over the past years, the broad community of language teachers, teacher educators and school leaders has become more collaborative. Some examples of sharing pedagogical and technical expertise today include team teaching, peer online observations, working closely with learning designers, sharing resources with colleagues, attending online webinars and professional development. English language teaching organisations across the world have continued to bring teachers together at online professional development events, such as conferences by the British Council, English Australia, Trinity College London, TESOL International, JALT, CamTESOL and NileTESOL. Many teachers have joined knowledge communities on social media (such as #AusELT in Australia) and have found these virtual networks to be a valuable form of professional development (Bruce & Stakounis, 2021). From an ecological perspective in education, individuals have the agency to relate to their institutional, cultural, personal and interactional ecologies (Mercer, 2021). Therefore, the learning and development of language teachers are social as much as they are individual. The past years have shown that increased social interaction and peer support lead to more creativity and innovation and create a stronger feeling of community among language teachers. The implication is that future LTE programs should not only develop individuals' skills for creating technologically enhanced teaching design solutions but also focus on the importance of teacher-driven innovations and collaboration.

Now that prolonged periods of forced shutdowns and emergency remote teaching are a thing of the past in many parts of the world, online education is here to stay, whether for individual support, in hybrid form or alongside the face-to-face mode of teaching. Time and resources have been invested in language course design and preparing teachers to teach online in the post-COVID era (Bawa, 2022; Choi & Chung, 2021, English Australia, n.d.). The positive developments stemming from emergency remote teaching now need to be sustained and become features of in-person and planned online teaching and LTE. These strengths include adaptability and creativity, increased self-reliance and autonomy, and collaboration with wider professional networks. Mavridi (2022) suggests that the transformative power of language teachers' collective experiences at the height of the pandemic will inform more robust and pedagogically sustainable approaches to teaching in the future.

To summarise, whilst the massive and rapid changes undertaken by teachers during COVID-19 can show us how resilient they can be, 'fighting fires' is not a sustainable approach to teacher education or practice. There is a risk that in times of crisis, a heightened focus on immediate skills (such as learning to use new technologies) eclipses student learning and experience and leaves teachers vulnerable to burnout. We suggest the concept of *sustainability* as a way to build on this idea in the context of LTE. We propose putting teacher autonomy at the forefront of the measures preparing them for the uncertain future. To achieve this, LTE should not be reactive but should aim to equip teachers to think proactively about changes in their teaching contexts, students' needs and professional development goals. We strive to encourage and sustain the ability to reflect on one's practice and identify professional development needs. Moreover, we believe that in the future, language teachers will continue to rely on their professional communities, both online and offline. Thus, in our view, *sustainability* in teacher education encompasses more than training and development aimed at technology-mediated teaching, important as it may be (Kessler et al., Chapter 14 of this volume). In the next section of this chapter, we discuss this new concept in LTE that encompasses equipping pre- and in-service teachers with the skills of critical reflection and adaptive expertise throughout their careers, fostering a reflexive mindset and a way of life.

Sustainability as a future-oriented approach

In this chapter, we introduce *sustainability* as a new way to conceptualise LTE, to think beyond developing teaching skills and towards a mindset that will equip teachers for their future careers. Sustainability in English language teaching has been defined as the endurance of systems and processes involved in learning and teaching (Musetti, 2018). This endurance is achieved through understanding fast-paced global and regional changes, drawing on local knowledge and responding to shifting trends and realities of English language teaching. Thus, we understand teachers to be working in a complex system that interacts with other complex systems, adopting an ecological approach to understanding LTE (Larsen-Freeman, 2019). In this chapter, sustainability in LTE means preparing graduates for change and uncertainty by equipping them with the ability to assess and understand their contexts, work with others and take charge of their own learning. It is also important to consider teacher well-being as part of sustainability, to counter the negative impacts of change as we have seen during the pandemic (Mercer, 2021). Like Mercer (2021), we acknowledge that well-being should not only be focused on individual characteristics, but societal factors. However, as our focus is on educating future teachers, and we cannot predict all of our student teachers' future working contexts or have the influence to affect change in them, we believe that focusing on the individual within the wider context is the best approach.

We see the key abilities of adaptability, critical and collaborative reflection, and autonomy needed for student teachers' futures. The term adaptability (sometimes interchangeably used with the term adaptive teaching) has been used in teaching to mean the skill and practice of changing a lesson plan to respond to the needs of students in the classroom (Parsons & Vaughn, 2016). This is possible through reflection-in-action (Schön, 1994) where the teacher is observing and reflecting on the students during the lesson to make decisions about its direction. Adaptability has also been used for other kinds of reflection on completed lessons, for future lessons and into practice more generally (Hoffman & Duffy, 2016). While reflective teaching practice is a key part of our teacher education program and philosophy as educators, and will be further discussed below, we use adaptability more broadly in this chapter to mean 'adjusting thoughts, actions, and emotions in response to novel, changing, or uncertain situations' (Collie et al., 2020, p. 351). These situations may occur in the classroom or a broader context as could be seen in rapidly changing working conditions for teachers internationally during COVID-19, which impacted teachers' working lives and well-being as well as classroom interactions (Schleicher, 2020). Adaptability has been shown to increase teachers' engagement and involvement at work and is also likely to be associated with teachers undertaking additional actions beyond their role (Collie et al., 2020). Our aim is to work with teachers to develop their *adaptive expertise*, which means that they can restructure competencies and beliefs over their careers as the need arises, making them more flexible in the face of change (Bransford et al., 2005). Adaptive experts are different from routine experts, who develop a set of skills that become increasingly more efficient over time (Bransford et al., 2005). We propose that an over-focus on skills at the expense of the mindsets required to adapt to change will lead to routine experts who are efficient provided the working conditions remain relatively stable: an unlikely scenario. To prepare future teachers, we need to do both: student teachers require a theoretical and practical understanding of teaching skills and methodologies. At the same time, they should have opportunities to challenge core beliefs, experiment with new ideas and have practical opportunities to experience changing conditions. The idea of uncertainty is key to preparing adaptable teachers: just as COVID-19 and its implications were unprecedented, we cannot foresee what situations student teachers will have to deal with at a micro level in their classroom or on a broader scale during their working lives. Therefore, to design *sustainable* LTE, we must make sure that our student teachers are adaptable.

There is an urgent need to widen the focus on reflective practice in LTE and beyond to help our teachers to be adaptable both in the classroom and beyond it. The reflective practice movement has been widely influential in LTE and practice (Farrell, 2016) and will undoubtedly be familiar to readers. However, there is often not enough thought given to how it is done, including the omission of contextual and emotional factors of teachers' working lives (Farrell, 2022). Understanding this from a Complexity Theory perspective, there is a constant interplay between individuals and their environment which is always dynamic and changing (Larsen-Freeman, 2019). We need to prepare teachers not only for changes in their classrooms but also for wider changes that may impact their working lives. What makes this difficult is that we cannot know all of the challenges our student teachers will face in the future. This is why we, as teacher educators, need to equip them with skills to critically reflect on the situation and contextual factors that may influence their practice and build their confidence to respond to changes as they arise. Farrell (2022) calls for this kind of widened approach to reflection, which would provide teachers with more understanding of what factors may influence their teaching, incorporating an understanding of the past, present and possible future.

At the same time, language teachers should deepen their reflection to interrogate their own beliefs about language and learning. The development of a teacher's Wisdom of Practice, their core understandings of language, language learning and language teaching, can be a good start for critical reflection, as these beliefs influence teacher decision-making (Chappell, 2017). Teacher cognition can influence classroom practice and outcomes as well as planning decisions, as was shown in Chappell et al.'s (2015) study on IELTS teachers in Australia. Articulating and challenging these beliefs, particularly when they are contrary to the student teacher's own practice, may 'lead to sustained innovation in their classroom practice' (Chappell, 2017, p. 434). In fact, this is a key quality of adaptive experts, who are able to examine and restructure their core beliefs through their career as their situations change (Bransford et al., 2005), preventing teachers from carrying beliefs throughout their careers which do not align with their contextual reality.

In addition, the power of collaborative reflection (Walsh & Mann, 2015) can help keep teachers connected and supporting each other, vital during periods of uncertainty and change. It allows for a deeper level of critical reflection, as teachers can broaden their own perspectives by working with others (Barfield, 2016). Student teachers can use self-inquiry to examine their journey towards becoming teachers both alone and together to understand how their developing knowledge is situated in context (Johnson & Golombek, 2020). Collaboration can counter the negative effects of isolation and make teachers feel more connected (Ostovar-Nameghi & Sheikhahmadi, 2016), which is important for teachers' well-being during times of uncertainty and change. If teachers can collaborate with a wider focus, they may be able to influence school or institutional policies, curricula and practice. Critical reflection as a community on whole school issues and design approaches to development and learning can result in broader changes than what is possible on the individual level (Diaz Maggioli, 2004).

To prepare student teachers to be able to make decisions and transform themselves and their environments, it is important to develop their autonomy. Autonomy in education usually refers to a learner's capacity to manage their own learning (Benson, 2011). Teacher autonomy can lead to increased motivation and self-confidence (Finsterwald et al., 2013). In terms of sustainability, autonomous teachers are likely to be better decision-makers (Vescio et al., 2008), which can increase their adaptability during times of change. Autonomy is also a factor in teacher well-being (Mercer, 2021). We acknowledge that autonomy in student teachers' future careers will be somewhat dependent on factors outside of the individual. However, teachers who understand their own agency within a wider context can transform their environments as well as be transformed by those around them in a process of co-adaptation (Larsen-Freeman, 2019).

To illustrate how sustainability can be applied in an LTE program, we provide some examples from our Graduate Certificate of TESOL and Master of Applied Linguistics and TESOL courses at Macquarie University. Firstly, we embed critical and collaborative reflection throughout the foundation study units. From the beginning of their course, student teachers are asked to critically reflect on their future teaching contexts. In their first assessment task in two of our core units, they are asked to consider factors in the classroom, school and wider context that may influence their teaching practice. Throughout these units, they analyse and prepare for potential problems that may arise, always including factors at both the classroom and the wider level, whilst being flexible in the moment. Following classroom activities that demonstrate English language teaching principles, student teachers collaboratively reflect on their experience undertaking the activity as a student and as a teacher, including any adaptations required for their contexts.

Online microteaching tasks allow students to provide peer feedback and collaboratively reflect on their developing teaching practice (Bodis et al., 2020). During microteaching, student teachers have an opportunity to practice new ideas in short activities in groups. Not only does this provide 'structured mediational spaces' for student teachers to be supported into their teaching careers (Johnson & Golombek, 2020, p. 117), but it also provides a good starting point for individual and collaborative reflection. Throughout the foundation unit focused on language teaching methodologies, student teachers upload microteaching videos to our online unit page using Voice-Thread (www.voicethread.com), a multimodal asynchronous interactive platform. Videos, interactive online tasks, peer feedback on VoiceThread and discussion forums on our learning management system scaffold students to integrate ELT methodologies in practice, learn how to provide constructive feedback to others and understand the principles of reflection. During the semester, students reflect collaboratively and individually on their teaching and work towards their own professional development goals through actionable steps. A culture of sustained reflection and collaboration is encouraged. Thus, our students do not merely demonstrate flexibility and adaptability to the new teaching mode but develop the habit of reflecting critically on their teaching and relating their observations to their future practice.

In the meantime, student teachers are supported to develop their confidence and autonomy. They are encouraged to manage their own learning, and are able to make choices about how they study and what they focus on, using key principles of autonomy (Benson, 2011). They can learn in any mode and can flexibly switch between modes according to their circumstances. There are options about how to complete tasks according to preferences. They can choose the context that they wish to focus on and design lessons for, allowing them to zero in on their area of interest. In addition, as student teachers learn to provide feedback to each other through modelling and scaffolded tasks, they gradually take control of the process of peer feedback until they are independent (Bodis et al., 2020). Classroom tasks are student-centred, and student teachers are supported over time to take on more leadership roles in the classroom. Developing teachers' autonomy prepares them to make decisions about teaching and learning in the future (Vescio et al., 2008) and is a key skill of sustainability in teacher education.

Recommendations for building sustainability

We propose the following ways to integrate sustainability into LTE programs although they may be more widely useful for teacher education in general. We direct these suggestions to teacher educators and include practical tips for embedding sustainability into their programs.

Adaptability

The aim is to develop student teachers' adaptive expertise at a micro level in the classroom, widening out to a macro level, with an ecological perspective.

- Focus on developing flexibility in lesson planning; ask student teachers to imagine potential issues that might occur during teaching, including

changing location, equipment available, student numbers, behavioural issues, etc. Students can make contingency plans to deal with change.
- Prepare students for flexibility that may be required during a teaching career, e.g., covering a class at the last minute without much preparation, changing modes at the last minute or teaching a hybrid class. Classroom activities and role plays can give students opportunities to experience these kinds of situations in a supported environment.
- Demonstrate and verbalise how you, as a teacher educator, are adapting in the classroom to unexpected events. This helps model your thought process and prepare them for flexibility in the classroom. For example, if there are fewer students in class due to a weather event, you can explain how you are changing the activity to make allowances for the smaller class size. While these kinds of in-the-moment decisions are often second nature to an expert teacher, novices are still developing this understanding of teaching and benefit from making the normally invisible processes visible (Bransford et al., 2005). This will also require teacher educators to be reflective.
- Incorporate the need to express adaptability in assessment tasks, e.g., assessing the skill to adapt an activity plan to a changed situation.

Critical and collaborative reflection

Student teachers should have ongoing opportunities to critically reflect on tasks, teaching practices and their wider contexts both individually and collectively in a supportive environment.

- Ensure that class tasks and assessment tasks include critical reflection, for example, analysing how contextual factors might affect the teaching and learning environment, challenging ingrained beliefs about teaching and learning and developing an openness to try new ideas.
- Provide ample opportunities for student teachers to engage in microteaching in groups, giving them practice in teaching skills as well as gradually constructing their teacher identities. These are an excellent start for individual and group reflection.
- Include opportunities for student teachers to reflect with each other, especially by giving feedback and working through teaching and learning problems. It is important to scaffold the kind of feedback that is expected from peers and monitor how this occurs, particularly in the initial stages, to ensure this is a supportive process.
- Give student teachers opportunities to utilise and build on feedback to create short- and long-term professional development goals. Encourage them to develop their own plans about how they will meet their goals.

- Discuss teacher well-being in class and consider ways in which teachers can look after themselves and others as a learning community. Understand the interacting factors that may affect teacher well-being, from an ecological standpoint (Mercer, 2021).

Autonomy

Student teachers should have opportunities to make choices about how and what they learn and take on leadership roles in the learning process.

- Provide choices for students to manage their own learning, whether this is through investigating topics of personal relevance, choosing how they wish to learn or how to use the learning resources.
- Facilitate student-centred classes where the student teachers can take leadership roles and work together. Giving students, individually or in groups, the chance to teach or lead the class is a valuable preparation for their future careers.
- Help student teachers develop a robust and dynamic Professional Learning Network to help them meet their future needs as teachers. This also assists student teachers to understand contextual factors that might affect them. Class tasks or projects could involve investigating organisations or professional communities in their context and what they could gain from by connecting with them.

Conclusion

We strongly believe that promoting *sustainability* is the best preparation of student teachers for their professional lives. We also acknowledge that there are limitations to the extent to which student teachers will be able to implement skills and mindsets developed in LTE in future practice. From an ecological perspective, well-being is both the responsibility of the individual and the system (Mercer, 2021), and contextual factors are likely to have an impact. Equally, teachers need space to be autonomous in their workplaces and classrooms as much as they need an understanding of autonomy in teaching and learning (Vieira, 2017). We acknowledge the emphasis in this chapter on the individual, and that systemic change is needed to support teachers in their working lives. However, this kind of macro change is beyond the scope of teacher education, and, as discussed, future events and challenges cannot be predicted. Therefore, the best way forward is to prepare student teachers to analyse and critically reflect on their own contexts, autonomously make decisions, create communities and adapt to changes as they arise. Preparing teachers to take on a role 'as agents of change' (Vieira, 2017, p. 694), who can work to improve conditions individually and collectively, may affect systemic change from the bottom up.

Considering the rapidly dynamic and changing conditions of English language teaching, we recommend that teacher educators implement more sustainable approaches to LTE. The focus on skills that are relevant in today's world alone will not adequately prepare student teachers for their futures in education, as evidenced by the COVID pandemic or changes in education induced by artificial intelligence. A broader ecological approach is needed, with an understanding of wider contextual factors and their influence on teaching and learning. In addition, teacher education should focus on mindsets which will assist student teachers to prepare for an unknown future. This is where the reflective mindset and adaptive expertise will converge. By the end of their training, student teachers should be able to make decisions autonomously as well as create communities: in fact, some of these may be established during teacher education which can be utilised in the future. As shown throughout this chapter, these mindsets will help teachers increase their efficacy, engagement and well-being in their future careers through change and uncertainty.

References

Barfield, A. (2016). Collaboration. *ELT Journal, 70*(2), 222–224. https://doi.org/10.1093/elt/ccv074

Bawa, P. (2022). *Preparing faculty for technology-dependency in the post-COVID-19 era*. IGI Global.

Benson, P. (2011). *Teaching and researching autonomy* (2nd ed.). Longman.

Bissessar, C. (2021). *Emergency remote learning, teaching and leading: Global perspectives*. Springer. https://doi.org/10.1007/978-3-030-76591-0

Bodis, A., Reed, M., & Kharchenko, Y. (2020). Microteaching in isolation: Fostering autonomy and learner engagement through VoiceThread. *International Journal of TESOL Studies, 2*, 1–12. https://doi.org/10.46451/ijts.2020.09.14

Bransford, J., Derry, S., Berliner, D., Hammerness, K., & Beckett, K. L. (2005). Theories of learning and their roles in teaching. In L. Darling-Hammond & J. Bransford (Eds.), *Preparing teachers for a changing world: What teachers should learn and be able to do*. Jossey-Bass.

Bruce, E., & Stakounis, H. (2021). *The impact of COVID-19 on the UK EAP sector: An examination of how organisations delivering EAP were affected and responded in terms of academic delivery and operational procedures*. BALEAP. https://www.baleap.org/wp-content/uploads/2021/06/BALEAP-Report-Covid-and-EAP-May-2021.pdf

Burns, A., & Knox, J. S. (2011). Classrooms as complex adaptive systems: A relational model. *TESL-EJ, 15*(1), 25.

Chappell, P. (2017). Interrogating your wisdom of practice to improve classroom practices. *ELT Journal, 71*(4), 433–444. https://doi.org/10.1093/elt/ccx004

Chappell, P., Bodis, A., & Jackson, H. (2015). The impact of teacher cognition and classroom practices on IELTS test preparation courses in the Australian ELICOS sector. IELTS Research Reports. https://www.ielts.org/for-researchers/research-reports/online-series-2015-6

Chen, J. (2021). *Emergency remote teaching and beyond: Voices from world language teachers and researchers*. Springer. https://doi.org/10.4018/978-1-7998-9538-1.ch008

Choi, L., & Chung, S. (2021). Navigating online language teaching in uncertain times: Challenges and strategies of EFL educators in creating a sustainable technology-mediated language learning environment. *Sustainability*, *13*(7664), 1–14. https://doi.org/10.3390/su13147664

Collie, R., Guay, F., Martin, A. J., Caldecott-Davis, K., & Granziera, H. (2020). Examining the unique roles of adaptability and buoyancy in teachers' work-related outcomes. *Teachers and Teaching, Theory and Practice*, *26*(3–4), 350–364. https://doi.org/10.1080/13540602.2020.1832063

Collie, R., & Martin, A. J. (2016). Adaptability: An important capacity for effective teachers. *Educational Practice and Theory*, *38*(1), 27–39. https://doi.org/10.7459/ept/38.1.03

Collie, R., Shapka, J. D., Perry, N. E., & Martin, A. J. (2015). Teacher well-being: Exploring its components and a practice-oriented scale. *Journal of Psychoeducational Assessment*, *33*(8), 744–756. https://doi.org/10.1177/0734282915587990

Diaz Maggioli, G. (2004). *Teacher-centered professional development*. ASCD.

English Australia. (n.d.). *Approaches to hybrid English language teaching*. Retrieved October 10, 2022, from https://www.englishaustralia.com.au/professional-development/online-courses

Farrell, T. S. C. (2016). Anniversary article: The practices of encouraging TESOL teachers to engage in reflective practice: An appraisal of recent research contributions. *Language Teaching Research*, *20*(2), 223–247. https://doi.org/10.1177/1362168815617335

Farrell, T. S. C. (2019). 'My training has failed me': Inconvenient truths about second language teacher education (SLTE). *TESL-EJ*, *22*(4).

Farrell, T. S. C. (2022). *Reflective practice in language teaching*. Cambridge University Press. https://doi.org/10.1017/9781009028783

Finsterwald, M., Wagner, P., Schober, B., Lüftenegger, M., & Spiel, C. (2013). Fostering lifelong learning – Evaluation of a teacher education program for professional teachers. *Teaching and Teacher Education: An International Journal of Research and Studies*, *29*(C), 144–155. https://doi.org/10.1016/j.tate.2012.08.009

Gravett, S., & Petersen, N. (2022). *Future-proofing teacher education*. Routledge.

Hockly, N. (2023). Artificial intelligence in English language teaching: The good, the bad and the ugly. *RELC Journal*. https://doi.org/10.1177/00336882231168504

Hoffman, J. V., & Duffy, G. G. (2016). Does thoughtfully adaptive teaching actually exist? A challenge to teacher educators. *Theory into Practice*, *55*(3), 172–179. https://doi.org/10.1080/00405841.2016.1173999

Johnson, K. E., & Golombek, P. R. (2020). Informing and transforming language teacher education pedagogy. *Language Teaching Research*, *24*(1), 116–127. https://doi.org/10.1177/1362168818777539

Larsen-Freeman, D. (1997). Chaos/complexity science and second language acquisition. *Applied Linguistics*, *18*(2), 141–165. https://doi.org/10.1093/applin/18.2.141

Larsen-Freeman, D. (2019). On language learner agency: A complex dynamic systems theory perspective. *The Modern Language Journal*, *103*, 61–79. https://doi.org/10.1111/modl.12536

Larsen-Freeman, D., & Cameron, L. (2008). *Complex systems and applied linguistics*. Oxford University Press.

MacIntyre, P. D., Gregersen, T., & Mercer, S. (2020). Language teachers' coping strategies during the Covid-19 conversion to online teaching: Correlations with stress, wellbeing and negative emotions. *System*, *94*, 1–13. https://doi.org/10.1016/j.system.2020.102352

Marks, H. M., & Louis, K. S. (1997). Does teacher empowerment affect the classroom? The implications of teacher empowerment for instructional practice and student academic performance. *Educational Evaluation and Policy Analysis*, *19*(3), 245–275. https://doi.org/10.3102/01623737019003245

Mavridi, S. (2022). *Language teaching experiences during COVID-19*. British Council.

Mercer, S. (2021). An agenda for well-being in ELT: An ecological perspective. *ELT Journal*, *75*(1), 14–21. https://doi.org/10.1093/elt/ccaa062

Moser, K. M., Wei, T., & Brenner, D. (2021). Remote teaching during COVID-19: Implications from a national survey of language educators. *System*, *97*, 1–15, https://doi.org/10.1016/j.system.2020.102431

Musetti, B. (2018). Project planning and sustainability. In J. I. Liontas (Ed.), *The TESOL encyclopedia of English language teaching* (pp. 1–7). John Wiley & Sons. https://doi.org/10.1002/9781118784235.eelt0134

Neilsen, R., Weinmann, M., & Arber, R. (2020). Editorial: Teaching and learning English in the age of COVID-19: Reflecting on the state of TESOL in a changed world. *TESOL in Context*, *29*(2), 1–13. https://doi.org/10.21153/tesol2020vol29no2art1427

Ostovar-Nameghi, S. A., & Sheikhahmadi, M. (2016). From teacher isolation to teacher collaboration: Theoretical perspectives and empirical findings. *English Language Teaching*, *9*(5), 197–205. https://doi.org/10.5539/elt.v9n5p197

Paesani, K. (2020). Teacher professional development and online instruction: Cultivating coherence and sustainability. *Foreign Language Annals*, *53*(2), 292–297. https://doi.org/10.1111/flan.12468

Parsons, S. A., & Vaughn, M. (2016). Toward adaptability: Where to from here? *Theory into Practice*, *55*(3), 267–274. https://doi.org/10.1080/00405841.2016.1173998

Pinner, R. S., & Sampson, R. J. (2021). Humanizing TESOL research through the lens of complexity thinking. *TESOL Quarterly*, *55*(2), 633–642. https://doi.org/10.1002/tesq.604

Rapanta, C., Botturi, L., Goodyear, P., Guàrdia, L., & Koole, M. (2020). Online university teaching during and after the Covid-19 crisis: Refocusing teacher presence and learning activity. *Postdigital Science and Education*, *2*(3), 923–945. https://doi.org/10.1007/s42438-020-00155-y

Schleicher, A. (2020). *The impact of COVID-19 on education: Insights from education at a glance 2020*. Organisation for Economic Co-operation and Development. https://www.oecd.org/education/the-impact-of-covid-19-on-education-insights-education-at-a-glance-2020.pdf

Schön, D. A. (1994). *The reflective practitioner: How professionals think in action*. Routledge.

Shin, D. (2020). Introduction: TESOL and the COVID-19 pandemic. *TESOL Journal*, *11*(3), 1–3. https://doi.org/10.1002/tesj.547

Sutton, R. E., & Wheatley, K. F. (2003). Teachers' emotions and teaching: A review of the literature and directions for future research. *Educational Psychology Review*, *15*(4), 327–358. https://doi.org/10.1023/A:1026131715856

Vescio, V., Ross, D., & Adams, A. (2008). A review of research on the impact of professional learning communities on teaching practice and student learning.

Teaching and Teacher Education: An International Journal of Research and Studies, 24(1), 80–91. https://doi.org/10.1016/j.tate.2007.01.004

Vieira, F. (2017). Task-based instruction for autonomy: Connections with contexts of practice, conceptions of teaching, and professional development strategies. *TESOL Quarterly, 51*(3), 693–715. https://doi.org/10.1002/tesq.384

Walsh, S., & Mann, S. (2015). Doing reflective practice: A data-led way forward. *ELT Journal, 69*(4), 351–362. https://doi.org/10.1093/elt/ccv018

Wong, J. O. (2020). A pandemic in 2020, Zoom and the arrival of the online educator. *International Journal of TESOL Studies, 2*(3), 82–99. https://doi.org/10.46451/ijts.2020.09.19

Yuan, R., & Yang, M. (2022). Unpacking language teacher educators' expertise: A complexity theory perspective. *TESOL Quarterly, 56*(2), 656–687. https://doi.org/10.1002/tesq.3088

3
UNDERSTANDING THE NEEDS OF INTERNATIONAL EAP STUDENTS

Adaptive progress

Justine Light, Denise Lo, and Martin Guardado

Background

English for Academic Purposes (EAP) is a branch of English for Specific Purposes (ESP) aimed at providing learners with the language skills required for success in post-secondary or institutional academic settings. EAP can be viewed as a singular form of ESL instruction as it is burdened by a high-stakes need for specific transitional skills development and maintaining a strong transactional currency, as it is often a gatekeeper of progression into terminal programmes. The specific nature of EAP provides a unique context for conducting needs analysis (NA). "Needs analysis" or "needs assessment" are terms used widely in EAP programmes and can be defined as a preliminary evaluation of teaching and learning objectives to aid in effective EAP programme curriculum development (Sönmez, 2019). Data from an EAP needs analysis can serve to inform the curriculum that successfully helps the learner to transition to a new context as well as to engage the learner through meaningful programming. Effective EAP instruction must begin with determining the academic context in which English will be used, prompting early course design to be conducted through an assessment of learner needs (Tajino et al., 2005). The term "need" may refer to components of language relating to either productive, such as spoken and written language skills, or receptive performance, reading, and listening skills (Generoso & Arbon, 2020) and represent perceived learner necessities in academic English language ability (Martins, 2017). The needs learners will encounter in their post-EAP programmes might vary greatly across programmes and disciplines, not to mention the dynamic and sometimes unpredictable nature of academic discourse practices and expectations (Duff, 2010). Thus, there needs to be recognition and awareness that any NA process will necessarily be incomplete. NA encompasses a range of objectives relating to curriculum development and renewal to ensure continued programme efficacy. Amirian and Tavakoli (2009) suggest NA to be a prerequisite of course development due to the diversity and highly situational nature of learner needs, achieved through the collection of information on preferred learning styles of students, specific skill acquisition, and the role of teachers and learners within classroom activities (Duddley-Evans & John, 1998).

Research has found NA to be advantageous in terms of learner outcomes and course efficacy (Smith et al., 2022), suggesting NA may support learner motivation as course material represents practical skills sought out by learners (Basturkmen, 2014; Hyland, 1997). Additionally, NA provides educators with insights into both immediate needs and idealized final behaviour (Ajideh, 2009) as well as a lens to view narrow and broad range needs within and outside of the scope of a restrictive course syllabus (Brunton, 2009).

While constituting an integral component of EAP course design and ongoing classroom assessment, how to generate robust and useful NA information from learners, educators, and stakeholders has been largely overlooked until recent years. Assimilation of technology into EAP classrooms has prompted rapid adaptation of computer use by learners and educators alike, which poses novel challenges in regions with low digital literacy (Eslami, 2010). Moreover, variability in access to digital technologies and high-speed internet, along with the freedom to access language learning applications, has expanded our understanding of how digital inequality may be defined. Similarly, the COVID-19 pandemic and transition to emergency remote teaching (ERT) urged scholars to more thoughtfully consider learner needs and the ways in which learners may be assessed. Thus, the first section of the chapter will provide an overview of current approaches to conducting needs analyses as well as propositions to improve the generalizability of such findings. It will also discuss some of the challenges to conducting NA, including regional variability in EAP learner needs, and finally differences related to the varied academic discourse patterns of different terminal programmes of study.

Current approaches to needs analysis

NA serves a foundational role in curriculum design by introducing the learner to the expectations of the EAP programme itself and the institution. For learners, NA is valuable in identifying how English will be used in their field of study (Riazi et al., 2020), while educators are provided with insights into prospective students' current or entrance academic language proficiency (Mackay & Mountford, 1978). Needs analyses are conducted via assessment tools that often include questionnaires, interviews, observation, self-ratings, and group discussion in isolation or in combination depending on researcher's methodological preferences or expertise and resource availability (Chegeni & Chegeni, 2013; Kohoutová, 2006). Data collection through observation of classrooms and exam marking sessions (if these sessions are part of the programme) is an integral component to determine how success is defined by individual educators and the variation which may exist between current and historical EAP curricula (Guardado & Light, 2020). Additionally, assessments of learners' GPA records and course completion rates are reflective of learner experiences in the course, and while not isolating problematic areas for learners, may be indicative of discrepancies between learners and educators perceived language needs.

When conducting NA, it is important to consider the demographics of learners relating to their current skills and competencies, potential areas of weakness, and cognitive styles (Tajino et al., 2005). However, as posited by Duddley-Evans and St. John (1998), the findings of NA depend largely on the interpretation of who is asking the questions. Such an inherent bias is further amplified in common data collection methodology as, most often, surveys are utilized by EAP course designers and researchers to collect responses from many individuals (Hyland, 2006). This is problematic in determining the reliability and validity of NA findings[1] as the open-endedness of survey responses or one type of data alone cannot provide researchers with a complete picture of actual learner needs (Long, 2005; Smith et al., 2022). Thus, recent research relating to NA has often employed a triangulated approach involving a variety of participants and measures, ranging from self-assessment survey responses to non-participant observation (Ahmadi & Afshar, 2020; Atai & Nazari, 2011). For instance, Smith et al. (2022) conducted a NA of EAP learners using a mixed method triangulated approach to data collection, suggesting that quantitative and qualitative data collection from multiple sources would serve to mitigate individual weaknesses of any individual approach conducted in isolation. Findings supported the importance of validation through data triangulation when conducting NA, a conclusion echoed by other scholars in EAP and NA (Huang, 2010; Önder Özdemir, 2014; Serafini et al., 2015; Sönmez, 2019).

Data triangulation involves responses from a variety of sources, including current and former EAP students, educators, administrators, and external stakeholders such as academic faculty partners (Guardado & Light,

2020). The inclusion of stakeholder responses offers insight into specific academic literacy skills required for success in the learner's field of study and future career, a necessary component of EAP curriculum design. Thus, understanding the academic literacy skills required for learner success is essential for consideration, as such skill demands may be misaligned with the perceived needs of the learners themselves. Standard qualitative consulting procedures for data elicitation, such as semi-structured interviews, offer an opportunity for comparisons to be drawn between educators and professionals in the learner's field of study (Mansur & Shrestha, 2015). Further differentiation of a learner's actual needs for academic skills development from educator pedagogical beliefs allows EAP course designers to narrow a course syllabus to reflect academic literacy needs more accurately. As data collection methodology has become increasingly sophisticated, utilizing combinations of stakeholder responses, previous EAP course material, assignments, and lecture or seminar observations becomes a necessity in the process (Guardado & Light, 2020). Long (2005) argues for the importance of pilot testing NA materials, a step often overlooked by EAP course designers (Serafini et al., 2015). This allows course developers and researchers to avoid repetition, complex writing, and leading or irrelevant questions, aiding in both reduction of researcher bias and accurately representing potential learner needs.

Interference or a lack of institutional support poses an additional challenge to EAP educators, as findings from learner NA may go beyond educator jurisdiction for curriculum reform. Such a challenge was identified by Fazel and Ali (2022) during a study of Canadian and Malaysian educators regarding how EAP students received summative and formative assessments. In the Malaysian context, assessment and guidelines for learners were referred to as "ready-made" or "fixed" in the educational institution, giving educators very little flexibility in curriculum implementation. In addition, regional discrepancies between the use of self-assessments between Canadian and Malaysian educators were brought to light, with no Malaysian educators reporting their use of learner self-assessment in the EAP classroom. Various studies have been conducted examining the NA of productive performance and receptive performance skills in regions across the globe. These include the importance of speaking skills for learners and educators in Taiwan (Chien & Hsu, 2011), difficulty in oral academic activities for learners in Malaysia (Mahfoodh, 2014), implications of reading comprehension on writing performance for learners in Korea (Moon et al., 2019), the learner needs for grammar and writing skill development in Ghana (Gborsong et al., 2015), and writing skill development in Iran (Pourshahian et al., 2012). This expansive global range of learner needs assessments provides insights into the areas in which learners often find their skills to be lacking and exemplifies how NA can inform educators of best practices for course design.

Responses of needs analysis to emergency remote teaching

As approaches to conducting NA have become more sophisticated over recent decades, the COVID-19 pandemic imposed a massive new challenge to both educators and learners following the transition to ERT. Not only did the EAP course transition to online delivery push teachers to reconsider their previous pedagogical approaches in the classroom, but it also forced the rapid acclimation of learners to course content delivery through a digital interface. Given that an essential component of language learning comes from interaction (Long, 1983), restrictions imposed upon learners by ERT, such as asynchronous lectures and lack of regular feedback, may hinder language development in an EAP classroom (Davies et al., 2020). Additionally, numerous learners reported limited computer or internet access in their homes, inhibiting their access to class materials, a finding echoed by emergent literature following educational institutions' rapid transition to online course delivery (McPhee & Lyon, 2020). As computer integration in EAP classrooms has increased dramatically in recent years, greater attention must be paid to the individual needs of learners regarding digital literacy and access during course design. As technology expands the options for EAP learning opportunities beyond those with the means and opportunity to be physically present in overseas locales, analysis of learner needs must also advance in its efficacy in digital formats. This new consideration during course design reiterates the importance of data triangulation and the emphasis on external stakeholder responses. Domain professionals in the learner's area of study represent responses of critical importance during curriculum design or reform, as their identification of technology proficiency for learner academic skill development should be reflected in the technology integration of EAP courses (Dashtestani, 2019). In addition, educator limitations regarding technology and computer literacy are indicative of the extent to which technology integration can be successfully implemented in EAP classrooms. Similarly, EAP instructors are often ill-equipped to act as technical support for students facing difficulties with their devices and must receive institutional support or training to adequately address challenges faced by learners (Kohnke & Jarvis, 2021). This is also compounded by the fact that educators can find themselves overwhelmed by the multiple additional demands posed by remote course delivery, including the lack of enough support from programme administration, pedagogical adjustments, and inadequate materials, to mention only a few.

Case study analysis

Introduction

The past few years have seen a number of transformative leaps forward in not only the delivery modality for EAP but also in how technology has been integrated into all aspects of teaching and learning, how post-secondary target programmes are changing approaches to undergraduate study, and more. In our chapter, we committed to considering the personal experience of an EAP instructor through an autoethnographic perspective on these changes. As Adams et al. (2015) describe, autoethnography is a research method that uses "personal experience to describe and critique beliefs, practices, and experiences" (p. 1). Moreover, they go on to posit that autoethnography values the researchers' relationships, reflections, emotions, and creativity. By including this instructor's autoethnographic story, we show that we value the instructor's personal narrative and identity in the midst of change on a global scale. As we go on to consider the future of EAP NA, we will reflect on emerging trends presented in the literature alongside the experiences of one instructor during the past few years of upheaval in EAP teaching and learning.

Instructor autoethnographic sketch

Prior to 2020, I (second author) had been teaching EAP for approximately 8 years in a face-to-face setting with a class size of 16–21 international students at a large university in Edmonton, Canada. I participated in the curriculum updates, which were based on needs identified through triangulated consultations with external and internal stakeholders (Guardado & Light, 2020). At that time, my definition of NA fitted with what Brown (1995) (as cited in Brown, 2009, p. 269) describes as a "systematic collection and analysis of all subjective and objective information necessary to define and validate defensible curriculum purposes that satisfy the language learning requirements of the students within the context of particular institutions that influence the learning and teaching situation." I relied heavily on the needs identified by the EAP programme through a target-situation analysis approach (Brown, 2009).

My dependence on the EAP programme to identify student needs gradually shifted as computer integration increased in the language classroom and the university. I began to become aware that the heavy focus on specific methods to assess language proficiency may not be aligned with the language skills expected of students in the undergraduate context. My feeling of this increasing gap only grew wider as dependence on educational technology grew rapidly over the course of the COVID-19 pandemic, and all classes transitioned to ERT almost overnight. The switch to online delivery allowed me to further examine the academic skills that would prove useful in an online classroom compared to a face-to-face one; moreover, I was pushed to rethink my approach to NA. The pandemic transformed the EAP classroom and the academic skills along with it. Consequently, substantial adjustments to the NA process were necessary to cope with it.

Emergency remote teaching

In March 2020, all the classes at the university were rapidly transitioned to online delivery over a weekend. I was halfway through a 2-month term working with a class of 19 students. During this transition, I focused on helping my students adjust to a completely new classroom experience. There was a lot of uncertainty for everyone. I felt I had to provide not only the academic support of my students but also their emotional support for all the upheaval they were experiencing. I switched into survival mode, doing what was needed as opposed to what was ideal. Now, reflecting back, I can see that prioritizing the students' mental health needs over academic needs in the initial weeks proved to be the right choice. As an instructor, creating a learning environment that factors in mental health and student well-being is equally as important as helping students develop their target language skills.

Despite the regular use of technology and devices in the face-to-face classroom, online delivery magnified the discrepancies in computer and internet access at home for students. For some, a stable internet connection proved to be a challenge both for those within Canada and abroad, while others did not have a computer or device at home that was compatible with the software used to live stream a synchronous online class or that was reliable for a 3-hour class. At the initial stage of the transition to remote learning, I felt the students' anxiety and frustrations as they tried to scramble to get the necessary equipment on their own and not miss hours of class with each passing day. Thinking back, I believe it would have relieved some stress for students to have access to recorded lectures at the start of the transition. I also now realize that as education depends more on technology and online delivery, digital inclusion (The Center for Digital Equity, 2022) is something I have to prioritize moving forward.

In addition to considering my student's access to technology, the abrupt shift to online delivery also exposed the varying degrees of digital literacy in my class. During the first three weeks, students required constant support through lengthy emails or after-class support. It was very draining and exhausting for me as I was also adjusting to the switch, but I felt they needed it at the time as everything had changed so quickly. This experience was eye-opening for me. I had often assumed that most of my students were digital natives and that their familiarity with technology would translate to digital literacy in the classroom. This did not seem to be the case when it came to software or applications they were not familiar with.

The new normal

After many terms teaching remotely, I now understand that there is a difference between delivering a class online using an in-person curriculum and activities and delivering an online class where the curriculum and activities reflect the needs and skills of students in an online environment. Unfortunately, it took a great deal of trial and error to reach this conclusion. This was in part because the abrupt switch to online left little to no time or resources dedicated to fully developing an online class.

One of my struggles was trying to meet students' online learning needs through activities and assessments originally designed for a face-to-face class. Often, it felt like trying to create a learning environment that was no longer authentic to the academic experience students would have post-EAP. The pre-pandemic learning objectives did not focus on preparing students to understand how to use online tools appropriately to assist their language learning, but based on the trajectory of technology in education, I knew I would be doing my students a disservice if I did not adapt my course materials. I also found that many of the issues I faced, like finding reliable assessment methods, were rooted in trying to replicate the face-to-face assessments instead of embracing assessments that would be more reliable in an online classroom, such as the use of translators, online grammar editing programmes, hired help, or keeping consistent timing for each student. I knew I would not be able to get an accurate sample of the students' language proficiency using the traditional methods, so I began to experiment with different approaches.

I decided to switch to a bi-weekly reading interview format by using a text we had previously discussed and had completed analytical activities as a class. This approach encouraged students to ask as many questions as they wanted about the text during the in-class discussion and generated authentic comprehension questions they had about the text as they knew I would then ask them about it. This also meant they would be less inclined to rely on translation software. The interviews were low stakes with a small grade. Feedback was given using a rubric using the learning objective in the curriculum. During the interview, students were asked comprehension questions reflecting the learning objectives and students were given time to explain their answers. The difficulty of the questions was based on each student's language proficiency. This approach allowed insight into each student's thinking process and offered a more accurate understanding of their reading, listening, and speaking abilities. After each interview, students were reminded to apply the reading strategies we had used in class, like annotated reading and vocabulary analysis, based on the depth of understanding of the text. While these interviews seemed time intensive, both the students and I found them truly valuable as they provided much-needed one-on-one time to build rapport and also to conduct a micro NA for each student. Once these interviews became part of the class routine, we all looked forward to the meetings. Towards the end of the term, they became weekly meetings with a focus on providing feedback and micro NA for other language skills, like writing and pronunciation.

Building rapport among students was just as challenging but necessary to build group cohesion. However, students were generally reluctant to turn on their mic to speak when in a large group in a virtual classroom. To facilitate more inter-student engagement, I encouraged students to use reaction buttons (clap, thumbs up, etc.) and use the chat box to ask and answer questions or leave casual comments. I did this by modeling using those functions when students were presenting or doing group work. With these functions, engagement increased substantially, and some even made jokes in the chat box. I soon realized that the chat box was a powerful tool for students to communicate with each other. This was a language skill that was not included in the pre-pandemic NA.

The journey from vulnerability to agency

As the pandemic progressed and online delivery for all university courses became the norm, it was clear that the needs identified with pre-pandemic assessment no longer reflected the demands for a fully remote or hybrid undergraduate experience. The ability to identify these needs became more difficult as the academic skills required to fully prepare students for their academic careers became a moving target as university courses were rapidly adapting their assessment and delivery methods. A handwritten five-paragraph essay became less relevant as some faculties were purchasing online grammar editing software for students to use on all assignments. This struggle was compounded by sudden policy changes, like mandatory exam monitoring tools and varying ad hoc approaches to online teaching, with some classes conducted entirely asynchronously or synchronously and everything in between. Having to respond to these rapid changes tested my flexibility and adaptability as an instructor and pushed me to be more digitally agile. It also changed my approach to NA and pushed me to regain instructor agency. I had to first look to my students for their mental health needs which was difficult for a large-scale NA to address. I learned that by doing more regular informal micro NA with my students throughout the term, I was able to generate useful needs information and tailor a more fitting course for my students, which in turn increased their intrinsic motivation. I also looked to other professors for insight into how they were adjusting their classroom practices by attending Learning Festivals to gain the most up-to-date insight, as it was logistically impossible for the EAP programme to conduct a traditional NA with the respective stakeholders at that time. The pandemic has expedited the integration of technology in the classroom and has created a remote learning environment that is now the norm for both students and instructors. Being mindful of digital inclusion will now be equally as important for me as an instructor to consider moving forward. While not all classes will remain remote post-pandemic, the role of technology in the language classroom will remain, and the importance of encouraging instructor-led NA will continue to be valuable and beneficial to student learning.

Future considerations for EAP and NA

What have we learned in this period of time when our perceptions of teaching and learning language mediated by technology have been dramatically propelled forward? Teachers for whom technology was often an afterthought or a compartmentalized tool for one specific aspect of EAP instruction have now taught courses, or indeed multiple courses, entirely online. Teachers and learners alike have found novel opportunities, efficacies, or conveniences in being able to access language learning solely through online modalities. How do we maintain this momentum and leverage what we have learned to improve access and equity for English language learners to opportunities to develop academic English skills and achieve success in an English language medium of instruction or post-secondary study in an English-speaking context? What can the instructor in our case study take from her experiences during a time of the pedagogical shift and apply in her "post-" or normal teaching life? Simply put, in terms of needs assessment for EAP students, what should we preserve from our experiences during our collective dramatically changed realities for teaching and learning, and what may not have longevity beyond its usefulness in an urgent and sudden response to the unknown?

Managing bias in NA

Discomfort with our dramatically changed modality of teaching and assessing needs forced us to shift away from normalized and routinized patterns of assessing needs. As we have broken our routines, perhaps it is time to reconsider how our previous needs assessments may have been prone to bias. To what extent did our bias inform the ways we constructed NA tools, how we asked the questions, and how we drove the agenda of our own inquiry? An emerging trend in NA has been described as the need for data triangulation (Ahmadi & Afshar, 2020; Huang, 2010; Önder Özdemir, 2014; Serafini et al., 2015; Smith et al., 2022; Sönmez, 2019). As we have opened ourselves to utilizing new methods of data collection for NA, the opportunity to consider how we can decrease the impact of bias on our NA should be addressed. Reducing the impact of bias through using the data triangulation technique (Huang, 2010; Önder Özdemir, 2014; Serafini et al., 2015; Sönmez, 2019) can enable us to collect needs assessment data that is more robust and represents learners' true language skill gaps and needs more effectively. Triangulating data by authentically exploring the post-secondary learning environment where EAP learners are headed will enhance the success of those learners as well as potentially result in higher levels of learner engagement as students see the relevance of courses, assignments, and feedback to their ultimate goals (Guardado & Light, 2020). Our case study instructor described how the existing approach to using a five-paragraph handwritten essay quickly emerged as an ineffective task for authentic assessment as the undergraduate target programmes of learners encouraged the use of grammar editing software and writing tools. As the educational world is shifting, NA that clings to past approaches and is rooted in teacher preferences over learner realities will be ineffective in developing meaningful teaching plans.

NA as a fundamentally cyclical process

It has been argued that the NA of EAP programmes should be viewed as cyclical in nature (Guardado & Light, 2020). Once a teaching plan is implemented as a result of an NA, gauging the impact on learners is critical. The NA should not be viewed as a one-off event. It is continuous and cyclical and represents a process some view as living. The notion of classroom learning as a balance between the plan and the lived experience of the classroom participants (Aoki, 1993) is not novel. This approach means that the NA will feed into the classroom plan and experience, but that the classroom experience will be part of the cycle of NA. While this concept of NA has clearly been evident for decades (Long, 2005), resource support from programmes and institutions, as well as recognition by instructors that NA is not a one-and-done event in their practice, may have been slower to coalesce (Guardado & Light, 2020). The impact of a sudden and dramatic shift in the modalities of teaching and learning may have reawakened awareness.

This notion of the iterative nature of NA was discernible for our case study teacher. As she tested and recognised that new ways of conducting NA were effective or ineffective, she worked to adjust her instructional approach to incorporate this feedback into her plan. Her plan clearly needed to be fluid, and as such, adapting that plan was a given. As dramatic shifts in modality and experience of teaching and learning occurred, novel approaches perhaps never previously considered have been attempted. Suddenly, the need to evaluate how this NA data was collected in novel ways was prescient. Maintaining this view of NA as a cycle, open to continuous adjustment and review, presents a new habit worth maintaining.

Digital literacy

Digital literacy has emerged as a pressing issue in NA (Dashtestani, 2019); once more, this is not an unforeseen or unknown issue among scholars, instructors, or learners themselves. However, the rapid and unrelenting shift to online instruction on a global scale has demanded a re-examination of digital literacy and its impact on needs assessment. This recognition has compelled us to consider how we can strive to conduct a needs assessment with learners who may have a wide range of digital proficiency skills. Dramatic changes in our ways of delivering learning have forced us to ensure our NA tools provide accurate data. Moreover, EAP instructors are uniquely positioned to scaffold learners as they prepare to embark on post-secondary studies. Our case study instructor described her growing awareness of the digital demands that would be placed on her EAP learners once they transitioned to their undergraduate studies. She was attentive to the plethora of digital demands emerging in the undergraduate context and knew that these elements needed to become part of her own teaching plan. She describes the need for digital agility on her part as well as on the part of her learners.

Digital inclusion and equity

A discussion of digital literacy and NA leads readily to a consideration of digital equity and inclusion. Are there takeaways from this transformative time in EAP and post-secondary education which can be leveraged to consider how technology could expand digital inclusion and promote more equitable access to EAP and post-secondary studies in English medium settings? Our initial gains in understanding how to conduct NA in digital settings and with hybrid modalities of instruction both in EAP and post-secondary studies have been largely centered on how to better serve the learners with whom we already work in a time of global crisis. Could we leverage these gains and new understandings in conducting NA in a digital setting to consider who we are choosing to include in these opportunities? Currently, EAP is an expensive undertaking, often preferred to be completed in the country of post-secondary study, meaning multiple years of overseas study and living expenses. As we have learned more about conducting NA and, ultimately, language learning delivery has harnessed technology through varied modalities, can we manage these costs, expand these learning opportunities, and broaden digital inclusion and equity? Our case study instructor described managing a complex online learning environment needing to pay attention to technological access issues, digital literacy, and digital confidence. She addressed these issues and implemented specific strategies to build group cohesion and conduct ongoing NA through micro NA. These advances in our perceptions of how learner needs can be met when mediated through technology could be used to expand access to those learners currently excluded from EAP study abroad options.

Note

1 Although a NA is meant to determine the needs of a particular group of learners, published results are sometimes used to understand or confirm the needs of learners in similar contexts.

References

Adams, T. E., Holman Jones, S., & Ellis, C. (2015). *Autoethnography: Understanding qualitative research.* Oxford University Press.

Ahmadi, M., & Afshar, H. S. (2020). Students' needs or teachers' wishes? A triangulated survey of medical EAP in Iranian context. *Iranian Journal of Applied Language Studies, 2*(12), 225–260. https://doi.org/10.22111/IJALS.2020.5965

Ajideh, P. (2009). Autonomous learning and metacognitive strategies essentials in ESP class. *English Language Teaching, 2*(1), 162–168. Retrieved May 3, 2022, from https://eric.ed.gov/?id=EJ1082227

Amirian, Z., & Tavakoli, M. (2009). Reassessing the ESP courses offered to engineering students in Iran (a case study). *English for Specific Purposes World, 8*(23), 1–13.

Aoki, T. T. (1993). Legitimating lived curriculum: Towards a curricular landscape of multiplicity. *Journal of Curriculum and Supervision, 8*(3), 255–268.

Atai, M. R., & Nazari, O. (2011). Exploring reading comprehension needs of Iranian EAP students of health information management (HIM): A triangulated approach. *System, 39*(1), 30–43. https://doi.org/10.1016/j.system.2011.01.015

Basturkmen, H. (2014). Ideas and options in English for specific purposes. https://doi.org/10.4324/9781410617040

Brown, J. D. (2009). Foreign and second language needs analysis. In M. H. Long & C. J. Doughty (Eds.), *The handbook of language teaching* (pp. 269–293). Blackwell Publishing Ltd. https://doi.org/10.1002/9781444315783.ch16

Brunton, M. (2009). An account of ESP – with possible future directions. *English for Specific Purposes, 8*(3), 1–15.

Chegeni, N., & Chegeni, N. (2013). Language curriculum development and importance of needs analysis. *ELT Voices - India*, *3*(4), 1–13.

Chien, C., & Hsu, M. (2011). Needs-based analyses of freshman English course in a Taiwan university. *International Journal of Humanities and Social Science*, *1*(11), 121–224.

Dashtestani, R. (2019). English for academic purposes instructors' use and acceptance of technology in EAP courses. *CALL-EJ*, *20*(1), 115–134.

Davies, J. A., Davies, L. J., Emerson, J., Hainsworth, H., & McDonough, H. G. (2020). Responding to COVID-19 in EAP contexts: A comparison of courses at four Sino-foreign universities. *International Journal of TESOL Studies*, 32–51. https://doi.org/10.46451/ijts.2020.09.04

Duddley-Evans, T., & John, M. S. (1998). The difference between present and required knowledge goes back to the gap between present know-how and the exigencies. *INTL. International Research Journal of Applied and Basic Sciences*, *4*(5), 1014–1020.

Duff, P. A. (2010). Language socialization into academic discourse communities. *Annual Review of Applied Linguistics*, *30*, 169–192.

Eslami, Z. R. (2010). Teachers' voice vs. students' voice: A needs analysis approach to English for academic purposes (EAP) in Iran. *English Language Teaching*, *3*(1), 3–11.

Fazel, I., & Ali, A. M. (2022). EAP teachers' knowledge and use of learning-oriented assessment: A cross-contextual study. *System*, *104*. https://doi.org/10.1016/j.system.2021.102685

Gborsong, P. A., Afful, J., Coker, W., Akoto, O., Twumasi, R., & Baiden, A. (2015). A needs analysis of undergraduate students of communicative skills: The case of tertiary institutions in Ghana. *Open Journal of Modern Linguistics*, *5*(5), 413–424. https://doi.org/10.4236/ojml.2015.55037

Generoso, J. C., & Arbon, A. M. (2020). Language needs analysis: An EAP curriculum design to develop foreign students' English skills. *The Journal of Asia TEFL*, *17*(2), 428–445. https://doi.org/10.18823/asiatefl.2020.17.2.8.428

Guardado, M., & Light, J. (2020). *Curriculum development in English for academic purposes: A guide to practice*. London, UK: Palgrave MacMillan.

Huang, L.-S. (2010). Seeing eye to eye? The academic writing needs of graduate and undergraduate students from students' and instructors' perspectives. *Language Teaching Research*, *14*(4), 517–539. https://doi.org/10.1177/1362168810375372

Hyland, K. (1997). Is EAP necessary? A survey of Hong Kong undergraduates. *Asian Journal of English Language Teaching*, *7*, 77–99.

Hyland, K. (2006). *English for academic purposes: An advanced resource book*. Routledge.

Kohnke, L., & Jarvis, A. (2021). Coping with English for academic purposes provision during COVID-19. *Sustainability*, *13*(15), 8642. https://doi.org/10.3390/su13158642

Kohoutová, I. (2006). *Teaching English to Adults: Needs Analysis*. [Unpublished master's thesis]. Charles University in Prague. Retrieved May 3, 2022, from http://hdl.handle.net/20.500.11956/4660

Long, M. H. (1983). Native speaker/non-native speaker conversation and the negotiation of comprehensible input1. *Applied Linguistics*, *4*(2), 126–141. https://doi.org/10.1093/applin/4.2.126

Long, M. H. (2005). *Second language needs analysis*. Cambridge University Press.

Mackay, R., & Mountford, A. (1978). *English for specific purposes: A case study approach*. Longman.

Mahfoodh, O. (2014). Oral academic discourse socialisation: Challenges faced by international undergraduate students in a Malaysian public university. *International Education Studies*, 7(2), 10–17. https://doi.org/10.5539/ies.v7n2p10

Mansur, S. B., & Shrestha, P. N. (2015). The EAP course design Quagmire – juggling the stakeholders' perceived needs. In P. N. Shrestha (ed), *Current Developments in English for Academic and Specific Purposes: Local innovations and global perspectives* (pp. 93–113). Garnet Education.

Martins, H. F. (2017). Revisiting needs analysis: A cornerstone for business English courses. *Journal of English Language & Translation Studies*, 5(1), 57–63.

McPhee, S., & Lyon, K. A. (2020). Student voices on remote education in the COVID-19 era: Recommendations for fall based on student self-reported data. *UBC Remote Pedagogy Report*, 1–16.

McPhee, S. R., Lyon, K., Briseno-Garzon, A., Varao-Sousa, T., & Moghtader, B. (2020). Student voices on remote education in the COVID-19 era: Recommendations for fall based on student self-reported data. Institute for the Scholarship of Teaching and Learning. *UBC Remote Pedagogy Report*, 1-16. https://doi.org/10.13140/RG, 2(28175.20641).

Moon, Y., Choi, J., & Kang, Y. (2019). Does reading and vocabulary knowledge of advanced Korean EFL learners facilitate their writing performance? *The Journal of Asia TEFL*, 16(1), 149–162. https://doi.org/10.18823/asiatefl.2019.16.1.10.149

Önder Özdemir, N. (2014). Diagnosing the EAP needs of Turkish medical students: A longitudinal critical needs analysis. *Ibérica, Revista De La Asociación Europea De Lenguas Para Fines Específicos*, 28, 35–57. Retrieved May 3, 2022, from https://www.redalyc.org/articulo.oa?id=287032049003

Pourshahian, B., Gholami, R., Vaseghi, R., & Kalajahi, S. (2012). Needs of an ESL context: A case study of Iranian graduate students. *World Applied Sciences Journal*, 17(7), 870–873.

Riazi, A. M., Ghanbar, H., & Fazel, I. (2020). The contexts, theoretical and methodological orientation of EAP research: Evidence from empirical articles published in the *Journal of English for Academic Purposes*. *Journal of English for Academic Purposes*, 48, 1–17. https://doi.org/10.1016/j.jeap.2020.100925

Serafini, E. J., Lake, J. B., & Long, M. H. (2015). Needs analysis for specialized learner populations: Essential methodological improvements. *English for Specific Purposes*, 40, 11–26. https://doi.org/10.1016/j.esp.2015.05.002

Smith, G. F., Jung, H., & Zenker, F. (2022). From task-based needs analysis to curriculum evaluation: Putting methodological innovations to the test in an English for academic purposes program. *English for Specific Purposes*, 66, 80–93. https://doi.org/10.1016/j.esp.2022.01.001

Sönmez, H. (2019). An examination of needs analysis research in the language education process. *International Journal of Education and Literacy Studies*, 7(1), 8. https://doi.org/10.7575/aiac.ijels.v.7n.1p.8

Tajino, A., James, R., & Kijima, K. (2005). Beyond needs analysis: Soft systems methodology for meaningful collaboration in EAP course design. *Journal of English for Academic Purposes*, 4(1), 27–42. https://doi.org/10.1016/j.jeap.2004.01.001

The Center for Digital Equity. (2022). *What is digital inclusion?* Retrieved June 25, 2022, from https://thecenterfordigitalequity.org/what-is-digital-inclusion/

4
SILENCE AS AUTONOMY

Case studies of Australian and international students

Dat Bao

Silence learning

Although silence as a theme in research has become visible in education since the early 1970s (Sharpley, 1997), the concept of 'silent learning' in the two following decades was hardly mentioned in the discourse (Bao, 2023). It was not until the late 1990s and early 2000s that 'silence' concerning how students learn began to enter the scope of many projects. When the theme was broadened from 'inner speech' to 'silence', researchers also started covering a broader spectrum of topics. New topics emerged, such as learner reflection (Bao, 2002; Niegemann, 2004; Wuttke, 2012), silent engagement (Obenland et al., 2012), and contemplative pedagogy (Owen-Smith, 2017), among many others. In unprecedented ways, silence research also made novel connections with affect, perception, experiences, cultural traits, physical settings, classroom dynamics and experimentation, task design, assessment innovation, and silence-related pedagogy. Together they form different patterns of development that will be identified in the coming section.

Students are inherently diverse in their learning behavior. While some prefer verbal modes, others employ reflective styles, that is, using silence in their learning. Others vary their behavior according to changeable classroom situations. This chapter focuses on *autonomously silent* learners who choose silence as a proactive part of learning rather than a delay in learning. Of course, the positive value of speech cannot be downplayed. However, since a large body of discourse in education has already addressed how excellent verbal interaction is, this chapter will not consolidate that further.

DOI: 10.4324/9781003361701-6

Instead, the chapter delves into the practical value of silence. This focus is because many introverted students are often misunderstood, neglected, or marginalized simply because their ways are often not every teacher's favorite. Teachers who do not appreciate silent students tend to believe such individuals are intellectually weak and need help. Through research efforts, this chapter argues that quiet students do not need help in many cases; they only need to be understood.

Definitions of silence and autonomy

Defining silence

Silence can be defined as a permanent trait, a part of one's personality, or as situational behavior resulting from changes in circumstances. Silence can be a meaningful communication strategy with clear motives such as defiance, objection, disagreement, and consideration, among other intentions, or it can be meaningless, simply suggesting, as Jaworski and Sachdev (1998) put it, an 'absence of noise' (p. 274).

According to Remedios et al. (2008), 'silence' among students does not necessarily refer to complete quietness but is employed loosely to denote minimal talk during classroom discussion. Scholars have tried to look at silence and talk in more complex ways than treating them as sound and muteness. Silence itself can be a form of talk. While talk is sometimes known as externalized speech (Ridgway, 2009) and interactive speech (Saito, 1992), silence is an 'articulatory rehearsal mechanism' (Ridgway, 2009, p. 49), subvocal articulation (Rayner et al., 2012), and internalization of speech patterns (Mitchell & Myles, 1998). If standard or accepted classroom talk is sometimes defined as 'the speech of educated people' (Edwards & Westgate, 1987, p. 28), then standard or accepted classroom silence can also be defined as the silence of educated people.

Defining autonomy

Student autonomy is an individual capacity to take charge of one's learning, a decision that significantly impacts personal growth and achievement. Autonomy involves freedom, choice, and negotiation, which are crucial environmental factors for learning development (Lamb, 2009; Raz, 1986; Sinclair, 2009). This ability, however, is not inborn but must be acquired through education practices (Holec, 1981). Silence signifies autonomy when one consciously chooses to remain silent for a learning purpose. When that happens, stopping students from productive thinking would mean disempowering their autonomy and denying them their most important learning space.

The discourse on silence in learning

The discourse on silence studies is highly complex and filled with mutual disagreement, with a history of at least 130 years starting in the nineteenth century in Europe within psychological research (see Bao, 2023). Within the humble scope of this chapter, which is about using silence as autonomous learning, it may be optional to unpack how silence for learning has begun and evolved. Instead, selecting what seems most relevant to the current study would be more practical. The literature, therefore, will be integrated into the entire chapter rather than being concentrated only in this section. A significant reason for doing this is for the relevant discourse to be closely connected with the content of the study. A second reason is to bring out the gap and the contribution of this chapter in the field. The gap is that a great deal of discourse on silence has criticized and marginalized silence as a weakness in student learning (Bao, 2023; Canary & MacGregor, 2008; Smith et al., 2005). The contribution is that this study needs to reveal a different angle on silence; that is, some students employ silence as a strength in their learning (Bao, 2014): without silence, and when forced to talk extensively, these students cannot learn effectively. For some, talking and learning simultaneously differs from what they are comfortable with.

This section looks at the hierarchy between silence and speech, the common view on silence as a disruption to learning (which this project aims to challenge), silence as a foundation of learning as much as speech, and some insights into what reflective students do.

The silence-speech hierarchy

Classroom hierarchy among peers has its complex dynamics. Psychologically, peers in the same classroom might influence one another's behavior. In a class I taught at an Australian University, most students were Anglo-white except two. During discussions, these two students felt so inhibited by their highly verbal Anglo peers that they could not participate much. Despite my efforts to involve the two by connecting discussions with their specific contexts, they lost interest in learning. Halfway through the semester, they dropped out of the course. The clash of learning styles made these students give up their sense of belonging in the class community.

Power hierarchy in the classroom, besides the dominant style of a class, also persists due to teacher attitudes toward silence and talk as well as teacher preferences for specific interaction dynamics. Such attitudes confirm the dominant structure of values in classroom practice and make students feel included in or excluded from the learning process. Arguably, students who are underprivileged for choosing to learn in the silent mode may become victims of classroom hierarchy and inequality. This situation can make introverted students develop more negative emotions toward the learning process than their extroverted counterparts. If the teacher is unaware of this tension, favoritism might occur and impede learning performance. When that happens, the classroom becomes a site of disempowerment. Treating silence and talk as unequal learning tools would perpetuate inequity in the educational setting. Unfortunately, students are not inherently in the position of power to challenge the dominant ideology of what constitutes good learning.

Silence as disruption to learning

In the discourse of education over the past six decades, the list of silence being captured as an obstacle to education has been endless. Such examples include silence as withdrawal behavior (McCroskey, 1977), failure of language (Tannen, 1985), inadequate ability in self-expression (Burns & Joyce, 1997; Chen, 1985; Wu, 1991), an impediment to communication (Foss & Reitzel, 1988), poor listening skills (Pearson & West, 1991), a state of idle ignorance or unlearning (Jaworski, 1993, p. 69), social withdrawal (Evans, 1996), fear of responding (Chesebro & McCroskey, 1998), communication breakdown (Yoneyama, 1999), low language proficiency (Nakane, 2005; Tatar, 2005), fear of incompetence (Prentice & Kramer, 2006), lack of initiative (Ping, 2010), to name a few.

Bean and Peterson (1998) even suggest that students who do not participate in class might need to be brought 'to an office conference where the instructor can speak honestly about the problem' and through supportive coaching. Hopefully, these 'students may begin to make small steps toward progress' (p. 39). These scenarios depict the silent student as an offender who undermines classroom learning and thus needs psychotherapy. In societies where talk is the norm, silence is connected with undesirable values (Tatar, 2005), and silent students might be seen as passive observers (Lieberman, 1984) who are 'inadequately educated', who lack 'independent thinking skills and who do not respect the teacher' (Liu, 2002, pp. 39–52). Petress (2001) reasons those who do not actively speak out during classroom processes 'are acting unethically' because 'silence impedes student learning' (p. 104).

Silence and speech as ways of learning

Despite the above, an alternative view by a humble number of scholars has recognized silence and talk as two legitimate modes of classroom performance. Caranfa (2004), for example, argues that 'silence is the very foundation of learning' (p. 211). According to Yang's (1994) social orientation theory, for a society to be culturally healthy, its members should be involved in the practice of reciprocity, shared responsibility, solidarity, and belonging. To apply these principles in educational settings, students should make reasonable choices to talk or keep silent to serve their learning and to benefit the learning of the community. Doing so is to make shared norms productive, build interpersonal acceptance, and work toward the group's welfare. Words are not to be thrown into the air and become lost, but they are meant to be a helpful substance for learning for others. Classroom time is too limited and valuable to be wasted upon the careless word from the casual mind. If everyone learns to be a considerate partner, every minute of learning will be more efficiently spent. Instead of being filled with social talk, the shared learning environment will be enriched with worthwhile thoughts, good-quality contributions, and well-deserved attention.

What reflective students do

The concept of reflective students in this discussion refers to those proactively thoughtful in the learning process and may or may not feel the need to speak much during classroom processes. The fact that these students tend to keep quiet does not necessarily mean they are not learning as enthusiastically as many of their peers. Instead, they process information as much as those who regularly participate in classroom discussions. Research by Bao (2014) has indicated that although many learners believe in the value of verbal output, some learners practice speaking in the mind and benefit from that process in ways similar to producing verbal output. Educators and scholars' views on silent students, especially students of East Asian background, are sometimes exaggerated by too much attention being paid to students' national backgrounds and traditional beliefs as the outright source of influence (Han, 2003; Kennedy, 2002; Li, 2003; Matthews, 2001; Moon, 2011; Tamai & Lee, 2002). The severe problem of such a view comes from an excessive interest in students' static, original culture rather than the complex dynamics of classroom factors that govern silent behavior. To assume silence primarily as the product of inherited values is to treat silence out of context and regard students as passive, powerless, and dependent individuals. To do this also means denying the reality that international students studying in Western countries are constantly exposed to different ways of thinking, learning, and behaving and have been trying to adapt to new academic settings.

Based on this realization, there is a need to rethink the learning nature of quiet students in the classroom. This is because holding on to cultural background to explain present-day classroom behavior would risk disempowering students' autonomy and undermining individuals' resourcefulness. Education research has shown that during their silence, many students share contribution space with others (Bao, 2014). They care about the quality of verbal contribution, consider others' viewpoints, save class time by whispering to peers, perform mental processing, attentively listen, and connect with others in their thoughts.

Misperception about the silent mode of learning does not uniquely apply to students of Asian backgrounds. Anglo-Western students are also subject to misunderstanding if prone to silent learning behavior. In a discussion on how silence serves as a learning strategy in a middle school classroom in the United States, Hall (2007) reports how silence was connected to students' learning disabilities and underperformance. In Hall's report, some American students who mainly employed silence as a way of learning to read had to go against the natural talking norm and suffered from being misunderstood as passive learners. While recognizing the learning value of silence to some extent, the report highlights silent American students as those with weaker abilities than others: they struggle and hold on to silence as if holding on to a crutch.

Methodology

Research design

My study, which is a case in point to bring knowledge about silence forward, rests upon a phenomenological qualitative design, with semi-structured in-depth interviews as the primary source of data. Data reveal how students employ the silent learning mode in their academic study in autonomous ways. Those ways include coping with cognitive challenges, practicing self-management of learning, and responding to learning conditions. The 20 students from the study cannot represent the learning culture of where these students come from. Instead, the participants offer an enriched discussion to demonstrate the fact that silence as a learning choice is not at all simple: individuals, based on their personalities and interaction with their learning contexts, exhibit various ways of employing silence to serve learning.

Research questions

The interpretive case study follows a bottom-up approach in which data mainly come from participants' experiences rather than from the researcher's knowledge and perception. The main research questions include the following:

How do you employ silence for learning?
What seem to be the strengths and weaknesses of student silence?
How do silence and talk, respectively, allow students to control their learning process?

Selection of participants

Twenty students from Australia, China, Japan, and Korea, who were university students in Australia, took part in this study. The reason for selecting these groups was to see whether those who were known to be verbally (Anglo-Australians) and those who were known to be verbally passive (East Asians) demonstrated a fundamental difference in the way they employed and perceived silent learning.

The participant selection method relied on the voluntary and available nature of participants in Australian universities. In the call for research participation, it was made clear that the study only recruited students who felt they had reasons to be silent in their learning process for purposes they knew well. Students who felt that they were silent due to fear, shyness, tiredness, unwillingness to communicate, and low competence were not recruited for this project simply because, up to the point of research, there had been too many studies of this type being conducted and published. For this reason, writing a chapter in this area would not expand the discourse.

Data collection method

The same questions above were then used to guide the semi-structured interviews. Overall, the focus of data collection was on the positive and challenging use of silence as well as how silence was employed intellectually and meta-cognitively.

To begin with, participants were given the questions and some time (15–20 minutes) to reflect on their responses in the absence of the researcher. During this time, participants could make their notes. After that, a semi-structured interview was conducted to capture an in-depth elaboration of those views as well as rich experience related to them.

The survey aimed to select students who employ silence for learning. Again, the scope of the project was to identify individuals who use silence as a way of learning. The voice of such students has been largely neglected in the education discourse until recently. Participants' responses to interview questions were of an individual, experiential, and subjective nature. The importance of individuals' experiences and opinions has been recognized by Knigge and Cope (2006). The project was conducted with sensitivity to the culture and learning circumstances of participants and the works of other scholars that might be linked to the data in this study. Trustworthiness was built through conscious attempts to be loyal to the words of participants.

Method of data analysis

Data analysis focuses on participants' intended voices rather than the verbatim word. Such methods are highlighted by Wellington (2000) and

Bryman (2004) as thoughtful ways to decode themes and meanings in empirical data. To explain participants' perceptions, transcriptions of their responses to interview questions were processed through content analysis. Their words were categorized, termed, and interpreted to capture thoughts, behavior, and viewpoints. Such a procedure of categorization combined with interpretation to produce research outcomes is well supported by Cohen et al. (2011), Creswell (2007), Hesse-Biber and Leavy (2004), and Maxwell (2005). This investigative approach reflected features of interpretative phenomenological analysis (Husserl, 1970; Moran, 2000), a tradition often found in qualitative psychological research.

Data analysis took great care to be interpretive more than literal in reporting participants' voices, which means looking beyond the surface of interviewees' words and exploring significant values. Wellington (2000) and Bryman (2004) highlight such caution and pursuit as thoughtful ways to decode themes and meanings in empirical data. To explain participants' perceptions, transcriptions of their responses to interview questions were processed through content analysis which involves detailed coding and categorization.

Main findings

The participants being interviewed feel that silence comes from their conscious decision rather than as subconscious passive behavior. The three findings presented in this section point to students' awareness of silence as intensive cognitive work, a natural part of learning, and an autonomous choice.

Silence as intensive cognitive work

In many cases, silence represents a conscious choice rather than intrinsic passivity. Most participants in the study express the need to work in silence, especially when learning content seems cognitively demanding. If the content requires mental processing, they find highly verbal peers' premature participation unpleasant as it interferes with their thinking space. Several students resent the fact that their natural silent learning behavior is often treated as going against the talking norm, and thus they suffer from being misunderstood as inactive learners. Two students elaborate:

> When I am silent, inside my head, it is very noisy. I can hear myself talk, translate, and complete input. Sometimes although the topic proves to be inspiring, I may not participate, but instead, there will be plenty of thinking processes and mental notetaking. It is possible to be engaged in silence. Often the more silent I am, the more the content has affected my thinking.
> *Candace, Australian*

It is difficult to say if you are in better control of what you learn through silence or talk. Some people can steer the conversation to their needs and thus control their learning, while others prefer to control through silent observation.

Michael, Australian

Silence helps students incubate abilities for future communication. Silence is also employed for monitoring language to avoid rushing toward premature performance. Inner speech and quiet observation allow learners to live the indirect experience of a verbal communicator without actually talking out loud.

In my estimation, my total talking time during every lesson during the last semester was only a few minutes, which seemed insufficient for my verbal skills to develop properly. To compensate for this, I decided to learn English by processing information in my head and imagining what I was capable of saying.

Nam-hee, Korean

Moving from thinking in a second language to actual verbalization is a real challenge for many students. Thus, an essential role of silence is that it allows students to focus on processing a large quantity of knowledge within a short time. Silence, therefore, can enhance the speed of learning more effectively than talk, which tends to be more time-consuming.

Silence is a natural part of learning

Silence, if well observed, guided, and managed, can become a robust foundation of learning on which many processing tools are exercised, including connecting knowledge, critical thinking of target content, comparing and contrasting views, gathering resources, talking in the mind, and taking notes of one's thoughts. Most students in the study believe that learning behavior is simply a response to what is going on in the classroom rather than a permanent style independent of the real classroom environment. One participant reflects:

It is hard to say whether every student participating is good or bad because it depends on different situations. If the class size is large, with more than sixty students, it is ridiculous for everyone to speak out, but if there are only 15 students, it is likely to happen under control. Besides, whether participation is appropriate also depends on the subject. If it is a debating or speaking class, being active is necessary and recommended. However, if we consider writing or reading classes, every student talking will not lead to a good outcome.

Lidan, Chinese

Several students identify various functions of silence in the learning process, such as expressions of agreement or disagreement, listening as vicarious participation, and preparation for speech:

I cannot say which type is better because silence itself does not matter, but its purpose does matter. If silence is used to show objection or dislike, it is unpleasant.

Manabu, Japanese

I generally show my consent by talking more than being silent. I use silence more as a form of disagreement because I do not want to offend others and tend to be careful about stating objections.

Maya, Japanese

By listening to others, I gain a lot of new information. I always enjoy listening to others, especially when they share what I have never thought of or did not expect to find.

Daichi, Japanese

I appreciate the quiet time given to me so I can prepare to present my idea because I can put quality into what I'm going to say rather than say it without careful thought, and the quality becomes so messy that nobody will like what I say.

Yukari, Japanese

To some, a well-utilized silence time can transfer ideas from internal processing to external output, which is likely a high-quality contribution to classroom learning after students have processed an issue of shared interest. Participants reveal that the practice of inner speech generates useful resources for the selective presentation of good ideas. As Rogers (1969) observes, students' internal processing skills, which are often overlooked, should be recognized as having creditability.

Silence as an autonomous choice

Silence and talk represent two modes of communication that exist in everyone's repertoire, and which one is to be used in what context should be the matter of personal choice rather than of lack of ability. As several students commented:

> A good teacher makes students feel that they can talk any time they want, without having to request permission, feeling they may be wrong, or being afraid that they are not accepted.
>
> *Kaiyi, Chinese*

> When raising a question, the teacher should give us some time to think, but this does not always happen. Many do not give us sufficient time to reflect after they ask a question.
>
> *Xincheng, Chinese*

> I'm quiet when my teacher asks me to describe something I have never experienced before.
>
> *Lingling, Chinese*

For some, collaborative learning is not just about incessantly talking with each other, which at times might become a form of abuse, but also about being verbally moderate and respectful of peer learning. One Chinese student decides to be quiet as a way of showing care for her peers:

> Silence can become a caring act. When I disagree with my classmates, I keep silent to avoid making them feel uncomfortable. When I have advanced knowledge to share, I'm afraid to show off and make my classmates feel bad, so I keep silent. Silence, for me, is not about saving my face or keeping me secure, but it is about saving the faces of others and making them feel secure. In other words, it is a strategy to keep a good relationship with others. Talk sometimes may destroy a lot of good feelings.
>
> *Biyin, Chinese*

According to some participants, silence signifies autonomy when one consciously chooses to remain silent and reflects passivity when one practices group norms. Silence may send a positive or negative message depending on individual learning styles and dispositions. For instance, some use silence to show acceptance and cooperation, whereas talk could mean disagreement or resistance to authority.

> For me, silence expresses communication functions such as approval or resistance. Some lecturers forced the class to accept their arbitrary views; others were unclear in explaining complicated concepts but pressured

students with many questions to test their understanding of those concepts.

Yung-won, Korean

I resort to silence as a way of resisting lecturers' ineffective pedagogies. If the lecturer inspired me more, I would try to share my ideas. Otherwise, I would keep my thoughts to myself.

Hye-in, Korean

Future directions

Interpretation of findings

The above presentation of data has captured what participants wish to say. This section will bring that meaning forward by connecting that understanding with some relevant discourse in education. The interpretation in this section covers four points:

- The need to recognize both speech and silence as legitimate learning modes
- The need to allow thinking space without pressurizing students to speak up at any cost
- The understanding that well-used silence supports high-quality verbal participation
- The understanding that verbal participation needs proper timing rather than happening at all times

Recognition of both learning modes

The findings presented in this chapter demonstrate how mental rehearsal provides conditions for self-directed learning. Verbal interaction and silent thinking should be recognized as the two equally important dimensions of classroom performance. While the former shows evidence of social involvement, the latter facilitates cognitive engagement. Besides, there is a need for teachers to respect students' learning modes. Some students can think and talk effectively at the same time; others may need help to combine spontaneous talk and cognitive thinking.

The quality of silence is as important as the quality of talk. Silence is of high quality when it is well-timed, leaves necessary space for others to speak, has a communicative intention, serves mental processing, and helps to prepare for further interaction. On the contrary, its quality can be low if silence happens due to absent-mindedness or undesirable emotions such as fear, shyness, or dissatisfaction. Observation and common sense show that we all make conscious efforts to move in and out of silence in various needs to modify how we communicate. Through efforts to break the silent routine or to refrain from a chatting desire, students' experiences become enriched, new skills are piloted, and their comfort zone is challenged. Both talk and silence have 'merits and demerits' in students' learning (Agyekum, 2002, p. 49). While silence allows space for reflection on talk, talk helps one to test the outcome of silence; in this way, one mode functions effectively thanks to the other.

Allowing the thinking space

According to Dolya (2010), both internalized monologue and thinking aloud form the basic speech structures of human thoughts. However, which mode to resort to depends on one's sociocultural experience. Because of this, the success or failure of language learning cannot be understood by looking at one single phenomenon and giving it one simplified interpretation. Instead, one needs to consider many social, cultural, political, historical, economic, educational, and psychological forces where learning occurs. Every student, consciously or subconsciously, is bound by these factors, which constantly play their roles in the educational process. Classroom preference and acceptance of learning styles are examples of these forces. For example, many silent students feel intimidated when sensing how eloquent peers tend to hold themselves above others. Some teachers tend to show more respect to students who speak willingly than those who speak minimally.

When complex ideas cannot be put into words, some participants put them in a silent space where people do not judge. In doing so, they assume the right to make choices of how to learn most comfortably. This individual capacity to self-regulate classroom performance is often considered a student agency (Duff, 2012; Wright, 2012). Assuming supreme ways of teaching and learning and then imposing them on students without consulting them would amount to erasing such agency. As defined and understood by Pavlenko and Lantoff (2000, p. 169), the agency is the foundation on which 'ultimate attainment' in learning is built. Forcing students to silently reflect when they wish to speak or making them verbally participate when they need quiet reflection would cause damage to their learning system.

How silence supports speech

Silence can be seen as the beginning and a portion of talk so that to think and talk might not be fundamentally different. As Ridgway (2009, p. 49) observes, 'thinking in a language provides practice which is arguably as good as speaking it. Processes as important as automatization continue to operate, and one's proficiency continues to develop'. Speech exhibits its virtue, such as when a good explanation is needed to save misunderstanding (Picard, 1952). Likewise, silence is a virtue when a good pause saves superfluous abuse of meaning. In many cases, silence takes over when language reaches the limit of its expressive capacity. When words fail, it is not the emptiness that is left behind, but sometimes an imperative space is proposed to build further understanding. Silence in this situation does not represent the loss of words but the replacement of words by a more expressive means of message delivery.

The timing of speech

Sometimes, when the desire to express one's view is not well-timed, when classroom discussion has not provided the proper gap for the right contribution, one might consider restraining that desire for a moment. Such delay does not mean communication is lacking but may imply that the person knows how to communicate. Blurting out words any time one wishes to do so is only sometimes the best policy. Sharing meaningful ideas requires preparation to ensure the message is entirely well-versed. If sociocultural competence is perceived as part of communication ability, knowing when and how to keep silent is a socialization acquisition process alongside language acquisition (Agyekum, 2002; Wardhaugh, 1992).

Silence, like talk, should always be employed differently, especially in cross-cultural contexts where members of various cultures hold different sociopragmatic values. Even within the same culture, ways of talking and behaving in silence must be adjusted to reflect the communicative intention and social dominance between interlocutors. It is commonly acknowledged that with relevant sociocultural understanding, students could vary their message to achieve nuances of meaning (Harlow, 1990; Leech, 1983; Thomas, 1983). For this reason, only learning how to speak would make interactive skills incomplete. However, a thoughtful communicator must also learn to refrain from speech on time to show interpersonal understanding and maintain a good relationship. Developing such ability entails both learning in the classroom and observing social interaction. Students who are forced to talk when they need silent thinking would not be learning effectively (Chalmers & Volet, 1997; Moust et al., 1987; Remedios et al., 2008; Wilson, 1995). Furthermore, selecting one's favorite learning mode and controlling how to learn is more important than simply following the teacher's instruction (Armstrong, 2012).

Pedagogical implications

Silence exists in every student's repertoire, and negating it, neglecting it, or not finding ways to utilize it would be a waste of learning resources. Many students employ silence in classroom learning whether the teacher is aware of such practice; some attempt to turn silence into speech production; others withdraw into themselves after realizing that their teacher cares more about verbal participation than organized reflection. Students need concrete classroom processes to strengthen their mental processing ability rather than merely receiving the teacher's sympathy. Along this line, it is essential to be aware that the proactive use of silence can support the production of high-quality speech. Teachers with this understanding will likely allow room for mental rehearsal to reach its optimum.

Education pursuing diversity in social, cultural, and academic ways must look at education from both pedagogical and learning perspectives and recognize this tension. While student silence makes it difficult for teachers to teach, low acceptance of silence makes it difficult for students to learn. If the relationship between talk and silence is unbalanced and denotes hierarchy, talkative students will feel superior and thoughtful students will feel inferior. To handle this dilemma, pedagogy will be revisited with the usefulness of silent processing in mind. Drawing from data on how students employ silence in processing information and rehearsing verbalization in mind, I would like to propose the following strategies for teachers to help students maximize their reflective learning potential:

- Being attentive to students' reflection time and space
- Refraining from encouraging untimely participation
- Considering task-related factors that might require silent thinking

Open-minded pedagogy can be a tool for social inclusion. Many educators' advocacy for verbal involvement has excluded classroom members who are highly intelligent but not highly verbal. Educational processes will be most meaningful when the teacher is aware of how talk and silence, respectively or collectively, can help students learn effectively as well as overcome learning challenges.

Teachers' verbal performance also plays a role in asserting power. Many teachers have an inherent tendency to keep talking at all times. They reiterate lecture content. They think aloud to fill class time at any cost. Classroom power can be easily thrown off balance: when students are busy thinking, they do not usually talk, but some teachers might misunderstand that such silence means that learning has stopped. The teacher then tries to talk so that students can listen and learn without knowing that such unnecessary words interfere with learning. When this happens, instruction becomes repetitive and takes up space that could otherwise be employed for student thinking.

Pedagogically recognized silence can liberate students from the constraint of having to produce impulsive, low-quality participation. Silence needs to be managed with an acute awareness of why, how, when, and how long one needs it to support learning and when the verbal mode of learning should take over. Obligatory talk can be frustrating when students are required to publicize their half-baked thoughts when they are unprepared to do so. Silence training should be organized for teachers to be aware of student needs for reflectivity, concentration, outcome, and avoidance of idle, unproductive moments. By the same token, speech needs to be directed to enhance learning rather than become a mere social time in the classroom. The learning structure will fundamentally change when this knowledge is applied so that students can employ silence and talk as learning tools in conscious, informed ways.

Conclusion

Conceptualizing silence as learner autonomy is an unusual and provocative act that challenges the view of silence as low ethics, disability, poor competence, and uncooperative behavior. The recognition of proactive silence in this chapter, however, does not come from mere ideology, assumption, or imagination. However, it derives from data whereby participants employ silence actively in these manners:

- They deliberately choose to silence as their conscious behavior (rather than suffering from shyness, anxiety, or apprehension).
- They use silence actively for learning purposes and outcomes (instead of relaxation or idleness). Such outcomes are not hidden forever but occur in thoughts, written notes, and a plan to verbalize such ideas when they feel the need to do so.

Autonomy involves clear objectives, freedom of choice, and active learning. Since these features are self-evident in the use of silence in this project, silence must be recognized beyond the common criticism as a dilemma that needs repairing.

Acknowledgment

The author would like to thank all the students who participated in this project. The individual names mentioned in the data are pseudonyms and no participant identity is revealed.

References

Agyekum, K. (2002). The communicative role of silence in Akan. *Pragmatics, 12*(1), 31–51.
Armstrong, J. S. (2012). Natural learning in higher education. In N. M. Seel (Ed.), *Encyclopedia of the sciences of learning* (pp. 2426–2433). Springer.
Bao, D. (2002). *Understanding silence and reticence: Action research in the Vietnamese EFL classroom* [Unpublished PhD thesis]. Leeds Beckett University.
Bao, D. (2014). *Understanding silence and reticence: Nonverbal participation in second language acquisition*. Bloomsbury.
Bao, D. (2023). *Silence in English language pedagogy: From research to practice*. Cambridge University Press.
Bean, J. C., & Peterson, D. (1998). Grading classroom participation. *New Directions for Teaching and Learning, 74*, 33–40.
Bryman, A. (2004). *Social research methods* (2nd ed.). Oxford University Press.
Burns, A., & Joyce, H. (1997). *Focus on speaking*. National Centre for English Language Teaching & Research (NCELTR).
Canary, D. J., & MacGregor, I. M. (2008). Differences that make a difference in assessing student communication competence. *Communication Education, 57*(1), 41–63.
Caranfa, A. (2004). Silence is the foundation of learning. *Educational Theory, 54*(2), 211–230.
Chalmers, D., & Volet, S. (1997). Common misconceptions about students from Southeast Asia studying in Australia. *Higher Education Research and Development, 16*(1), 87–98.
Chen, I. M. (1985). Elimination of student's fear towards English learning. In C. Chen, H. Huang, L. Hsiao, J. Kuo, M. Chen, & G. Wang (Eds.), *Papers from the second conference on English teaching and learning in the Republic of China* (pp. 87–96). The Crane Publishing.
Chesebro, J. L., & McCroskey, J. C. (1998). The relationship of teacher clarity and teacher immediacy with students' experiences of state receiver apprehension. *Communication Quarterly, 46*, 446–456.
Cohen, L., Manion, L., & Morrison, K. (2011). *Research methods in education* (7th ed.). Routledge.
Creswell, J. W. (2007). *Qualitative research design: Choosing among the five approaches*. Sage Publications.
Dolya, G. (2010). *Vygotsky in action in the early years: The 'Key to Learning' curriculum*. Routledge.
Duff, P. (2012). Second language socialization. In A. Duranti, E. Ochs, & B. Schieffelin (Eds.), *Handbook of language socialization* (pp. 564–586). Blackwell Publishing.
Edwards, A. D., & Westgate, D. P. G. (1987). *Investigating classroom talk* (1st ed.). Falmer Press.
Evans, M. A. (1996). Reticent primary grade children and their more talkative peers: Verbal, non-verbal, and self-concept characteristics. *Journal of Education Psychology, 88*(4), 739–49.
Foss, K. A., & Reitzel, A. C. (1988). A relational model for managing second language anxiety. *TESOL Quarterly, 22*(3), 437–54.
Hall, L. A. (2007). Understanding the silence: Struggling readers discuss decisions about reading expository texts. *Journal of Educational Research, 100*(3), 132–41.
Han, S. A. (2003). Do South Korean adult learners like native English-speaking teachers more than Korean teachers of English? Paper presented at the AARE conference in Auckland, New Zealand, November 30.

Harlow, L. (1990). Do they mean what they say?: Sociopragmatic competence and second language learner. *The Modern Language Journal, 74*, 328–351.
Hesse-Biber, S. N., & Leavy, P. (Eds.) (2004). *Approaches to qualitative research: A reader on theory and practice.* Oxford University Press.
Holec, H. (1981). *Autonomy in foreign language learning.* Pergamon.
Husserl, E. (1970). *Local investigation.* Humanities Press.
Jaworski, A. (1993). *The power of silence: Social and pragmatic perspectives.* Sage Publications.
Jaworski, A., & Sachdev, I. (1998). Beliefs about silence in the classroom. *Language and Education, 12*(4), 273–292.
Kennedy, P. (2002). Learning culture and learning styles: Myth-understanding about adult (Hong Kong) Chinese learners. *International Journal of Lifelong Education, 21*(5), 430–445.
Knigge, L., & Cope, M. (2006). Grounded visualization: Integrating the analysis of qualitative and quantitative data through grounded theory and visualization. *Environment and Planning A, 38*(11), 2021–37.
Lamb, T. (2009). Controlling learning: Learners' voices and relationships between motivation and learner autonomy. In S. Toogood, R. Pemberton, & A. Barfield (Eds.), *Maintaining control: Autonomy and language learning* (pp. 67–86). Hong Kong University Press.
Leech, G. (1983). *Principles of pragmatics.* Longman.
Li, J. (2003). The core of Confucian learning. *American Psychologist*, February, 146–147.
Lieberman, P. (1984). *The biology and evolution of language.* Harvard University Press.
Liu, J. (2002). Negotiating silence in American classrooms: Three Chinese cases. *Language and intercultural communication, 2*(1), 37–54.
Matthews, B. (2001). The relationship between values and learning. *International Education Journal, 2*(4), 223–232.
Maxwell, J. A. (2005). *Qualitative research design: An interactive approach* (2nd ed.). Sage Publications.
McCroskey, J. C. (1977). Classroom consequences of communication apprehension. *Communication Education, 26*, 27–33.
Mitchell, R., & Myles, F. (1998). *Second language learning theories.* Edward Arnold.
Moon, S. (2011). Expectation and reality: Korean sojourner families in the UK. *Language and Education, 25*(2), 163–176.
Moran, D. (2000). *Introduction to phenomenology.* Routledge.
Moust, J., Schmidt, H., De Volder, M., Belien, J., & De Grave, W. (1987). Effects of verbal participation in small group discussion. In J. Richardson, & W. Eysenck (Eds.), *Student learning: Research in education and cognitive psychology* (pp. 147–154). Open University Press.
Nakane, I. (2005). Negotiating silence and speech in the classroom. *Multilingual, 24*, 75–100.
Niegemann, H. (2004). Lernen und Fragen: Bilanz und Perspektiven der Forschung [Learning and questions: Research results and perspectives]. *Unterrichtswissenschaft, 4*(33), 345–56.
Obenland, C. A., Munson, A. H., & Hutchinson, J. S. (2012). Silent students' participation in a large active learning science classroom. *Journal of College Science Teaching, 42*(2), 90–8.
Owen-Smith, P. (2017). *The contemplative mind in the scholarship of teaching and learning.* Indiana University Press.
Pavlenko, A., & Lantoff, J. P. (2000). Second language learning as participation and the (re)-construction of selves. In J. P. Lanto (Ed.), *Sociocultural theory and second language learning* (pp. 155–177). Oxford University Press.

Pearson, J. C., & West, R. (1991). An initial investigation of the effects of gender on student questions in the classroom: Developing a descriptive base. *Communication Education*, 40, 22–32.

Petress, K. (2001). The ethics of student classroom silence. *Journal of Instructional Psychology*, 28(2), 104–104.

Picard, M. (1952). *The world of silence*, S. Godman (trans.). Henry Regnery.

Ping, W. (2010). A case study of an in-class silent postgraduate Chinese student in London Metropolitan University: A journey of learning. *TESOL Journal*, 2, 207–214.

Prentice, C. M., & Kramer, M. W. (2006). Dialectical tensions in the classroom: Managing tensions through communication. *Southern Communication Journal*, 71(4), 339–361.

Rayner, K., Pollatsek, A., Ashby, J., & Clifton Jr, C. (2012). *Psychology of reading*. Psychology Press.

Raz, J. (1986). *The morality of freedom*. Clarendon Press.

Remedios, L., Clark, D., & Hawthorne, L. (2008). The silent participant in small group collaborative learning contexts. *Active Learning in Higher Education*, 9(3), 201–16.

Ridgway, A. J. (2009). The inner voice. *The International Journal of English Studies*, 9(2), 45–58.

Rogers, C. R. (1969). The increasing involvement of the psychologist in social problems: Some comments, positive and negative. *The Journal of Applied Behavioral Science*, 5(1), 3–7.

Saito, H. (1992). Interactive speech understanding. *Proceedings of Coling-92*, Nantes, 23–8 August 1992.

Sharpley, C. F. (1997). The influence of silence upon client-perceived rapport. *Counselling Psychology Quarterly*, 10(3), 237–46.

Sinclair, B. (2009). The teacher as a learner: Developing autonomy in an interactive learning environment. In R. Pemberton, S. Toogood, & A. Barfield (Eds.), *Maintaining control: Autonomy and language learning* (pp. 175–198). Hong Kong University Press.

Smith, K. A., Sheppard, S. D., Johnson, D. W., & Johnson, R. T. (2005). Pedagogies of engagement: Classroom-based practices. *Journal of Engineering Education*, 94(1), 87–101.

Tamai, K., & Lee, J. (2002). Confucianism as a cultural constraint: A comparison of Confucian values of Japanese and Korean university students. *International Education Journal*, 3(5), 33–49.

Tannen, D. (1985). Silence: Anything but. In D. Tannen, & M. Saville (Eds.), *Perspectives on silence* (pp. 93–111). Ablex.

Tatar, S. (2005). Why keep silent? The classroom participation experiences of non-native English-speaking students. *Language and Intercultural Communication*, 5(3 and 4), 284—293.

Thomas, J. (1983). Cross-cultural pragmatic failure. *Applied Linguistics*, 4(2), 91–112.

Wardhaugh, R. (1992). *An introduction to sociolinguistics* (2nd ed.). Blackwell.

Wellington, J. (2000). *Education research: Contemporary issues and practical approaches*. Continuum.

Wilson, S. A. (1995). Conformity, individuality, and the nature of virtue: A classical Confucian contribution to contemporary ethical reflection. *Journal of Religious Ethics*, 23(2), 263–89.

Wright, L. (2012). *Second language learner and social agency*. Multilingual Matters.

Wu, Y.-H. (1991). Why don't they speak up? A study of factors that affect classroom participation in English language learning. In L. Yaofu, H. Huang, H. Jeng, & A. Hadzima (Eds.), *Papers from the seventh conference on English teaching and learning in the Republic of China* (pp. 159–187). The Crane Publishing Co.

Wuttke, E. (2012). Silence is silver; talk is gold? Analysis of classroom talk in a learner-centred setting. In E. Hjörne, G. van der Aalsvoort, & G. de Abreu (Eds.), *Learning, social interaction and diversity: Exploring identities in school practices* (pp. 103–117). Sense Publishers.

Yang, K. S. (1994). Chinese social orientation: A social interactional approach. In K. S. Yang, & A. B. Yeu (Eds.), *The psychological behavior of the Chinese* (pp. 82–142). Kuei-Kuan. [In Chinese].

Yoneyama, S. (1999). *The Japanese high school – Silence and resistance*. Routledge Japanese Studies Series.

SECTION II

ELT assessment, feedback, and managing classrooms in new circumstances

5
NEW APPROACHES TO THE ASSESSMENT OF ENGLISH AS AN ADDITIONAL LANGUAGE

Graham Seed, Angeliki Salamoura, and Nick Saville

Introduction

Assessment is often used for high-stakes purposes, such as proving English ability in order to obtain a visa for access to an English-speaking country. It is, therefore, rightly expected that institutions which use candidates' results ensure the tests are of sufficient quality to be fit for purpose.

Quality ensures the test is reliable in that the candidates obtain an accurate result that reflects their English ability and that this result can be replicated across different test versions. But the tests also need to demonstrate validity; for example, the candidates are tested in the language that is useful to their actual or future *target language use* (TLU). At the same time, a balance must be struck against the practicality of actually being able to carry out an assessment. For instance, a reliable, valid, and authentic listening test may be too costly or take too much time to deliver. Achieving an appropriate balance between the quality features relevant to the context will result in a quality assessment that is fit for its purpose and uses.

The quality can be demonstrated by presenting a *validity argument* (e.g., Chapelle & Lee, 2021; Davies & Elder, 2005), where a testing body presents the evidence that its test(s) is of sufficient quality. The argument can be measured against industry standards, such as the Association of Language Testers in Europe (ALTE)'s Principles of Good Practice (ALTE, 2020).

The need to demonstrate quality is, therefore, a constant in language assessment even though the contexts and uses of assessment have been evolving over time. This chapter will therefore consider two key changes happening in recent years: the increasing use of digital technology in assessment and the changing perceptions about language proficiency and assessment. We set these out in terms of what has happened up to now (Past), what the current state of play is (Present), and possible ways in which these areas may develop further (Future).

Past: Using digital technology

Since the beginning of the 21st century, the use of digital technology has been of growing importance in English language testing. For many large-scale testing organisations, technological innovation traditionally meant computerising their paper-based tests to benefit from the financial and environmental efficiencies of avoiding physically transporting tests to and from the test centre.

Computer-based (CB) testing began in earnest in the 1990s in large-scale English language testing, although with limited infrastructure, paper-based tests continued to dominate. In fact, many of the CB tests were simply replicating an existing, linear, paper-based test using a different medium. Some technological solutions were created to respond to the prompts, such as 'drag and drop' for a matching activity. The test as a whole was delivered by post to the test centre on a CD-ROM or similar format. This later morphed into an online-delivered test, either to be downloaded or to be accessed directly online using a permanent internet connection. In the latter case, it is possible for the test to be sent, taken, and marked almost instantaneously.

Task types and the whole user experience (UX) have developed to use technology, resulting in on-screen timers, different windows, an online notepad to replicate a real-life one, and other facilities. Productive skills have also been replicated in a CB environment, with typing replacing handwriting as the medium of written production. The question of authentic, communicative speaking tests has been more of a challenge. Some test providers simply focus on elements such as pronunciation and fluency in read-aloud activities. In contrast, others enable open-ended responses that are recorded and sent electronically to examiners. Still, others have tried to replicate spoken interaction by providing audio or video of other 'speakers' to whom the candidate must respond in pseudo-conversation.

Adaptive testing CB adaptive testing was another innovation that took off in the first decade of this century, particularly for objectively marked tests such as those focusing on grammar, vocabulary, reading, and listening. This type of test uses an algorithm that presents items to the candidate based on their score in the previous item(s); i.e., the following item is automatically chosen to be harder or easier depending on whether the candidate answered the previous one correctly. This means the test can provide a more accurate overall result, and the algorithm can also target particular topics or foci of interest as well as levels of difficulty. It also means each test version can be unique for every single candidate.

The prerequisites are a large bank of test items, each tagged with difficulty values, usually measured by item response theory (IRT)—a psychometric paradigm to evaluate overall performance in a given ability (a 'latent trait') against performances of test items of unequal difficulty. Depending on the number of candidates and their ability levels, and in particular the number resitting the test, the bank of items must be large enough and frequently refreshed to minimise security issues of test questions being memorised or leaked.

Past: Approaches in language assessment

Models of language proficiency assessment have developed over time. Where grammar-translation techniques were the norm for much of the first half of the 20th century, the evolution of assessment constructs developed to reflect the paradigm shift to the communicative approach in language learning and assessment in the 1980s and 1990s and the subsequent expansion of this to include the socio-cognitive dimension (Weir, 2005) following constructivist theories (Vygotsky, 1978). The communicative approach highlights the need for assessments to replicate a TLU domain with task-based communicative requirements to fulfil, thus having both *situational* and *interactional* authenticity (Bachman & Palmer, 1996; Douglas, 2000) as far as is practically possible within the constraints of an assessment context. This has been the leading driver of many English assessments over the last thirty or so years.

Present: Using digital technology

CB or digitally delivered tests are nowadays very common, achieving accurate numerical grades and also providing qualitative feedback.

The advantages of the shift to online tests have been several. The speed, reduced printing and shipping costs, and improved testing conditions (such as listening using headphones). Also, not having fixed dates for the test session and the increasingly more authentic medium as many everyday communicative tasks are performed using a device connected to the internet. The challenges, however, have included a high set-up cost and the need for creativity and innovation to create relevant computer-delivered task types. Language testing tended to be slower in implementing digital technology than in other spheres of life, and some attempts were only successful because of the technological infrastructure. Teaching and learning still often take place in the classroom and on paper, and assessment has continued to reflect that. Even in technologically advanced countries such as Japan, there has been some resistance to assessment technology because exams are traditionally pen and paper.

But COVID-19 lockdowns during 2020 and 2021 proved, to some extent, a catalyst to speeding up digital adoption in language assessment (Taylor, 2021), and such adoption has been of increased interest in research publications and conferences since 2020, discussing the positive and negative aspects (Saville & Buttery, 2022).

Remotely-delivered tests and automarked responses are two digital tools that the language assessment industry uses nowadays and these are discussed in brief below.

Remotely-delivered assessment

A face-to-face speaking test is often seen as a useful assessment in an overall language proficiency test. However, it is also the most expensive to administer. One candidate will need the attention and expertise of one or more examiners in a confined, dedicated space for an appropriate length of time. Remotely-delivered speaking tests began as Simulated Oral Proficiency Tests (SOPIs) in the 1980s on tape recorders and then on computers. Online speaking tests nowadays have two major advantages. Firstly, this would eliminate the cost of the examiner(s) and the candidate travelling to a test venue. Secondly, this replicates the authenticity of modern technologically-enhanced communication, which has become even more prevalent in daily life since COVID lockdown restrictions necessitated the increased use of video-conferencing calls.

Inoue et al. (in press) researched the practicalities of such a test. They found that the examiner and/or interlocutor needed specific training to handle the format efficiently, particularly with potential technical issues such as 'delayed synchronization of audio and video, exaggerated movement … restricted view of gestures … and less obvious cues for turn-taking'. These issues will likely lessen over time as familiarity with the format grows, but the challenge of potential malpractice by candidates taking the test at home needs to be considered.

Remote test taking can also be applied to the English testing of other skills (e.g., writing, reading), enabling candidates to take the test electronically from home at their chosen time. To prevent the various forms of malpractice that could ensue outside the security of an invigilated exam centre, systems need to be set up to mitigate attempts at cheating. These could include preventing the candidate's device from displaying anything other than the test, turning on the device's camera as well as the need for a camera on an additional device to relay live images of the candidate, the instruction not to wear headphones, and for the device's microphone to pick up any sound in the room, and other measures. All this data can be fed back to the testing organisation to review during the test, where an invigilator (or 'proctor') is reviewing the data in live time and can step in and deal with potential security issues as they come up or after the test has taken place. A number of testing organisations now employ these remote proctoring methods for their assessments (e.g., IELTS Online, TOEFL).

During the COVID lockdowns, many assessment providers amended their existing CB tests to be delivered remotely with remote proctoring. Isbell and Kremmel (2020) welcomed the flexibility this offered at the time of need, and no doubt this trend will continue. However, while the potential benefits of remote proctoring should not be dismissed, current systems still need to be improved. It is acknowledged that the risks of malpractice remain, especially in the case of high-stakes assessments, and so users need to be aware of this. Additionally, using remote proctoring with children raises specific logistical and ethical questions.

Automarking

The marking of language tests requires trained assessors, and thus there is a cost and time element to providing candidates with their results. Objectively marked paper-based tests can be automated by Optical Mark Readers (OMR), e.g., for multiple-choice items, or optical character readers for handwritten short answers with limited correct answers. For CB tests, machines do this very simply.

Subjectively-marked language tests, usually in the form of free-response speaking or writing, are more complex to be automarked because of the unpredictability of the responses. Nevertheless, over the last two decades, online automated assessment and feedback systems have been successfully developed for both spoken or written performance or, more exactly, to 'predict the score that a human examiner would assign to oral [or written] test responses under the same construct' (Knill & Gales, in press) and therefore award the response with, e.g., a CEFR-benchmarked score (Yannakoudakis et al., 2018). Advances in natural language processing (NLP), artificial intelligence (AI), and machine learning have facilitated this.

In the case of spoken responses, there are additional challenges compared with writing. An automated speech recognition (ASR) system first has to transcribe audio recordings of non-native speech from many different L1 backgrounds (i.e., differences in pronunciation and stress, as well as grammar and vocabulary errors) and at varying levels of English proficiency. It also has to cope with background noise on the recording. The text of the transcribed speech can then be used to train an AI using *machine learning* in a similar way to writing assessment. Ultimately the trained automarker can award marks to unseen performances and may also be able to provide qualitative feedback to the candidates. Learning and assessment providers are now using these technologies in products such as Cambridge's Speak & Improve and Pearson's PTE.

Current advances in machine learning have come a long way, but there is still much ground to be covered. For now, hybrid automarking provides satisfactory ways to combine the benefits of using humans and machines to deliver fairer outcomes (Xu et al., 2020). The combination can provide more reliable results and allay the fears of end users who have negative perceptions of machines in charge of the assessment process. This points to the importance of *hybridity* in language assessments and keeping humans 'in the loop' when developing and deploying AI-based systems (Saville & Buttery, 2022).

Present: Changing constructs in language assessment

The second major trend in more recent approaches to assessment is distinct from the technological changes but complementary to the overall drive towards the personalisation and contextualisation that technology offers (Saville, 2017).

Even if many aspects of the communicative model have not changed, the way people communicate has changed over the last thirty years, as have the TLU situations. To give one example, Weir and Chan (2019, p. 243) note that the construct of academic reading has changed in that we find information and gain understanding frequently through reading and watching videos on the internet, rather than looking in a physical book. The COVID-19 pandemic has shifted communication practices further, particularly with oral communication skills, as Taylor (2021) noted. Nowadays it is commonplace to interact via video-conferencing, and thus the constructs that language assessors measure may develop as a result. This section therefore focuses on some of the shifts in thinking about the nature of language proficiency that are currently being debated. These include the shift to talking about *modes of communication* rather than skills, the *multilingual turn*, using English as an additional language within other school subjects and skills, and the integrated approach between learning and assessment.

Skills and modes of communication

The original Common European Framework of Reference for Languages (CEFR) (Council of Europe, 2001; p. 14) categorised language activities into four main types—reception, production, interaction, and mediation.

However, despite the emphasis on interaction and the integration of skills, a more traditional four-skills approach has persisted in communicative language assessment—with speaking, writing, listening, and reading tested separately. The CEFR's Companion Volume (Council of Europe, 2020) therefore has revisited the activities and presents them as four modes of communication: reception (usually listening, reading, or watching), production (oral and written), interaction (oral and written), and mediation.

Whereas interaction involves taking one piece of content and responding to it with new content, mediation often involves taking one piece of content and keeping that same message but changing its register, mode, tone, language, or other dimension so that a third party can understand the message better. Mediation also involves other situations where a language user needs to facilitate others' communication. Relatively few language assessment bodies directly assess mediation skills through a component dedicated to that mode. There has however been much research on the topic (e.g., Stathopoulou, 2015), so it is expected that a greater emphasis will be placed on it by language assessment bodies too in the coming years.

In addition, *multimodality* is a term broadly encompassing 'multiple medias', whereby non-linguistic features are integrated into language assessment. Examples are the use of audio-visual input in listening tests (Wagner, 2008) and growing calls to 'expand the construct of L2 listening by including the ability to understand visual information' (Suvorov, 2015, p. 479). This is reflected in the CEFR Companion Volume, as both a feature of and a resource for technologically-mediated communication: 'A rigid separation between written and oral does not really apply to online transactions, where multimodality is increasingly a key feature and resource, and the descriptors therefore assume the exploitation of different online media and tools according to context' (Council of Europe, 2020, p. 86).

The main influence of the Companion Volume and its renewed focus on modes of communication is that assessment tasks will become more complex to reflect authentic scenarios involving the integration of skills across several phases of a communicative event. In other words, there is an opportunity to expand the constructs of language ability in this way, and in order to do so in a feasible way, digital technologies of the kind mentioned above will be needed.

Multilingual turn

As part of the 'multilingual turn' (May, 2014) in language education, there is recognition of the multilingual realities of English learners who know the language they use at home, plus potentially additional languages such as their language of schooling, regional dialect or variant, as well as other languages they have learnt, even only in part. This leads to English interacting with the various other languages that its users have some proficiency in, rather than English being considered a separate entity (Kunnan & Saville, 2021).

These factors lead to practices of plurilingualism, whereby the learner can use all the known or partially known languages to maximise the value of a communicative act. This may result in code-switching and translanguaging, where a language user will change language within a communicative act depending on the usefulness of the context or even pay no attention to the languages used. While this practice is commonplace in many parts of the world, there has been a particular paradigm shift in Europe and North America. The increased recognition and promotion of the usefulness of plurilingual repertoires in learning is now coming to light, and there is support for this in educational policy settings (Gutierrez Eugenio & Saville, 2017).

Applying this to language assessment is a new task (Saville & Seed, 2021). Seed (2020) categorises plurilingual assessment into four areas which include cross-linguistic mediation (Stathopoulou, 2015), whereas Seed and Holland (2020) provide some examples of what this might look like in practice.

English within other subjects and skills

We have seen that the expansion of the communicative model to include social and cognitive competences has been expanded by considering multimodality and multilingualism. With the real-life context of English use being increasingly recognised as important within the assessment, it is, therefore, right to involve other non-linguistic skills. Bespoke assessments, therefore, may be required to demonstrate competences such as computer skills, cultural understanding, problem-solving, and critical thinking (among others), which measure the linguistic knowledge within and alongside a particular non-linguistic skill. Frameworks to guide the learning and assessment of these areas have started to emerge. Two examples are the Cambridge Life Competencies Framework[1] and the Framework of Reference for Pluralistic Approaches to Language and Cultures (FREPA).[2] Content and Language Integrated Learning (CLIL) is another medium that has had much focus in the last few decades, with thought being extended to assessment and learning (e.g., De Boer & Leontjev, 2020).

Move towards integrated learning and assessment

For most of its history, language assessment has seen a division between summative and formative assessment. In the past two decades, however, a strong trend for a joined-up approach among the different types of assessment as well as between assessment and learning has emerged: learning-oriented assessment (LOA). A number of models have been proposed in this space in the context of general education for adult university learners (Carless, 2007), in the L2 classroom (Turner & Purpura, 2015), in the context of standardised assessment (Green & Hamp-Lyons, 2015), or in aligning classroom learning and assessment with external standards and tests (Jones & Saville, 2016).

Salamoura and Morgan (2021) identified four common denominators in this LOA movement. The first one is the integration of assessment *for* and *of* learning in that all forms of assessment should be designed and administered to support learning and teaching inside and outside the classroom. Assessment tasks truly become learning-oriented if they share the same high-level learning objectives as the course of study. Similarly, integration of assessment *for* learning (e.g., diagnostic assessments) and assessment *of* learning (e.g., proficiency tests) is typically achieved through their common link to the same external criterion (e.g., the CEFR), their alignment to the same high-level learning objectives set for the course, and their common construct (cf. Jones & Saville, 2016; Salamoura & Unsworth, 2015). The second one concerns the systematic collection of evidence for learning and record-keeping. A key function of LOA is to elicit evidence about learning, which can be collected systematically over a period of time and used to inform further actions, such as checking student understanding and monitoring progress against objectives.

The third denominator and cornerstone of LOA is the provision of timely, feed-forward, constructive feedback (see also Lam, 2021). Appropriate feedback can make a critical contribution to learning, and it is conceptualised in mainstream educational literature as information given to the learner, which they can then use to narrow the gap between their current and desired stage of learning (Black & Wiliam, 1998; Hattie & Timperley, 2007). These three LOA denominators—the use of assessment as a learning tool, collection of learning evidence, and feedback – can be seen as stepping stones for the fourth one, which is the development of learner autonomy. In the LOA context, ensuring that students think about and understand their learning and progress is important because learners who take more responsibility for their learning tend to progress more. (See Gebril, 2021 for different perspectives on LOA and Salamoura & Morgan, 2021 for examples of application of LOA practices in an English classroom setting.)

Implemented appropriately, an LOA approach to learning helps teachers and learners achieve better planning of learning, understanding of where the learners are now in their learning journey and what they need to do next to improve, as well as providing ongoing evidence that learning has taken place. The AI developments of the past two decades can play a pivotal role in adopting LOA because technology can now significantly facilitate the development and implementation of LOA features that are labour-intensive.

Future directions

This section will discuss some of the new approaches to English language assessment that utilise digital technology or take on board new constructs, and how these methods can create a more personalised and motivating experience for the test taker. It has also shown that, despite the first computer-assisted language tests being more than twenty years old, there is still so much that can be done in this area, which somewhat lags behind the use of technology in other fields. Nevertheless, future success is expected to be dominated by the use of educational technology (EdTech) and the use of AI in educational assessment (EdAI).

This leads to an increase in available *data*. A digitally-driven future of assessment, taking place more often and in more various, dynamic, and personalised formats, allows a constant gathering of richer data on what the learner can do in the target language through assessment. The learners' development over time can be longitudinally tracked. With good data capture mechanisms, this data collection can be used to better support learning, learners, and teachers (EDUCAUSE, 2021). The output may make use of AI, but it needs to be accessible and interpretable for all users: candidates, their teachers, schools, parents, and recognising organisations.

A major challenge to the use of digital technology in assessment is the question of whether there is the appropriate digital *infrastructure* to support this at the national level (e.g., providing internet connectivity to all social and geographical areas), the institutional level (e.g., schools investing in robust technology), and the household level (e.g., having the right equipment and the right knowledge to access the technology). Lack of access at any of these points will lead to inequality between countries or groups of people; this is known as the *digital divide*, which increased during the COVID-19 pandemic (Saville & Buttery, 2022). This challenge applies to digital assessment just as to other areas of life.

Another future direction that is slowly but steadily emerging is automatic test construction. For example, a machine does not select from a pre-existing item bank but searches the web for reading texts gauged to be at the candidate's ability level and creates appropriate test items unique for the candidate. Or using generative AI, such as ChatGPT, a machine creates its own text suitable for the target ability level and other characteristics of the test taker. These measures could reduce security risks, though the quality of the AI-generated texts and items needs to be assured.

The final part of this chapter first looks at two areas in which research has already begun, but real assessment products will emerge in the future: gamification and eye-tracking. Essential for the future is the consideration of ethical issues, as well as issues of fairness and social justice.

Gamification

As stated above, many CB tests have relied on paper-based tests and replicated them with existing technology. Conversely, 'digital first' assessments necessitate the synthesis of user experience (UX) principles with assessment expertise to ensure the test and the way the test appears on screen makes sense from a usability perspective while also upholding essential assessment requirements (e.g., related to working memory, cognitive load, etc.). UX and assessment specialists need to work with the technology developers to understand what is technically feasible.

Examples of this are digital gamification or games-based assessment, whereby a language assessment is conducted within the context of video gaming. This is a newer trend to 'increase student engagement, motivate and promote learning' (Weir & Chan, 2019, p. 249). Research on applying digital gaming in second language learning has shown the benefits (e.g., Reinhardt, 2020). Many language learning apps have emerged on the market that use game-style formats that can be applied in formative assessment contexts. However, very little research has been done on applying this in more formal assessment contexts. Pickles (2019) talks about a prototype digital game-based LOA and found lower levels of test anxiety.

There is still considerable work to be done on implementing language assessments using gaming contexts, and it can be seen how the use of virtual and/or augmented reality-enhanced devices and headsets could enable the authentic feel of an assessment, just as they are starting to be used in language learning (e.g., Seely, 2020).

Eye-tracking

The use of eye-tracking in language assessment is in its infancy but has the potential to provide innovative solutions. Eye-tracking 'is a non-invasive method in which participants' eye movements are recorded as they carry out a task' (Schmidt & Pastorino, in press). Eye-tracking may therefore allow the evaluation of receptive skills more directly rather than indirectly through comprehension questions. So far, in the L2 assessment context, the technology has been used mostly as a research tool to investigate cognitive processes involved in test taking for validation purposes (e.g., Bax & Chan, 2019) to provide useful information about the design of the content and on-screen layout of the task, rather than as a direct measurement tool of language skills (Brezak et al., 2018). The latter is an aspirational goal: for a candidate to read and answer questions on a text while eye-tracking software picks up on their eye movements to ascertain how fully the candidate has comprehended the text.

Ethics

As the use of AI and accompanying data collection in language assessment grows, so do voices that advocate the need for the *ethical use* of AI in the field. The Institute for Ethical AI in Education (2021) has recently published a framework that aims to address this issue. According to it (ibid., our emphases added), AI systems should be used to:

- achieve *well-defined educational goals* based on strong societal, educational, or scientific evidence that this is for the benefit of the learner.
- *assess* and recognise a broader range of learners' talents.
- promote *equity* between different groups of learners and ... not discriminate against any group of learners.
- increase learners' level of *autonomy* over their learning and development.
- balance *privacy* and the legitimate use of data for achieving well-defined and desirable educational goals.
- enable *transparency and accountability*. Humans are ultimately responsible for educational outcomes and should therefore have an appropriate level of oversight of how AI systems operate.
- allow *informed participation*. Learners, educators, and other relevant practitioners should have a reasonable understanding of AI and its implications.

The *ethical use* of AI and data in language assessment is an area that will grow in importance, and we actively call for test providers and researchers to engage in its development and sound implementation. Two immediate needs are the upskilling of teachers and assessment practitioners so that they actively engage in this process and reap the benefits; and the updating of the *codes of practice* of language assessment professional bodies to acknowledge and offer guidance around AI use.

Fairness and social justice

Of late, greater attention is paid to issues of fairness and social justice, including notions such as *equality/equity, diversity, and inclusion* (represented in the acronym JEDI). These will play an increasing role in assessments in the future. Respecting the rights of individuals in their own contexts reflects the shift in assessments towards increased personalisation and contextualisation but also calls for greater consideration of the issues of fairness. This can manifest itself in many different ways.

Firstly, one challenge is how to respect and promote diversity in assessment settings where standards and standardisation play such key roles. An

English test used globally can give candidates a standardised experience, creating greater reliability because each test taker sees the same content. But some candidates may be unfairly biased if the test uses less familiar content for them personally. Secondly, the use of English in a multilingual world means that the native speaker's prestige, previously seen as the height of attainment in proficiency, is no longer valid in real-world communicative situations. This results in the testing of English as a language for international communication and the importance of 'world Englishes' or non-L1 models within English assessment. It was also a specific focus in the updated Companion Volume of the CEFR (Council of Europe, 2020). Furthermore, the assessments themselves may need to be 'decolonised' (Greatorex et al., 2021), in order to shift the actual content of the tests away from focusing on the culture of the English native speaker. This might be achieved by reducing the number of reading texts used in a global test that are written by British authors who describe the natural world when travelling in Asia with the 'locals'; or the American culture implicitly expected to be inferred when being asked a speaking test question about eating out.

One additional challenge in this area is the importance of score interpretation and use. Central to the validation argument is the issue of fit-for-purpose to the context. As an example, language tests may be used to prove sufficient language ability to obtain a visa or access a particular country's higher educational institutions. But policymakers should be wary of using test results as a gatekeeping mechanism by setting arbitrarily high test score expectations in order to reduce immigration or deter immigration by certain groups of people (ALTE, 2016; Rocca et al., 2020).

Conclusion

What might the future of language assessment look like?

Given the far-reaching technological and AI advancements of the past two decades and the parallel evolution of our thinking about the nature of language proficiency and the role of assessment, we are at a unique crossroads. Technology and AI can accelerate the implementation of many ambitions around the design, administration, and use of language assessment that a couple of decades ago seemed out of reach.

In the future, language assessment could:

- give simultaneous information on learners' proficiency, learning progress so far, feedback on how to improve, and recommendations about next steps.
- provide evidence about the test's quality, validity, ethical use of AI, and its impact on stakeholders in various contexts.

- cater better to 'non-linear' learning pathways and assess the *process of learning* as much as the outcomes by offering different types of assessment for different purposes (OECD, 2019).
- offer a more authentic language experience and construct—by adopting, for instance, multimodal and skills-integrated tasks or assessing online language use.
- be informed by data gathered longitudinally (not just from a one-off session) and from a range of contexts (e.g., assessment events, learning tasks, real-life use).
- become more personalised and contextualised to learner requirements with content and format appropriate to the candidate's context, age, linguistic background, learning and assessment needs, motivation, and other requirements.[3]
- be accessible and inclusive for all test takers, embracing the multilingual and multicultural realities of many learners.
- become increasingly integrated with learning and part of wider *ecosystems of learning and assessment*, which will combine a range of materials and tools that collectively cater to all the needs of a learner.

The above possibilities come with an important caveat, though. These exciting developments can be truly impactful only if a clear assessment purpose and sound assessment principles guide technology choices and implementation. The ultimate challenge for language assessment providers in the future will still be maintaining the validity, reliability, and positive impact required for high-quality, personalised digital assessments.

Acknowledgments

Thanks to the 'Think Tank' team at Cambridge English for their help in discussing and formulating many of the ideas that have ended up in this chapter. The authors wish to thank Amy Devine, Marianne Pickles, and Nicholas Glasson in particular.

Notes

1. https://www.cambridge.org/gb/cambridgeenglish/better-learning-insights/cambridgelifecompetenciesframework
2. https://www.ecml.at/Portals/1/documents/ECMl-resources/CARAP-EN.pdf
3. In the future, it may be possible for a test taker to ask for, e.g., a medium-stakes test of speaking for the hospitality industry, a sample of speech or a target CEFR level, and a perfectly personalised test generated for them to take.

References

ALTE (2016). *Language tests for access, integration and citizenship: An outline for policy makers.* Council of Europe/ALTE.

ALTE. (2020). *Principles of good practice.* Retrieved from: https://www.alte.org/Materials

Bachman, L. F., & Palmer, A. S. (1996). *Language testing in practice.* Oxford University Press.

Bax, S., & Chan, S. (2019). Using eye-tracking research to investigate language test validity and design. *System, 83,* 64–78.

Berzak, Y., Katz, B., & Levy, R. (2018). Assessing language proficiency from eye movements in reading. In *Proceedings of the 2018 Conference of the North American Chapter of the Association for Computational Linguistics: Human Language Technologies, Volume 1 (Long Papers)* (pp. 1986–1996). Association for Computational Linguistics.

Black, P., & Wiliam, D. (1998). Assessment and classroom learning. *Assessment in Education, 5*(1), 7–73.

Carless, D. (2007). Learning-oriented assessment: Conceptual bases and practical implications/innovations. *Education and Teaching International, 44*(1), 57–66.

Chapelle, C. A., & Lee, H. (2021). Understanding argument-based validity in language testing. In C. A. Chapelle, & E. Voss (Eds.), *Validity argument in language testing: Case studies of validation research* (pp. 19–44). Cambridge University Press.

Council of Europe (2001). *Common European framework of references for languages: Learning, teaching, assessment.* Cambridge University Press.

Council of Europe (2020). *Common European framework of references for languages: Learning, teaching, assessment. companion volume with new descriptors.* Council of Europe.

Davies, A., & Elder, C. (2005). Validity and validation in language testing. In E. Hinkel (Ed.), *Handbook of research in second language teaching and learning* (pp. 795–813). Lawrence Erlbaum.

De Boer, M., & Leontjev, D. (Eds.) (2020). *Assessment and learning in content and language integrated learning (CLIL) classrooms.* Springer Nature Switzerland.

Douglas, D. (2000). *Assessing languages for specific purposes.* Cambridge University Press.

EDUCAUSE (2021). *EDUCAUSE Horizon Report.* Teaching and Learning Edition. Retrieved from: https://library.educause.edu/-/media/files/library/2021/4/2021hrteachinglearning.pdf?la=en&hash=C9DEC12398593F297CC634409DFF4B8C5A60B36E

Gebril, A. (Ed.) (2021). *Learning-oriented language assessment: Putting theory into practice.* Routledge.

Greatorex, J., Coleman, T., Johnson, M., & Mouthaan, M. (2021). Decolonising the Curriculum: Decolonising OCR's areas of influence. In *ICERI2021 Proceedings* (pp. 3504–3513).

Green, A., & Hamp-Lyons, L. (2015). *Introducing opportunities for learning-oriented assessment to large-scale speaking tests.* Unpublished report, Cambridge English Language Assessment.

Gutierrez Eugenio, E., & Saville, N. (2017). Policy review: The role of assessment in European language policy: A historical overview. *Languages, Society & Policy.* Retrieved from: https://doi.org/10.17863/CAM.9801

Hattie, J., & Timperley, H. (2007). The power of feedback. *Review of Educational Research, 77*(1), 81–112.

Inoue, C., Nakatsuhara, F., Berry, V., & Galaczi, E. (in press). Video-conferencing speaking tests: An investigation of context validity related to test administration. In G. Yu & J. Xu (eds), *Language Test Validation in a Digital Age*. Studies in Language Testing volume 52. Cambridge University Press and Assessment.

Isbell, D. R., & Kremmel, B. (2020). Test review: Current options in at-home language proficiency tests for making high-stakes decisions. *Language Testing, 37*(4), 600–619.

Jones, N., & Saville, N. (2016). *Learning oriented assessment: A systemic approach*. Studies in Language Testing volume 45. UCLES/Cambridge University Press.

Knill, K., & Gales, M. (in press). Building an Auto-marker for Assessing Spontaneous L2 English Speech. In G. Yu & J. Xu (eds), *Language Test Validation in a Digital Age*. Studies in Language Testing volume 52. Cambridge University Press and Assessment.

Kunnan, A., & Saville, N. (2021). Setting standards for language learning and assessment in educational contexts: A multilingual perspective. In W. Ayres-Bennett, & J. Bellamy (Eds.), *Cambridge Handbook of language standardisation* (pp. 496–516). Cambridge University Press.

Lam, D. (2021). Feedback as a learning-oriented assessment practice: Principles, opportunities and challenges. In A. Gebril (Ed.), *Learning-oriented language assessment: Putting theory into practice* (pp. 85–106). Routledge.

May, S. (Ed.) (2014). *The multilingual turn: Implications for SLA, TESOL and bilingual education*. Routledge.

OECD (2019). *OECD Future of Education and Skills 2030: OECD Learning Compass 2030. A Series of Concept Notes*. Retrieved from https://www.oecd.org/education/2030-project/teaching-and-learning/learning/learning-compass-2030/OECD_Learning_Compass_2030_Concept_Note_Series.pdf

Pickles, M. (2019). *Gamification versus game-based* learning [Blog post]. Summit of Education 2019. Retrieved from: https://www.cambridgeassessment.org.uk/summit-of-education-2019/afternoon-sessions/gamification-versus-game-based-learning/

Reinhardt, J. (2020). Digital gaming in L2 teaching and learning. In C. A. Chappelle, & S. Sauro (Eds.), *The handbook of technology and second language teaching and learning* (pp. 202–216). Wiley Blackwell.

Rocca, L., Hamnes Carlsen, C., & Deygers, B. (2020). *Linguistic integration of adult migrants: Requirements and learning opportunities*. Council of Europe.

Salamoura, A., & Morgan, S. (2021). Learning-oriented assessment from a teacher's perspective. In A. Gebril (Ed.), *Learning-oriented language assessment: Putting theory into practice* (pp. 182–206). Routledge.

Salamoura, A., & Unsworth, S. (2015). Learning oriented assessment: Putting learning, teaching and assessment together. *Modern English Teacher, 24*(3), 4–7.

Saville, N. (2017). Digital assessment. In M. Carrier, K. Bailey, & R. Damerow (Eds.), *Digital language learning and teaching: Research, theory, and practice* (pp. 198–207). Taylor and Francis.

Saville, N., & Buttery, P. (2022). Interdisciplinary collaborations for the future of learning-oriented assessment. In K. Sadeghi, & D. Douglas (Eds.), *Fundamental considerations in technology mediated language assessment*. Routledge.

Saville, N., & Seed, G. (2021). Language assessment in the context of plurilingualism. In E. Piccardo, A. Germain-Rutherford, & G. Lawrence (Eds.), *The Routledge handbook of plurilingual language education* (pp. 360–376). Routledge.

Schmidt, E., & Pastorino, C. (in press). Eye-tracking and EEG in language assessment. In G. Yu & J. Xu (eds), *Language Test Validation in a Digital Age*. Studies in Language Testing volume 52. Cambridge University Press and Assessment.

Seed, G. (2020). What is plurilingualism, and what does it mean for language assessment? *Research Notes*, *78*, 5–15.
Seed, G., & Holland, M. (2020). Taking account of plurilingualism in Cambridge assessment English products and services. *Research Notes*, *78*, 16–25.
Seely, J. (2020). *Teaching and learning with augmented reality*. Cambridge Digital Learning paper. Retrieved from: https://www.cambridge.org/files/1916/3669/1819/Teaching_and_Learning_with_Augmented_Reality_V2.pdf
Stathopoulou, M. (2015). *Cross-language mediation in foreign language teaching and testing*. Multilingual Matters.
Suvorov, R. (2015). The use of eye tracking in research on video-based second language (L2) listening assessment: A comparison of context videos and content videos. *Language Testing*, *32*(4), 463–483.
Taylor, L. (2021, April 30). *What challenges might there be for language assessment in the 2020s?* [Conference presentation]. ALTE 1st Digital Symposium. alte.org/DigitalSymposium2021-videos
The Institute for Ethical AI in Education. (2021). *The ethical framework for AI in education*. Retrieved from: https://www.buckingham.ac.uk/wp-content/uploads/2021/03/The-Institute-for-Ethical-AI-in-Education-The-Ethical-Framework-for-AI-in-Education.pdf
Turner, C. E., & Purpura, J. E. (2015). Learning oriented assessment in second and foreign language classrooms. In D. Tsagari, & J. Banjeree (Eds.), *Handbook of second language assessment* (pp. 255–274). DeGruyter Mouton.
Vygotsky, L. (1978). *Mind in society*. Harvard University Press.
Wagner, E. (2008). Video listening tests: What are they measuring? *Language Assessment Quarterly*, *5*(3), 218–243.
Weir, C. J. (2005). *Language testing and validation: An evidence-based approach*. Palgrave Macmillan.
Weir, C. J., & Chan, S. (2019). *Research and practice in assessing academic reading: The case of IELTS*. Studies in Language Testing volume 51. UCLES/Cambridge University Press.
Xu, J., Brenchley, M., Jones, E., Pinnington, A., Benjamin, T., Knill, K., Seal-Coon, G., Robinson, M., & Geranpayeh, A. (2020). *Linguaskill: Building a validity argument for the speaking test*. Cambridge Assessment English internal report: unpublished.
Yannakoudakis, H., Andersen, Ø, Geranpayeh, A., Briscoe, T., & Nicholls, D. (2018). Developing an automated writing placement system for ESL learners. *Applied Measurement in Education*, *31*(3), 251–267.

6
FEEDBACK TO STUDENTS IN ELT

Maddalena Taras

Background (the past)

Feedback has always been and continues to be considered a panacea for learning despite numerous caveats: a present from expert tutors to less experienced students; a magic formula to enhance student learning; and increasingly a burden for students to shoulder and carry. Despite new discourses about dialogic feedback (Merry et al., 2013; Taras, 2023, chapter 4), 'dialogues' are generally unidirectional from tutors to students.

My academic and research development on assessment, student self-assessment (SSA), and feedback has progressed through different contexts, beginning with ELT (including EFL and ESP), then the teaching of French as a foreign language, and ESOL. These (relatively minor) differences in context confirmed that to move from specific to generic and *vice versa*, it is important to consider and clarify basic principles and theories. This was brought home to me when a University Teaching Fellowship required me to use my SSA model across faculties and subjects. I had resisted using SSA with oral language production, believing that students could not do this. Working with the drama department showed me that this is a basic principle for them and that it was my job to challenge my preconceptions and try it with my students, which I did successfully. My initial reticence led me to use oral SSA in the language laboratory when students self-assessed their recordings. Becoming braver, I used SSA with oral presentations in class.

My theoretical background focused essentially on learning theories and language learning and acquisition theories to inform pedagogies.

Assessment was an important adjunct to represent and highlight what had been learned. SSA became increasingly important as a reflection of learner-centred pedagogies.

A defining moment in my thinking was reading the work of Scriven (1967) and Sadler (1989), on the one hand, and the Assessment Reform Group (ARG, 2002) and Black and Wiliam (1998), central figures in Assessment for Learning discourses, on the other. The latter was a negative defining moment because it became clear that too many anomalies and contradictions in the research on Assessment for Learning were not conducive to helping tutors or students (Taras, 2007, 2009, 2010).

Perhaps the most important realisation was that lack of theoretical coherence was the greatest deficit in Assessment for Learning discourses, and Taras (2005) was a milestone in my understanding of assessment theory. Taras' article clarifies summative (SA), formative (FA), and SSA and, importantly, how they interrelate. This theoretical framework has formed the basis for understanding practices, particularly feedback and SSA practice. Thus, two researchers have particularly influenced my understanding of assessment positively, Scriven and Sadler, and two have influenced them negatively, Black and Wiliam (1998) and, especially, Black et al. (2003).

Moving to assessment discourses in education from a background of ELT was also very challenging, which is perhaps why I focused obsessively on details and discovered many anomalies and contradictions overlooked by education specialists.

What is important is to link concepts across subject divides. For example, corrective feedback (CF), from a cognitive theories' perspective in the ELT literature, focuses on immediate corrections in oral language. Zhao and Ellis (2022) 'contribute to the body of research that has investigated the relative effectiveness of implicit and explicit CF'. They briefly summarise current thinking and permutations on CF in a classroom-based study. Cognitive theories are used to describe different viewpoints. From the tutors' viewpoint, CF can be considered either implicit or explicit. The impact on learners is that the former may not register as correction, whereas the latter is more likely to be noticed as such. ELT refers to 'corrective feedback' (CF), educational assessment, in general, refers to SA and FA, and CF is probably closer to FA, or to what is currently being called classroom assessment. If this CF process is examined through a theoretical assessment lens rather than a linguistic one, we unearth new issues, as will be seen below. This chapter focuses on complex multi-criterion contexts, e.g., essay assignments that require content input in addition to language input. Discourses clarify SA, FA, and SSA theories within educational discourses.

Clarifying assessment theories and situating feedback within them

Perhaps the first questions to ask are where does feedback originate, and will its origins change the feedback? Educational feedback is assumed and presumed to be accurate and useful, particularly if it comes from tutors. This is different from opinions and decisions because feedback is formalised and focused. In any context, formal or informal, feedback is information that results from a judgement. A judgement by any other name is assessment. Therefore, all feedback we provide has its origins in assessment. This assessment may be explicit according to shared, transparent criteria and standards; this enables it to be questioned and ascertain to what degree it is accurate and ethical. Or assessment may be implicit and take place in the assessors' heads with the feedback being the only means of extrapolating the process. Educational assessment is required to be explicit for quality assurance purposes, and it may be timely to discuss milestones in assessment theories that currently frame feedback.

Summative and formative assessment

Scriven (1967) was the catalyst for changing discourses of assessment when he made the distinction between summative assessment (SA) and formative assessment (FA) assessment. Scriven (1967) says the following: first, SA and FA are processes and thus refer to what we do. Whatever anyone wishes to do with the results of these assessments cannot change the processes and, importantly, cannot be controlled. The functions or purposes to which these assessment results may be put are dependent on individual or group vagaries. Thus, separating discourses that focus on processes and those that focus on functions or purposes is crucial. Processes are the realities of what we do, and functions or purposes are wishes and hopes of what we would ideally like to happen: that is reality versus pie in the sky.

Second, SA is an assessment of *completed* work, be it by students, tutors, or anyone, and links to the literal meaning of summative. We would expect clear, shared, and explicit criteria and standards, and if the relative weightings of the criteria are not specified, then it could be assumed that the weightings are equal.

SA may be defined as the process and product of a judgement using explicit, shared criteria and standards in order to decide and express the quality of a process or product. Because there are explicit, shared criteria and standards, the SA will also be explicit. Generally, in (final) exams, part of the results, that is, the number or letter grade, are used as part of another comparative judgement classifying students. The comments explaining and justifying the number or letter grade may also be communicated. This complex and time-intensive process and product might end here. This is a judgement where a very narrow use of the product serves a specific purpose, often validation, accreditation, or selection and classification of candidates. That is SA. SA provides a judgement and justifies it.

If the comments explaining and justifying the number or letter grade are communicated, this is generally termed 'feedback'. Logically, this feedback is 'information' and no more (Sadler, 1989; Scriven, 1967). SA and feedback stop here. Since this feedback has been formally produced and is open to scrutiny, the likelihood of it being accurate and ethical is high. If the terminology used is accessible to students as well as tutors, then it should be useful information to guide them as to the quality of their work and for future improvements.

FA is totally separate from SA and usually involves the student/producer of the work.

FA is using the process and product of SA to

1 understand how a judgement has been reached against explicit, shared criteria and standards, and importantly
2 using this knowledge and understanding explicitly to update and improve the work.

Therefore, FA requires students/learners to engage and be cognisant of SA processes and products to be able to move to FA.

Taras (2005, 2012, 2013, 2023) goes a step further and requires students to situate this SA information into their production context. This includes volition, intentions, and all the emotional and self-regulated learning factors which were involved in creating the work (Panadero, 2017). In clearer speak, students must want to change their work, see the point in doing this, and importantly, accept the 'feedback' as being appropriate, relevant, and useful. This is generally the missing link in our assessment chain which might lead to students accepting and using comments.

Therefore, and crucially, the literature claims that FA + feedback = SA is making the initial assessment (SA) implicit. Making SA implicit means that it cannot be replicated in students' minds so that they can follow tutors' decisions. Also, it will inevitably lead to a lack of transparency and accountability, which is generally where most problems with assessment arise.

Technically, assessors can also carry out FA on others' work if they actually update this work themselves, turning it into a collaborative enterprise. It is the person updating the work who carries out FA, not the giver of information.

Self-assessment, whether for students (SSA) or for anyone, is an essential skill required to carry out FA (Panadero, 2017; Taras, 2002, 2015c, 2018, 2023). Taras' body of work on SSA has demystified what is available in the literature by making it explicit and how and to what degree the different models include and empower learners.

For Scriven (1967), FA is the ongoing process of updating any document, for example, when students use feedback from one student assignment to improve their next one, or when students have discussed ideas with peers and/or tutors and adjust their work. Ideas are gradually added and adjusted, and the changes form part of the progressive coming together of the whole. It is formative in the sense that it is forming into a whole from smaller ideas and constituent parts. The feedback which this type of assessment produces is constantly reused and recreated. However, as signalled above, for any information to be produced, SA is required. These FA steps and processes which Scriven describes are all preceded by SA. Therefore, Scriven does not differentiate between explicit and implicit SA. This is also the case for Sadler.

Since Scriven sees FA as continual updating and tweaking, logically, feedback could be seen as an internal dialogue with oneself on an ad hoc micro-level of thinking. Thus, this is continued SSA of our individual thinking and ideas, although in his seminal article, Scriven does not mention SSA, and it is Sadler who builds up the arguments explicitly for FA, albeit he mentions SA in passing: this creates two disconnects which Taras (2005) addresses. These descriptions go some way towards linking the very simplistic classifications of SA and FA, which have currently become the norm, with SA being considered final for accreditation and thus carrying a mark or grade, and FA being considered 'for learning' because it involves updating work.

Logically, even FA, as ongoing updating of work in progress, will also require constant SA closely followed by FA, whether this be explicit or implicit, conscious or unconscious. This reasoning makes FA impossible without constant SA preceding it, particularly when the same person is carrying out the FA as the SA. For example, self-correction during oral production is an important skill for each EFL/ESL or language learner to eliminate errors and develop fluency. I came as close to native speaker (NS) French as I was ever going to when I lived in Paris, and constant repetition and auto-correction were central to improving my fluency so that it became automatic. I also trained my friends and colleagues to correct me, and this feedback was invaluable.

Product feedback versus process feedback

Assessment is ubiquitous and takes place all the time with everyone: every decision, opinion, like, or dislike involves assessment implicitly. And there the problem lies; most of the assessment is implicit, and thus it becomes extremely difficult to clarify what we do when we assess. Yet, clarifying and making assessment explicit is a key aspect of learning, as further supported by self-regulated learning literature (Panadero, 2017).

To reiterate, Scriven makes the SA-FA distinction, and Sadler explains FA in detail and links it to SSA. Taras uses both Scriven and Sadler to link and explain SA, FA, and SSA. There is no polemic surrounding Sadler's work; however, Scriven (1967) was interpreted by Bloom et al. (1971), who wrote four years later, basing SA and FA on assessment functions, despite Scriven's expressed warnings. That is, Bloom et al. did not look at the processes within assessment, but claimed that SA and FA were distinguishable by their functions. This has two forms of impact: the processes of assessment, that is, what actually happens tends to be ignored, and noting that an assessment (for example, using a formative function) may lead to thinking that this makes it formative. The same argument is used for SA when based on functions. In reality, as noted, a function is the use which is made of the results of assessment. If an assessment is carried out, the function cannot be predicted or established beforehand. Also, as noted, any given assessment may be used in numerous and diverse ways by different people; therefore, it is impossible to establish or ring-fence a function. For example, if students are told in class that they will be given a FA, when tutors correct and/or grade the work, they can use the grade as a SA, which may be shared with other staff, parents, or stakeholders. What is then the function of that piece of work? Over time, when Black and Wiliam (1998) and the ARG (2002) from the UK had adopted Bloom et al. (1971), Scriven (1991) reframed his thinking and followed the crowd. In this chapter, all discussions, including the above, refer to processes unless it is specifically stated otherwise.

As noted above, engaging tutors in SSA across subjects was an important means for my understanding of the limitations that I was placing on my thinking and practices. Similarly, exploring and developing theoretical understandings, in addition to engaging with new thinking and terminologies, helped me to clarify why practices were working. In ELT, for each language skill, assessment, and SSA are as relevant as for any other educational subject. Taking the example of CF above and evaluating it through this theoretical lens clarifies a number of processes. Taras' theory notes that every assessment process requires (explicit or implicit) SA (Taras, 2005, 2012, 2023). Because CF is oral, conflating SA and FA may make it appear that there is no assessment, i.e., SA, when in fact it is the first crucial step. CF is a form of feedback; for it to be FA, it requires SA, followed by SSA and the student's decision to use the feedback. For example, if misleading or ambiguous syntax is used, providing the correct answer to replace this will circumvent the first (SA) step which notes implicitly that this is inaccurate because of inappropriate use. The same process applies when providing feedback in written production.

With CF, it is generally tutors providing the correction, and when this happens, students must first recall what they said, then compare tutor corrections with this and, through the comparison, decide what is going on linguistically. Using SSA, I would stop students at an appropriate place so they do not completely lose the thread of their thinking and ask them to think back to the potential mistake they made. If students could not find their own errors, then peers would be included. If it was a presentation rather than a discussion, then students were given indicators retrospectively of the contexts where they had made mistakes. It was surprising how often students remembered and were able to identify their own errors. It might take longer to carry out than tutor interventions, but the advantages were numerous, among which were creating good SSA and peer assessment habits, awareness, and skills. Thus, with SSA, as with all assessments, an original summative judgement, whether implicit or explicit, is followed by FA, which is students finding their own solutions. If peers or tutors were required to come to the rescue, at least, students had the chance to think first. Furthermore, the discussions became exciting in themselves.

Thus

FA = SA + feedback USED or considered by learners
Or SA + feedback used = FA
CF may be reconfigured as:
SA (implicit) produces (CF), i.e., the correction from SA = conveyed to learners
Learners receive CF without understanding the above steps but need to reconstruct the assessment comparison in their heads to make sense of it.

As terminologies of SA and FA become mainstream, potentially serious issues are best clarified. The first tripwire is confusing processes with functions, that is, what we do with a vague notion of what may be done with assessment results. Thus, SA, FA, and SSA are processes to be made explicit to all for all to be assessment literate. Second, the temptation to make SA implicit: all assessment requires SA as a starting point, especially FA and SSA. Third, making each SA explicit, that is, using explicit criteria and standards is central to ethical assessments.

Thus, if we really wish to support students' learning, this is best done, as the truism states, by helping them to understand their own thinking and beliefs and allowing them to reason their answers rather than making bland, bald, unsubstantiated statements. Only students can learn; therefore, let us let them learn. Understanding the difference between comments and commentary and reasoned thinking, which develops expertise, is critical in the contemporary world. As will be seen below, this is as important during language learning as in any other learning context.

Relationship between assessment, learning, and teaching

Two tree metaphors will be used to illustrate the relationship between assessment, learning, and teaching.

Banyan tree

Taras (2018) uses the metaphor of the banyan tree to explain the relationship between assessment, learning, and teaching. It presents the roots as assessment, which anchors the tree, and collects the basic nutrients and water from the ground so that the tree may develop. Generally, especially in Europe, the greater part of the roots is hidden and, like assessment, the extent of their influence and impact are not evident. An example is the banyan tree where the roots are partly in view in often magnificent displays. The canopy of leaves represents the learning which feeds, develops, and enriches the tree and society as a whole. The trunk and branches, teachers and teaching, are the support and conduits for basic minerals and water from the roots and the food which enable the tree to grow and develop. Thus, the tree as an ecosystem represents the socially supporting elements of educational contexts. This metaphor illuminates assessment as the key link to the leaves and development and growth and notes that the trunk, while an important support, can nevertheless be absent in some plants. These do not grow to the same size or magnificence as trees with strong supports, but they can nevertheless exist. This is likened to autodidacts.

Baobab tree

The baobab tree is a wonderful metaphor for the old-fashioned view of the role of the teacher as the font of all knowledge. In the banyan tree metaphor (Taras, 2018), the trunk or stem of a plant is likened to teachers who support and sustain learners and learning. The roots provide water and nutrients for the tree, as well as anchoring the plant. With the baobab tree, the context is different. The ground does not always have enough water and nutrients available; therefore, the trunk will store these so they can be used as required. This results in a massive trunk with a tiny canopy of branches and leaves, which can produce enough nutrition to keep the plant alive without depleting its large reserve of water in the trunk more than is necessary.

In the banyan tree, the leaves or canopy are likened to student learning, and they can feed themselves using sunlight, water, and minerals absorbed through the root system. Thus, in this system, the canopy, i.e., student learning, and the roots, i.e., the assessment system, are the main active components in a student-centred learning paradigm. However, where learners have their learning limited, as in the baobab tree context, and where teachers have the sole access to knowledge and information, then their growth will be limited and dependent on what teachers can provide. Although, technically, the ecosystem works in a similar way in the baobab, in reality, the trunk storing the water and minerals will balance the output to the leaves depending on the input from the roots. The roots of baobab are some of the longest tap roots known because they drill down to access any potential water table. Thus, the baobab tree is apposite in landscapes where water is scarce or arrives rarely. Educationally, this could be in places where books and/or internet access are not readily available, and teachers become 'the font' of knowledge.

The banyan tree metaphor demonstrates the crucial importance of making assessment visible and explicit (and, as we shall see, of SSA) for students' understanding and relating it to their learning. ELT students have extra dimensions to their learning journeys: in addition to grappling with two language systems, they also need to think and manage the content of their discourses and arguments. This is particularly difficult for oral production, but it is also taxing for other language skills. The banyan tree is a complete ecosystem of cyclical support and the creation of learning. With ELT and all language learning, this ecosystem necessitates relationships with peers and tutors, which is less notable with subjects like maths and history. Therefore, shared communicative practices and assessment literacies are particularly important in any language learning context.

Any tree is a complete assessment ecosystem, but in the banyan tree, the roots are visible and thus make assessment visible. In the baobab tree metaphor, the harmony of the contextual ecosystem is broken by extreme conditions, namely, the lack of water and the adaptation of the trunk to store any water when it is available. The all-powerful trunk, or teachers, can only support the canopy or students within the limitations of their own and available resources. If the teachers' language skills are limited, it is particularly impactful if there are limited ancillary materials to compensate. The type of tree which evolves depending on the climate and resources available. Likewise, in assessment, learning, and teaching, the way the processes are put in place will look different depending on the different contexts to achieve the best growth. The next section will relate how different SSA models can be adapted to these different contexts.

Current trends in SSA practices

Whilst the previous section highlighted the importance of theory and separating processes and functions, this section will focus on the different processes and how practices may be developed.

To clarify, self-assessment sometimes also refers to student assessment of tutors and teaching, or tutors assessing their own teaching. Although these may also be self-assessments, this chapter focuses only on SSA, that is, students' assessment of their own work.

SSA has long been recognised as being key to supporting student learning. Discourses of Assessment for Learning have reinforced this on a global scale. Relatively recently, research on self-regulated learning has further consolidated the central part SSA plays in learning.

Since SSA is central to respecting and achieving educational goals of self-regulated learners (Panadero, 2017; Taras, 2023), it is timely to clarify explicitly what is available in the literature to inform these current trends and enable our discourses and wishes to become realities.

All the SSA models can be adapted to most assessment types with some creativity and imagination. The following examples provide suggestions for ELT as a starting point. Using peer assessment alongside the SSA models would usefully encourage dialogue around assessment queries and develop assessment literacies. These discussions will also provide independence from tutors and extend students' understandings on a different level.

For all these models, as for all assignments and work given to students, certain basic processes are discussed and negotiated prior to students doing the work to be self-assessed. These include the details of the tasks required, how they will be assessed, and which criteria and standards will be used for the grading. Developing student assessment literacies requires discussion of the above so that the terms used are understood and used in similar ways across the group. This basic premise is true for all contexts, no matter the age or level, and the terminology and vocabulary used for the discussions can be adapted accordingly. The greater the involvement of students in decision-making, the greater the potential for student empowerment (Dann, 2014, p. 159). Taras and Wong (2023) provide practical examples of SSA from primary school to HE.

SSA models shadow tutors' processes of assessment, beginning with knowledge and thus quality of criteria and standards. Exploring rubrics and comparing their or others' work to exemplars also enables the building and consolidation of assessment literacies. These are all aspects which support learning because assessment uses the mechanisms which highlight how, why, what, and when learning happens. If these are not visible to tutors, we can enable learners to be clearer about themselves.

These criteria and standards may be in tutors' heads when they are assessing, but if these are to be shared as part of an assessment community, then making them explicit is crucial. Furthermore, with far less experienced students, they may require additional support in the form of checklists, exemplars, and rubrics which guide them as to what to look for. Carrying out these assessment processes explicitly with students will allow clarification, explanations, and sharing of assessment literacies. These are part of the reasons why peer and SSA are conducive to helping students' learning.

Self-assessment and feedback

Involving students in peer and self-assessment is an efficient means of inducting them and including them in assessment protocols and literacies so that a common language and comprehension of processes and products build a shared forum of understanding for discussion and development. Available self-assessment practices will be evaluated, and how these may be used to develop students' expertise in assessment, feedback, and assessment literacies. In its simplest form, SSA may be rubrics or checklists against which learners may compare their work (Panadero & Jonsson, 2013; Tan, 2020). This chapter focuses on available SSA models, including Taras' three SSA models, and how each may support students' understanding of their work and promote learning (Taras, 2023).

Taras (2018, 2023) identifies three basic groups of SSA models.

1 **Standard model,** which is the basic model used in discussions across the literature and, as such, is the default model.
2 **Self-marking** with Cowan's (2006) **Sound Standard** as a version of this.
3 **Three Versions of Taras' models with integrated feedback.**

Each will be discussed in detail in turn.

Standard SSA

The definition of SSA in the literature, generally seen as the Standard model, is uncontentious. It is students assessing their own work using (agreed) criteria and standards and submitting the SSA at the same time as their work. How the SSA is communicated may vary according to individual tutors, and grading is also optional. I have been persuaded that grading is an important means of understanding and appreciating standards (Sadler, 1989).

The Standard model was first developed in the 1930s in the USA and is the one referred to in the literature unless it is otherwise specified. There are claims that it empowers students by including them in assessments (Boud, 1995). However, since tutor assessment processes and SSA are totally separate, the result is that tutors and students each have a double workload, and there is no discussion forum for ideas or power sharing. The main reproach is that this model disadvantages students by being a confessional which may inadvertently reveal areas of confusion (Reynolds & Trehan, 2000; Taras,

2008, 2015a). Also, the SSA itself may 'confirm' any erroneous or mistaken ideas they may have. The main advantages are that it acts as a useful checklist for students and requires them to review their work.

In ELT, this model would benefit all models as a checklist for students, especially for oral presentations and written work. In oral production, it would encourage learners to monitor their own spoken language, which is a difficult task, and an important skill for improving proficiency and fluency. This applies similarly for written work.

Self-marking

Self-marking or self-correction provides students with a model answer with which to compare their work. This can be a clear and explicit step by step explanation of assessment for students. If students are involved in preparing the criteria and model answers, this will be additionally empowering for them, as will be the case for all models. Self-marking may be a simple tick box exercise where only the grade or mark is submitted to tutors, as with a vocabulary test, or it too can be a complex multi-criterion assessment with grading, where tutors are moderators of standards across the class.

Cowan's Sound Standard (Cowan, 2006) is similar to self-marking in all aspects except for the points of comparison: instead of using a model answer for comparison, it uses 55%, that is, a 'sound standard' or an average. The rationale is that most students are at this level and that models of excellence may be off-putting and demotivating. Therefore, students are provided with models for comparison which are just above and just below the 55%. The downside is that students are not offered aspirational levels, which may be particularly damaging for stronger students.

For both self-marking and the sound-standard variation, use with students in listening or reading comprehension would be a good introduction. A mark-sheet either provided by tutors or developed with student input would enable students to self-mark and peer-check, or peer mark their work. The self-marking should technically be easier since students would remember what they have written. Peer-marking could perhaps begin with anonymised work to enable students to separate the work from the emotional link with their friends. This might also benefit younger and less experienced students. Creating or participating in creating the marking scheme would benefit older and more experienced students. Sound standard is especially appropriate with weaker or more nervous learners who require more support and encouragement.

The immediacy of Standard SSA, self-marking, and Sound Standard has the advantage of their work being fresh in students' minds, although Taras found that waiting for tutors' correction and grading of their work created a positive distancing which generally demonstrated to students that they had already learned a lot since producing the work and that the distancing allowed more impartial assessment (Taras, 2003).

Taras' three versions of model with integrated feedback

Taras' three versions of SSA with integrated feedback all focus on the importance of feedback which may focus differentially on the tutor or students' own feedback. It is empowering in that students and peers disentangle their own understandings before receiving the tutor grades, which will inevitably impact their emotional reactions to the feedback (Taras, 2008, 2015a). All of Taras' versions encourage a focus on developing an understanding of grades, grading, and standards, as well as criteria.

Version 1: (V1) Student work returned with **tutor** feedback and no **grade**, peer discussion, and grading prior to tutor grades (Taras, 1999, 2001, 2002, 2007, 2010, 2015a, 2015b, 2015c, 2018)
Version 2: (V2) Students correct and grade (a) their original work and (b) peers' work prior to tutor grades and feedback (Taras, 2003, 2010, 2018)
Version 3: (V3) Students correct (a) their original work and (b) correct and grade peers' work, then receive tutor feedback and grades, and finally students grade their own work (Taras, 2015c)

Taras' original SSA models are the first new models since the Standard model was developed in the 1930s. Taras' SSAs follow student-centred learning discourses and, importantly, QAA regulations in HE where they were developed. The models differ in process, timing, and integration of feedback, whether it is tutors' (Taras, 1999, 2001, 2002) or students' (Taras, 2003). Taras (2010) evaluates and classifies the models according to students' degree of involvement in assessment, and Taras (2015a) and Taras (2018) focus on power differentials in the reclassified models. Taras' SSA versions are distinguishable by using accredited, graded work, as this is when students invest maximum time and effort. Also, students do not receive tutor grades until they have completed their SSAs to minimise their emotional impact. For V2 and V3, peer and tutor comments and grades are only received after they have corrected and graded their own work. Finally, the SSA processes take place just prior to receiving peer and tutor feedback and grades, for accredited work, generally 3–4 weeks after submission.

The three Taras SSA versions focus on helping students understand feedback related to their accredited work, whether from tutors, themselves, or peers. V1 prioritises tutor feedback, and students rethink and update their work on receiving this. V1 might thus be better suited for students beginning a course or of relatively low proficiency in either subject or language. Subsequent peer-assessment, grading of own and peer work, and discussions precede the final awarding of their grade by tutors.

V2 and V3 change the focus and are based on the rationale that the time-lapse taken by tutors to correct and grade their assignments has enabled students to gain a distancing from their work and be able to reread, correct, and grade it. This would help older and more advanced students develop their thinking. Peer-assessment and discussions follow allowing a thorough evaluation of the assignments before they receive tutor comments and grades. Anything students may have missed can then be discussed with tutors. This is an efficient use of student time in that they are the ones doing the thinking and assessing, and likewise for tutors, because they are not endlessly repeating the same things to different students. The difference between V2 and V3 is that V3 provides tutor comments and grades after students have updated their work but before their grading, whereas V2 provides tutor comments and grades when student updating and grading of themselves and their peers is complete. V3 may provide additional support from tutors if students are nervous about grading their own work.

V1 was originally developed with ELT students for them to be able to engage systematically with tutor comments on their work, particularly complex multi-criterion written work, without the initial emotional impact of grades. V1 might also be usefully used for oral production or translation work. V2 may usefully support more experienced students, particularly used alongside Standard SSA, or V1, of written or oral work, as it will require a greater understanding of comparing their work with their own thinking after a time gap. V3 is more supportive of student grading if they feel nervous or insecure about sharing their opinion about this prior to trying V2.

All SSA models allow students to work with criteria and clarify standards and induct them into assessment processes. Self-marking and the integrated models also allow students to develop expertise in focusing on the product so that even if students' grades do not count for accreditation, they can still become their own and their peers' double markers. Understanding criteria and standards should make it easier to use and attain them.

The Standard model is the least empowering because it separates tutors' and students' assessments and grading, although, as with all models, it is more empowering if students are co-creators of criteria. It is sometimes difficult to explain something which is relatively simple. The processes of these three versions of SSA are a case in point.

Although in all three Taras versions tutor grades are the ones that count as the official grade, if students can demonstrate that a higher grade is more just and appropriate, then this evidence will require tutors to change the grade. We can all learn from each other.

Future adaptations and developments

Educational discourses have moved learner and learning-centred pedagogies forward considerably in the last 30 years, although assessment is far less so. In general, our discourses do not match our practices, and a million and one reasons justify our inertia, especially since it is so difficult to swim against the current.

As educators, it can thus be argued that one of the major tasks, and the most difficult, for the future or the present is to scrutinise what we know and put these innovations into practice. Through practice and research, a clearer understanding will inform how these developments influence learning and learners in their contexts, and how these may also be generalised. One of the major challenges is epistemologies and ontologies which may lock us inside our own prejudices and narrow beliefs. As noted, one of the greatest and continuing challenges personally was adapting my initial innovation to other people and other contexts during a University Teaching Fellowship.

Also noted, an important failing has been the contradictory discourses, particularly in theory, which has made it difficult for educators to align practices with theory and to have coherent epistemologies. A number of researchers have demonstrated that despite learning and learner-centred discourses, teacher-led, teacher-controlled, and teacher-dominated beliefs predominate, both in HE (Haggis, 2009; Lau, 2016; Maclellan, 2001) and within the compulsory school sector (Biesta, 2022; Dysthe, 2008; Hargreaves, 2005).

Cognitive psychology has demonstrated that as humans we live with contradictory concepts, perhaps because it is impossible to ever know everything (Lakoff & Johnson 1980; Johnson, 1987). However, contradictions do not make for efficient and useful processes.

Being in a position to make an informed decision is a basic human right of a civilised world. Education helps to ensure that decisions may be informed and assessment is the primary tool.

The Convention on the Rights of the Child states:

Article 12 "1. States Parties shall assure to the child who is capable of forming his or her own views the right to express those views freely in all matters affecting the child, the views of the child being given due weight in accordance with the age and maturity of the child." (www. ohchr.org)

Being capable of having clear views and opinions and the courage to express these requires SSA at its heart and ethical, explicit, and shared assessment processes at all stages of education.

Conclusion

This chapter has presented learner-inclusive assessment processes which empower learners without disempowering tutors. These assessment processes are to everyone's benefit because they enlighten and educate. These processes can be adapted to suit all contexts if we have the courage to work with our students.

My unique perspectives on assessment, feedback, and SSA are firmly grounded in my eclectic background of ELT with the addition of educational discourses from education in general. The richness and diversity of ELT and educational contexts all provide rich pickings for us to understand principles and theories to develop and adapt our processes, none more important than those relating to assessment and feedback in general and theories in particular. Breaking down silos in different subjects is why most of my work became generic. SSA, as discussed here, might not be new, but much is new to ELT and many other contexts.

The single step of the SSA journey was first recorded in the USA in the 1930s. One of the reasons that this journey has moved so far in the last 25 years must surely be attributed to greater transparency and accountability of both processes and products of assessment. As importantly, the linking and mutual support of discourses relating to theory, practices, and empirical evidence provide coherent and logical discourses of assessment and SSA (Taras, 2015b). Developments also need to be pertinent to their time, and recent developments in self-regulated learning (Panadero, 2017) further demonstrate the centrality of SSA to educational, social, and emotional aspects, in sum, what makes us human learners.

The SSA models presented provide efficient ways for students to access inclusive, ethical, and empowering assessment processes that enable tutors to support students' learning. Long may we continue to learn from each other.

References

ARG (2002). Assessment for learning: 10 principles. Research-based principles to guide classroom practice. Assessment Reform Group.Downloaded from: http://www.assessment-reform-group.org

Biesta, G. (2022). The school is not a learning environment: How language matters for the practical study of educational practices. *Studies in Continuing Education*, *44*(2), 336–346. 10.1080/0158037X.2022.2046556.

Black, P., Harrison, C., Lee, C., Marshall, B., & Wiliam, D. (2003). *Assessment for learning: Putting it into practice*. Open University Press.

Black, P., & Wiliam, D. (1998). Assessment and classroom learning. *Assessment in Education. Principles, Policy and Practice, 5*(1), 7–68.

Bloom, B. S., Madaus, G. F., & Hastings, J. T. (1971). *Handbook on Formative and Summative Evaluation of Student Learning*. McGraw-Hill.

Boud, D. (1995). *Enhancing learning through self assessment*. Kogan Page.

Convention on the Rights of the Child. https://www.ohchr.org/en/ohchr_homepage

Cowan, J. (2006). *On becoming an innovative university teacher: Reflection in action* (2nd ed.). Oxford University Press.

Ruth Dann (2014) Assessment as learning: blurring the boundaries of assessment and learning for theory, policy and practice. *Assessment in Education: Principles, Policy & Practice, 21*(2), 149–166, DOI: 10.1080/0969594X.2014.898128

Dysthe, O. (2008). The challenges of assessment in a new learning culture. In A. Havnes, & L. McDowell (Eds.), *Balancing dilemmas in assessment and learning in contemporary education* (pp. 213–224). Routledge.

Haggis, T. (2009). What have we been thinking of? A critical overview of 40 years of student learning research in higher education. *Studies in Higher Education, 34*(4), 377–390.

Hargreaves, E. (2005). Assessment for learning? Thinking outside the (black) box. *Cambridge Journal of Education, 35*(2), 213–224.

Johnson, M. (1987). *The body in The mind: The bodily basis of reason and imagination*. University of Chicago Press.

Johnson, M., & Lakoff, G. (1980). *Metaphors we live by*. University of Chicago Press.

Lau, A. M. S. (2016). 'Formative good, summative bad?' – A review of the dichotomy in assessment literature. *Journal of Further and Higher Education, 40*(4), 509–525.

Maclellan, E. (2001). Assessment for Learning: The Differing Perceptions of Tutors and Students. *Assessment and Evaluation in Higher Education, 26*, 307–318. http://dx.doi.org/10.1080/02602930120063466

Merry, S., Price, M., Carless, D., & Taras, M. (2013). *Reconceptualising feedback in higher education*. Routledge.

Panadero, E. (2017). A review of self-regulated learning: Six models and four directions for research, *Frontiers in Psychology, 8*, 422. https://www.frontiersin.org/articles/10.3389/fpsyg.2017.00422/full

Panadero, E., & Jonsson, A. (2013). The use of scoring rubrics for formative assessment purposes revisited: A review. *Educational Research Review, 9*, 129–144.

Reynolds, M., & Trehan, K. (2000). Assessment: A critical perspective. *Studies in Higher Education, 25*(3), 267–278.

Sadler, D. R. (1989). Formative assessment and the design of instructional systems. *Instructional Science, 18*, 145–165.

Scriven, M. (1991). *Evaluation thesaurus* (4th ed.). Sage Publications, Inc.

Scriven, M. (1967). The methodology of evaluation. In R. Tyler, R. Gagne, & M. Scriven (Eds.), *Perspectives on curriculum evaluation (AERA monograph series – Curriculum evaluation)* (pp. 39–83). Rand McNally & Co.

Taras, M. (1999). Student self-assessment as a means of promoting student autonomy and independence, in: M. TARAS (Ed.) *Innovations in Learning and Teaching: teaching fellowships at the University of Sunderland*. University of Sunderland Press.

Tan, K. H. K. (2020). *Assessment rubrics decoded: An educator's guide* (p. 140). Routledge.
Taras, M. (2001). The use of tutor feedback and student self-assessment in summative assessment tasks: Towards transparency for students and for tutors. *Assessment and Evaluation in Higher Education, 26*(6), 606–614.
Taras, M. (2002). Using assessment for learning and learning from assessment. *Assessment & Evaluation in Higher Education, 27*(6), 501–510.
Taras, M. (2003). To feedback or not to feedback in student self-assessment. *Assessment & Evaluation in Higher Education, 28*(5), 549–565.
Taras, M. (2005). Assessment – summative and formative – some theoretical reflections. *British Journal of Educational Studies, 53*(3), 466–478.
Taras, M. (2007). Machinations of assessment: Metaphors, myths and realities. *Pedagogy, Culture and Society, 15*(1), 55–69.
Taras, M. (2008). Issues of power and equity in two models of self assessment. *Teaching in Higher Education, 13*(1), 81–92.
Taras, M. (2009). Summative assessment: The missing link for formative. *Assessment Journal of Further and Higher Education, 33*(1), 57–69.
Taras, M. (2010). Back to basics: Definitions and processes of assessments. *Revista Práxis Educativa, 5*(2), 123–130. http://www.revistas2.uepg.br/index.php/praxiseducativa/article/view/1829/1386
Taras, Maddalena (2012) Assessing Assessment Theories. *Online Educational Research Journal,* 3 (12). Downloaded from: http://sure.sunderland.ac.uk/id/eprint/3321/
Taras, M. (2013). Feedback on feedback: Uncrossing wires across sectors. In S. Merry, M. Price, D. Carless, & M. Taras (Eds.), *Reconceptualising feedback in higher education* (pp. 30–40). Routledge.
Taras, M. (2015a). Situating power potentials and dynamics of learners and tutors within self-assessment models. *Journal of Further and Higher Education.* (39), 1–18.
Taras, M. (2015b). Student self-assessment: what have we learned and what are the challenges? *RELIEVE,* 21(1). ENGLISH and SPANISH. ISSN 1134-4032. (1) ENGLISH https://ojs.uv.es/index.php/RELIEVE/issue/view/396. (2) SPANISH https://ojs.uv.es/index.php/RELIEVE/issue/view/396
Taras, M. (2015c). Innovative pedagogical practices: Innovations in student-centred assessment https://www.advance-he.ac.uk/knowledge-hub/innovations-student-centred-assessment
Taras, M. (2018). Transgressing power structures in assessment: Not a step too far, just far enough. In S. Jackson (Ed.), *Developing transformative spaces in higher education: Learning to transgress* (pp. 162–181). Routledge.
Taras, M., & Wong, H. M. (2023). *An essential guide for teaching, learning and reflection at school and university.* Routledge. https://www.routledge.com/Student-Self-Assessment-An-Essential-Guide-for-Teaching-Learning-and-Reflection/Taras-Wong/p/book/9780367691677
Zhao, Y., & Ellis, R. (2022). The relative effects of implicit and explicit corrective feedback on the acquisition of 3rd person -s by Chinese university students: A classroom-based study. *Language Teaching Research, 26*(3), 361–381. https://journals.sagepub.com/home/ltr

7
ELT CLASSROOM MANAGEMENT IN TIMES OF CHANGE

Christopher Graham

Classroom management – Definitions and past contexts

There are two challenges with any attempt to explore classroom management as an area of professional competence for English language teachers. One challenge is the variety of definitions of the content and scope of 'classroom management'. The other is the fact that it is not a discrete area of knowledge and skills, being so directly connected with methodological approaches, the specific teaching and classroom context, the prevailing educational culture in a given setting and an individual teacher's beliefs about language learning. Indeed, it could be said that classroom management is the most significant manifestation of a teacher's belief sets and teaching philosophy. The manifestation of these beliefs, at least to the eyes and ears of the learners, would be the 'key teacher interventions' (Scrivener, 2012), and these, perhaps above all, shape the foreground of the experience the learner has. The background to the learners' classroom experiences would be shaped by resource management, classroom layout, the often almost invisible rules and procedures, rapport and relationship-building techniques, the planning for a range of eventualities and the gentle self and peer-reflective practices that are visible only perhaps in their enforcement as the teacher sees appropriate. These background activities will reduce disruptions and facilitate learning (Cevallos & Soto, 2020).

As alluded to above, and not widely explored in the literature, is the idea that classroom management in effect is a tool of methodology (and arguably vice versa too) and totally interlinked with it. This is perhaps best

DOI: 10.4324/9781003361701-10

seen as an elastic and yet symbiotic relationship. For example, one of the legacies of COVID-19 and the move to remote teaching has been a change in the group dynamics of a classroom. It is harder to form meaningful working groups online with a psychological bond between learners, and teachers have had to adjust their methodological approach to activities that in face-to-face contexts would have been conducted in working groups. This change in approach will have classroom management challenges in that learners' levels of motivation may drop when in virtual working groups, meaning discipline may be an issue, and instructions especially in the early days of the remote approach need to be even clearer. Methodology and classroom management are inexorably linked.

Another extension to the perceptions of classroom management is the relationships that teachers have with other stakeholders, especially parents. The Covid pandemic has brought teaching into learners' home environments, and in many cases this has required or inspired greater parental intervention. Parents have needed to learn about the need for quiet environments conducive to learning that ELT can be noisy, that learners may use L1 and that teachers use a wide range of topics to motivate learners. The return to face-to-face may reduce the parental role, and teachers will likely have mixed views on this, but parents have certainly been more dominant stakeholders than they were.

Building on this idea of stakeholder influence, the core concept underpinning this chapter is that approaches to classroom management are constantly subject to myriad influences that can require classroom practitioners to adapt some or all of their approaches to changing circumstances.

These influences can be classified as:

1 External to ELT institutions and non-negotiable, such as the recent COVID-19 pandemic (explored in this chapter below) or the climate crisis. These influences are out of the hands of classroom practitioners and have to be managed as best as they can be.
2 External to ELT institutions and negotiable. These might include broad directives on methodology or curriculum that a ministry of education imposes on teachers, but that teachers can interpret in their practices, and in some circumstances engage in discussions and consultations around. Equally, initiatives, trends and classroom ideas gathered from conferences and professional publications would be examples of these types of influence.
3 Internal and non-negotiable. Examples of these would be a school changing disciplinary policies for students or examination procedures that teachers must adhere to.

4 Internal and negotiable. Included here would be topics and approaches explored in in-house professional development workshops, trends, research findings and feedback that teachers can experiment with in class, reflect on and then adapt to their contexts.

The impact of influences of these types will be discussed in the following section with some discussions around future developments in the section "Classroom management in evolution".

Classroom management – Present contexts

The resilience shown around COVID-19 and similar crises

COVID-19 has arguably been the biggest global challenge to the resilience of ELT practitioners, and their ability to adapt and adapt quickly, since the establishment of ELT as a profession. Regional and local conflicts and natural disasters have also created the need for similar resistance and adaptation in specific geographical areas.

If one of the characteristics of resilience is the ability to adapt to changing circumstances, then Covid has tested the global ELT community considerably. A degree of academic resilience (Capstick, 2018) has been shown by communities of teachers who may never have delivered a lesson online, yet found themselves at short notice working with Zoom and other platforms to deliver material not designed to be delivered online, to learners who had never attended a virtual class. This journey has been described as a transition from emergency remote teaching (Mavridi, 2022) to remote teaching and the sense that the global community has made the adaptation and remains motivated can be seen by the topics and themes from recent global conferences.

The skills of virtual classroom management can be said to include:

- the need to adapt non-digital teaching resources to online use, where the core course books did not have extensive digital components. Where the materials did have digital components, the management challenge was more around orientation and familiarity;
- the fact that many ELT classes are quite paper-heavy and that the shift online has meant many activities have had to be adapted to the paper-free context. For example, teacher-generated worksheets had to be made available for learners in a completely digital format, or replaced;
- the impact digital learning has on class cohesion and collegiality is a difficult outcome to measure but the rapid move online will have disrupted inter-student working relations and informal student mutual support

relationships. Teachers will have explored the use of Zoom breakout rooms, and other platforms such as Slack or Basecamp or Facebook groups, to replicate some of these relationships but this will have taken time as part of a learning curve and efficacy will have varied with the IT skills sets of individual teachers.

Other Covid-related issues include the following:

a The impact on high stakes testing, by these tests either not being taken at all or, increasingly, being 'e-proctored'. Many learners in high schools will have missed the opportunity to take public examinations and though many will have experienced in-school assessments, the sense of importance of a public, high stakes exam will have been lost for them. This will have an impact when they actually do a public examination and even if they do not, their experience of education may feel somewhat diluted. The tentative moves towards e-proctoring have been accelerated by Covid, and learners will have felt unfamiliar with the processes, and with the uncertainties around cheating and validity (Giller, 2021, p. 13), and again may feel the experience has been diluted. Equally, the digital divide is a significant challenge in the global rollout of e-proctoring (Giller, 2021, p. 41). Chapter 5 extensively elaborates on the issues of validity, reliability and practicality of e-tests.
b Physical classroom changes became a challenge for classroom management as Covid restrictions eased and learners began to return to schools, or in contexts where remote teaching was not widely used. Social distancing and in some cases the use of Perspex screens between learners will impact the ability of learners to work in collaborative groups, diminish the feeling of collegiality by the erecting of literal barriers and interfere with the ability of learners to have conversations and hear the responses of their colleagues. Teachers have needed to develop mechanisms to maintain that collegiality and those communication channels while avoiding the lesson becoming excessively teacher-centred. They will also have needed to develop devices that maintain discipline – likely to be an issue due to a feeling of isolation amongst learners – but also provide support to learners feeling vulnerable.

The impact of social media on students' knowledge of the world, and approaches to learning

The seemingly endless rise in social media use – especially amongst younger generations – is well-documented, as is the uneven distribution of access, the so-called digital divide.[1] The usage of different platforms seems to fluctuate with trends, the age ranges of user groups, and geography and cultural setting. This will have an impact on ELT classrooms.

In terms of ELT classroom management, the impacts of social media can perhaps best be subdivided into positive and negative.

Positive

Learners of all ages have become used to communicating across borders with ease and rapidly and these dynamics must surely impact upon their expectations for ELT classrooms and teaching. These expectations are likely to be around:

- the degree of autonomy they have in their learning – social media is, after all, about the user's ability to make choices;
- the extent to which they feel their learning is self-directed, again social media offers options and 'paths' for users;
- how much social media platforms are incorporated into their learning process. The fact that these platforms play significant roles in the lives of so many suggests that their use in ELT classes would be a motivator for learners;
- opportunities to enhance and develop their intercultural skills. Social media allows users to exchange ideas with people from a range of cultures and this is something that learners may expect to see reflected in classes. A monocultural context for language learning is becoming less and less appropriate;
- an awareness of English as a Lingua Franca has been enhanced by the use of social media, and the Anglocentric native speaker model would seem a long way from the experience of many users and thus English learners.

Negative

Social media can of course be a distraction both when used in class and as part of a broader psychological impact with the way it appears to influence attention spans (Harii, 2022; Mahalingham et al., 2022).

Digital equity, both in terms of access to devices and in terms of connectivity, comes to the fore when the use of social media within class and at home becomes commonplace, and teachers need to have a strategy in mind suited to their context (Hockly & Dudeney, 2018).

A range of levels of ITC literacy, information literacy and media literacy (Dudeney, 2020) amongst learners needs to be considered, and a strategy developed for their management, as social media and broader digital applications are used more and more widely in ELT classes. These issues can also apply to teachers, and CPD may be needed to alleviate teacher anxiety and the perceived stigma attached to this.

The implications of increasing equity for non-native speaking teachers and changing views of learning expectations and language models

The movement away from the native speaker teacher and language model hegemony has been slow in coming. The speed of progress towards equity for, and recognition of the value of, all qualified English teachers regardless of mother tongue is increasing, but there is still much work to do across the global ELT community. The bases for the discrimination against teachers who do not have English as their mother tongue vary with context, but they seem to be firmly embedded into the beliefs of those concerned. These include alleged commercial considerations, for example, that parents of young learners want native speaker teachers; related to accent and pronunciation models; around their perceived knowledge of idiomatic language, and sometimes the objections appear to be more related to the ethnicity of teachers.

The rationale behind equity for English language teachers regardless of mother tongue is explored comprehensively by Peter Medgyes (Medgyes, 2021), while Robert Lowe and Marek Kiczkowiak (Lowe & Kiczkowiak, 2016) discuss the impact of native speakerism on two language teachers, one native and one non-native. A recent case in Europe did clarify the legal status of non-native speaking teachers in terms of employment rights, at least within the EU and this will contextualise ongoing discussions.[2]

This movement towards recognition of something beyond the mother tongue either as a 'qualification' to teach English or as a reasonable aspiration for English language learners has some influence on ELT classroom management. The implications of this debate for classroom management include the following:

1 Student and parental or sponsor attitudes are important to the debate and the wider move towards a more equitable approach to English language teaching. Parents and sponsors in particular are often seen as the stakeholders most likely to resist learners being taught by non-native speakers. Teachers (of all language backgrounds) can take opportunities in parents' evenings, for example, to discuss the issue, and in class with learners to mention that, as appropriate, they themselves have also been learners of English (Medgyes, 2021, p. 69). This can help to demonstrate real empathy with the learners.
2 The ability to use the L1 of the learners can be an important classroom management tool for reassuring learners who feel over-challenged by

English or have developed a sense that others are making more progress. A few words in the L1 from the teacher, and specifically a teacher with an understanding of the learning culture, can be very valuable to an anxious learner and develop the empathy mentioned above.

3   Where teachers are working with learners from their own native language group, they can take opportunities to use their shared knowledge of L1 to develop the learners' abilities in L2. This could be comparisons between two items of language structure (something learners will quite naturally do in any case), or re-focussing a course book activity to take account of likely interference from the L1. Resistance to the use of L1 in classes can be institutional or ministerial (possibly being prohibited) or from colleagues or parents. Stakeholder education, as mentioned above, is a key part of ensuring the continuing move towards equity for all ELT teachers, and while not strictly classroom management, the teacher can have a pivotal role in cross-stakeholder education around the use of L1.

4   The commonly long-held aspiration of attaining native-like competence or command of the sound system in L2 has been losing credibility for some time now but there does remain a need to generate an understanding amongst stakeholders of the likely attainability and indeed desirability of a native level of competence (however that is defined) amongst learners. Teachers certainly have a role in creating that understanding, specifically in classroom management, explaining to learners the importance of how, for example, listening comprehension covering a range of accents (native and non-native) is critical to equipping them to engage with English in the outside world. Equally, reassuring them that a level of English that ensures their comprehensibility (albeit accented) is both an achievable and desirable goal. The mirage of native-speaker competence is not.

The growing global influence of translanguaging

An all-encompassing definition of translanguaging is offered by Ofelia Garcia. 'Translanguaging is the act performed by bilinguals of accessing different linguistic features or various modes of what are described as autonomous languages, in order to maximize communicative potential' (García, 2009). Developing on Garcia is 'translanguaging is about *communication*, not about *language* itself' (original author's emphasis) (Anon, 2016).

Although its roots are in EAL, translanguaging has the potential to change the methodological approaches and thus classroom management techniques employed in ELT classrooms radically (Conteh, 2018). The rationale behind the use of more than one language (likely, but not exclusively to be the mother tongue, and the language being studied) as part of the learning process is based upon the fact that for many learners, this use of two languages is part of their present or future study or workplace realities. Equally, for bi- or multilingual individuals, it is an entirely natural thing to do.

For example, young learners studying in a CLIL environment or students in an EMI university setting will often switch between languages as a part of the learning process and as part of their day-to-day communication. Equally, adults working in international corporations or organisations will find themselves communicating with local colleagues in both L1 and L2 while L2-only international colleagues are present. This hybrid real-life use of language is likely to become more and more the norm with increased globalisation and easier virtual communications.

Slightly beyond the scope of this chapter, but as mentioned above, EAL has been leading the use of translanguaging, notably moving away from the context where bilingual learners are 'encouraged' to use the centred language (Farrell, n.d.), English in this case. This can engender feelings of isolation from and offence about the status of their other, often mother, languages. There are surely benefits in the ELT classroom in this regard too.

The impacts of this on classroom management and their considerations are likely to include the following:

1 The need for teachers to develop approaches to delineating the uses of the relevant languages in class, communicating these to learners and ensuring they understand these delineations. While the 'real life' contexts that learners will find themselves in almost certainly will not have these delineations, they are needed in the pedagogic context.
   For example,
   will classroom instructions always be in English?
   when can learners ask questions in L1?
   do learners need to mark when they are going to transition to the other language?

2 As discussed above in the section about native speakerism, an extension to classroom management in the area of translanguaging would include developing strategies to pre-empt and manage resistance from external stakeholders such as parents and ministries of education; this might include discussions with parents and activity within local teacher associations. These same strategies would need to be applied to managing resistance from colleagues and other stakeholders whose beliefs around learning include using only L2 in the classroom.

3 Resource management has additional opportunities in a classroom where translanguaging forms part of the pedagogy. One of the benefits of

translanguaging in a monolingual classroom is that where complex issues such as climate change science, economic policy or cryptocurrency form part of the theme of a lesson, the use of L1 background resources can support learners. They can expedite the learners' understandings of an unfamiliar topic. Once these complex ideas are more fully understood by learners, the L2 discussions, language work and skills development activities can take place in a more meaningful way. The selection of appropriate L1 resources on these conceptually complex topics is a time-consuming classroom management activity but will yield learning benefits.

The higher profile being given to both teacher and student wellbeing

Wellbeing can be a complex concept to define. Sarah Mercer (2021) suggests that 'well-being is defined as the dynamic sense of meaning and life satisfaction emerging from a person's subjective personal relationships with the affordances within their social ecologies'. This is interesting as it suggests that wellbeing is centred around our interactions with our environment – our workplace, our colleagues, other students in our class, the students we teach, parents and so on. This 'social ecology' seems to include all the ELT stakeholders.

The awareness of wellbeing in ELT pre-dates COVID-19. That said, the pandemic and the move to emergency remote teaching was one of the drivers that put learner and teacher wellbeing in focus, as it became increasingly clear that both the transition and the virtual environment itself, new as it was, could be psychologically challenging for both students and educators. In particular, the loss or perceived loss of collegiality and the mutual support mechanisms inherently inbuilt, that virtual learning can create, have led to wellbeing concerns for both learners and teachers. Equally, 'learning loss' has raised wellbeing issues.

Teachers in particular, although other stakeholders have a responsibility here, increasingly need to develop strategies to create an atmosphere of safety and security within and without classrooms, both 'real' and virtual. While many learners have now returned to face-to-face learning, the psychological legacy of the COVID-19 pandemic lives on in the minds of many learners. Equally teachers and other institutional stakeholders need to work together to create mechanisms to ensure the wellbeing of the entire institutional community.

Some implications for classroom management include the following:

1 The facilitation of one-to-one discussions (face-to-face or online) via a 'surgery' system, that is agreed times and dates when the teacher will be available to talk to learners by appointment. The policies around the use

of the 'surgery', including booking processes and duration of meetings, confidentiality, and the parameters of discussion need to be shared with learners in advance. Teachers also need to be aware that the first session may be awkward for both parties and that it will only be in later sessions that the underlying challenges the learner faces will be offered up for discussion. As such, this is a change in the typical teacher-student dynamic and both stakeholders need to be cognisant of this.
2 Above and beyond the surgery approach suggested above, teachers need to be aware of all other support services available within their institution and able to judge which of these services might suit a given individual learner best.
3 A device that teachers might consider to manage learner wellbeing issues is a class-level, non-personalised reflection on potential concerns to pre-empt them. This might involve learners sharing possible anxieties and concerns that might occur, and discussing ways of managing them. On the basis that wellbeing issues are often fuelled by a feeling of isolation, a simple awareness that others have the same concerns may help to alleviate some of the learners' anxieties. A rider to this approach might be that obvious non-participation by a specific learner might indicate a more serious concern that needs addressing.
4 Where a teacher feels there are wellbeing concerns in a given class, (temporary) differentiation in class to respond to concerns can be a useful tool. This approach requires learners to be put into carefully selected mutual-support groups where learners can be encouraged to develop a short-term 'buddy' system. This is designed to be integrated into the daily teaching activities, not to be free-standing, and to be a short-term measure above all perhaps to demonstrate the idea that 'it's ok to talk'. A cliché perhaps, but for learners an important one.
5 Most classroom teachers are neither psychologists nor indeed psychiatrists, although aspects of both disciplines can form part of their daily experiences. Specialist professional development around the management of learner wellbeing is becoming more and more common and this is to be encouraged, perhaps the most important element of it being for teachers to understand the most common symptoms of a wellbeing issue that require them to call for outside medical support.
6 Classroom-based approaches to wellbeing can be made more powerful when they are linked to cross-school awareness campaigns and cross-stakeholder involvement. This broader aspect of classroom management outside of the classroom is key to creating the 'atmosphere of safety and security around wellbeing' referred to at the beginning of this section, although institution-wide wellbeing approaches are beyond the scope of this chapter.

The increasing inclusion of 'global issues' and social justice topics in coursebooks

Recent trends in the ELT publishing community and the broader materials development community have been to incorporate global issues into ELT teaching content, reflecting perhaps an increasing international awareness of them, outside ELT. These topics challenge the basis of the long-held acronym for taboo topics, 'PARSNIPS'.[3] The issues might include gender identity, gender roles, sexuality, immigration, poverty and equity, climate, human rights, the arms trade, health poverty, etc.

The rationale behind integrating these issues will tend to consider the positive motivational impact of introducing 'real' topics into the ELT classroom, the responsibility that educators have to increase awareness of these topics and the fact that they can give learners a 'voice' to express their feelings on the issues (Sciamarelli, 2017).

There are a number of classroom management issues and challenges around incorporating global issues into ELT teaching content, and these issues and challenges are not universal as they can often be geopolitical-context-specific.

1 Teachers need to have an awareness of the local cultural and political context as they introduce certain topics. Sexuality, immigration, and the arms trade can be unacceptable topics in certain countries and regimes, and while local teachers will be able to 'read' the context quite easily, this can be a challenge for non-local teachers. There may be settings where an international coursebook has some contentious topics that may be awkward to use in class. More commonly perhaps a learner might raise a global issue, and the teacher needs to be able to make a quick judgment call as to whether to simply suppress the topic immediately, or if they decide to pursue the discussion, what the acceptable parameters may be. This type of event is more and more common because of internet access and social media exposure, and again, more of a challenge for non-local teachers.

2 As well as geopolitical considerations, teachers need to have awareness of individual sensitivities amongst learners and any possible resistance from those learners and potentially other stakeholders, such as parents. Schools should have guidelines in place to manage this, and in particular if they are encouraging teachers to explore global issues, the rationale should be explained in advance to parents in an attempt to pre-empt any challenges.

3 Managing motivation can be a concern with global issues, especially with teenage classes. One of the reasons for this is that the topics can seem

remote and not relevant to them, and in some cases, they may have very little knowledge of the topics in L1. One approach to this, possibility as part of an intersectional approach (El Gharib, 2022), in a high school or university setting, is to develop cross curriculum links so that the global issues are explored, possibly in both L1 and L2 and in the spotlight of different disciplines. For example, poverty, educational inequity and gender issues are tightly interlinked and layered, and a cross curriculum approach might involve geography, history, economics and political science teachers as well as the ELT department.

4   Perhaps the most challenging decision an educator needs to make is whether to be a maverick or an activist. Whether to be the person who introduces controversial issues because they are relevant to the overall education of the learners. Whether to be the change maker. Estimates of the number of people studying the English language at any one time vary, as do what constitutes a 'learner of English', but the scale of the community gives teachers, materials writers and teacher educators the potential to be a huge force for good. Topics that might be integrated into ELT classes can vary with the context from being simply awkward for teachers and learners to having potentially dangerous consequences for them. Classroom management requires judgment calls on a daily basis and decisions to 'stretch the envelope' to include global issues are some of the hardest calls.

The integration of 21st century skills such as collaboration and critical thinking into ELT classrooms

'21st century skills' is a misnomer perhaps, now that period of history has arrived, but the commonly quoted taxonomy is the one developed by P21[4] that suggests four skills: creativity, collaboration, critical thinking and communication and, in addition, information, media and technology skills, and life and career skills.

Perhaps other new core skills can be added to the 'four Cs' outlined above. These new skills might include intercultural awareness, eco-literacy (Goleman et al., 2013) and empathy. Translanguaging, explored elsewhere in this chapter, could also be considered a 'new' 21st century skill, although it may not be universally applicable.

The rationale behind the integration of 21st century skills into the ELT classroom is driven by the fact that these skills are perceived as developing some of the requirements for the workplace context, for higher education study purposes, and as broader life skills. In that regard, they can be seen as a practical application and extension of the learners' English studies.

There are several implications for classroom management of the integration of 21st century skills.

1. A classroom that is developing and practising 21st century skills such as collaboration and critical thinking will, almost by definition, be more learner-centred and less teacher-centred. Underlying 21st century skills are the core ideas of learner autonomy and cooperation, and these cannot really be achieved in a teacher-centred classroom environment. A teacher's approach may need to vary to facilitate this.
2. One of the challenges for teachers working on 21st century skills in ELT is the distinction that needs to be made in terms of 21st century skills during their 'performance', between language and character. For example, if we take the skill of collaboration, the manifestation and demonstration of the skill may most commonly be seen as a linguistic performance. The measures of success might be seen as how a learner shares opinions and expresses agreement or dissent. But this is not necessarily a measure of the skill. The good collaborator may be the learner who has the lowest level of English or who is less confident about engaging in English, even though in L1 they are the most collaborative of individuals. Teachers need to be aware that behaviours are as much markers of success as are language performances, although the latter might overshadow the former.
3. The ease with which learners can comprehend and ultimately employ 21st century skills is likely to be dependent upon the transferability of the pre-existing skills amongst the learners. In this regard, teachers need to be aware of the extent to which the skills are taught – likely in L1, in the learners' home education systems – as this will ease the management of the development of these skills.
4. Teacher awareness and self-confidence can be a barrier to the development of 21st century skills in that some teachers themselves may feel that they do not have a grasp of the skills and their application, and equally because some teachers may be reluctant to work with the different, less teacher-centred, dynamics mentioned above. CPD solutions may be needed to resolve this.
5. It can be difficult to assess progress in the delivery of 21st century skills as there is no 'right' answer, different conclusions by different groups of learners to the same problem-solving activity may all be valid, for different reasons. Learners can find this lack of rigidity in the assessment of these skills frustrating and demotivating, so teachers need to consider approaches to its management. One thing to explore might be using the steps or the process of applying a 21st century skill as something to evaluate, rather than evaluating the end result (Graham, 2020, p. 142).

6 The best example of 21st century skills in action might, creating a virtuous circle, be the teacher's approach. A teacher asking learners to work in a collaborative and communicative way on 'noticing' some grammar or discussing some pre-listening questions to stimulate schemata could be seen as using 21st century skills. Thus, exemplification through the approach used by the teacher becomes a teaching tool.

Educational reforms with methodological implications such as the migration to a more learner-centred classroom

In recent years, many major government reform projects (self and donor-funded) around ELT methodology have focused on the evolution of the classroom dynamic from a teacher-centred to a learner-centred model.

Rationale for reforms of these types often revolve around the belief that learning is a student-centred journey (Jacobs & Renandya, 2016), and more specifically the belief that learners need to take responsibility – at least in part – for the learning process (Larsen-Freeman, 1987, p. 8).

Some of the elements of a learner-centred classroom that might create classroom management implications are:

- less teacher talking time and more use of learners working in pairs and groups, and collaboratively online beyond their classrooms;
- a higher degree of learner autonomy, with learners asking each other or checking online before reverting to the teacher for clarification;
- techniques such as 'noticing grammar' (Schmidt, 2010) or the 'flipping' of the classroom will also become more prevalent.

The implications for classroom management of the implementation of a more learner-centred approach might also include:

1 Resistance from both teachers and learners, very often centred on feelings of insecurity, are common reactions towards a progression to a more learner-centred classroom. The 'new' approaches are more public for learners so they can feel 'exposed'. Equally, the move towards a more autonomous learning style can leave learners feeling unsupported.
2 Teachers can sometimes have a sense of no longer being in control and the shift from being the centre of the classroom's focus to a more consultative and guiding role can be a challenge. More prosaically perhaps, a fear of silence as learners think and analyse ideas alone or in small groups can be of concern to teachers. The transition to a learner-centred classroom would seem to call for personal role reappraisals across the stakeholders.

3 The physical layout of the classroom may need re-evaluation to allow for working groups of learners and a higher degree of learner physical movement. Classroom environments with, for example, fixed desks and chairs may provide (surmountable) challenges in this context.

Classroom management in evolution

A reflection

The Covid pandemic will inevitably overshadow the third decade of the 21st century, and that shadow will extend into the ELT community and the way we manage our classes. It is probably unhealthy and not especially constructive to spend too much time analysing the impacts of Covid on ELT, but it seems reasonable to assess the pandemic as some sort of catalyst for change, and in terms of online delivery of classes, rapid change. At worst, it has destroyed the livelihoods and job security of many in our community and had a significant impact on the wellbeing of many people, while at best it gives us a chance to reassess as we regroup and move forward.

In the spirit of reassessment, the proposals for action below, based upon some of the themes explored in the body of this chapter, are intended to provoke debate across all the stakeholders. The word 'all' should be emphatic in that sentence, as the first proposal is that more cross-stakeholder cooperation and idea sharing about what goes on in classes and the challenges teachers face will be a key part of the development of the profession. Parents, teachers, publishers, exam authorities, school authorities and teacher educators would be on that list of stakeholders.

The impact of social media is something that needs to be embraced, albeit with some circumspection around the concentration span issues it seems to present. But that embrace needs to be inclusive and all educators as part of their classroom management need to be aware that digital equity is not only a problem 'elsewhere', but there are also learners in almost all communities who do not have internet access, and they must be provided for equally.

The move towards increasing equity for non-native speaking teachers is a movement that has grown because of campaigns by teachers and other stakeholders, but the battle is far from won. All members of the ELT community need to remind those many people who have doubts of why equity is important not just in terms of learning, but also as a moral imperative.

The encouraging of translanguaging is potentially a very significant change in the way we manage our classrooms but as with equity for all teachers, discussion across stakeholder groups will be needed to counter 'English only' policies.

The higher profile being given to wellbeing is perhaps (with remote teaching practices becoming embedded) the most significant of the COVID-19 'dividends'. The sustainability of wellbeing for students may require the overt teaching of wellbeing strategies as part of our classroom management and their integration into course books. Wellbeing for teachers and other staff requires cross-institutional initiatives.

The inclusion of 'global issues' can perhaps be best facilitated by an intersectional approach. Seeing the connectivity between issues can spotlight relevance (sometimes a challenge) and thus increase learner engagement.

The success of large-scale educational reforms and the classroom management implications thereof depends very often as much on how reforms are implemented as they do on their content, and excellent communication, consultation and change management practices will help to cement success. Again, the involvement of all stakeholders is vital.

Notes

1 Statista, 2022 https://www.statista.com/statistics/282846/regular-social-networking-usage-penetration-worldwide-by-country/
2 https://www.elgazette.com/eu-law-and-the-non-native-speaker-teacher/?fbclid=IwAR1EOLOd6Sl3J62tlK6cMyiuYSt4Nuz0ecGseNH4kC0VNO28uGGIOtGtV0k
3 https://scottthornbury.wordpress.com/2010/06/27/t-is-for-taboo/
4 https://www.battelleforkids.org/networks/p21

References

Anon (2016). Translanguaging is about *communication*, not about *language* itself. https://ealjournal.org/2016/07/26/what-is-translanguaging/

Capstick, T. (2018). Resilience. *ELT Journal*, 72(2), 210–213. https://doi.org/10.1093/elt/ccx068

Cevallos, L., & Soto, S. (2020). EFL classroom management. *Mextesol Journal*, 44(2).

Conteh, J. (2018). Translanguaging. *ELT Journal*, 72(4), 445–447. https://doi.org/10.1093/elt/ccy034

Dudeney, G. (2020). *Information, media and technology skills in 21st century skills in the ELT classroom: A guide for teachers*. In C. Graham, (Ed). Garnet Education.

El Gharib, S. (2022). What is intersectionality and why is it important? https://www.globalcitizen.org/en/content/what-is-intersectionality-explained/

Farrell, A. (n.d.). *The importance of a translanguaging approach in education*. City University of New York, Manifold Scholarship. https://cuny.manifoldapp.org/read/0bb3817a17dce4a174c5f92f9f2a37bd/section/14c83721-2815-4cad-8a3a-fdd8e93ace72

García, O. (2009). Education, multilingualism and translanguaging in the 21st century. In A. Mohanty, M. Panda, R. Phillipson, & T. Skutnabb-Kangas (Eds.). *Multilingual education for social justice: Globalising the local*. Multilingual Matters.

Giller, P. (2021). *E-proctoring in theory and practice: A review*. Quality and Qualifications Ireland.

Goleman, D., Bennett, L., & Barlow, Z. (2013). *Five ways to develop eco-literacy*. Greater Good, University of Berkeley.

Graham, C. (2020). 21st century skills in the ELT classroom: A guide for teachers. In C Graham (Ed.) (p. 142). Garnet Education.

Harii, J. (2022). Your attention didn't collapse. *It was stolen*. The Guardian 2 January 2022.

Hockly, N., & Dudeney, G. (2018). Current and future digital trends in ELT. *RELC Journal*, 49(2), 164–178. https://doi.org/10.1177/0033688218777318

Jacobs, G., & Renandya, W. (2016). Student-centred learning in ELT. In *English Language teaching today: Linking theory and practice*. Renandya, W. & Handoyo P. Springer. Pages 13–23.

Larsen-Freeman, D. (1987). From unity to diversity: Twenty years of language-teaching methodology. *English Teaching Forum*, 25(4), 8.

Lowe, R., & Kiczkowiak, M.. (2016). Native-speakerism and the complexity of personal experience: A duoethnographic study. *Cogent Education*, 3(1). https://doi.org/10.1080/2331186X.2016.1264171

Mahalingham, T., Howell, J., & Clarke, P. (2022). Attention control moderates the relationship between social media use and psychological distress. *Journal of Affective Disorders*, 297, 536–541. https://doi.org/10.1016/j.jad.2021.10.071

Mavridi, S. (2022). Emergency remote teaching and me: An autoethnography by a digital learning specialist during COVID-19. *Studies in Technology Enhanced Learning*. https://doi.org/10.21428/8c225f6e.960f4016

Medgyes, P. (2021). *The non-native teacher*. Swan Communication.

Mercer, S. (2021). An agenda for well-being in ELT: An ecological perspective. *ELT Journal*, 75(1), 14–21. https://doi.org/10.1093/elt/ccaa062

Schmidt, R. (2010). Attention, awareness, and individual differences in language learning. In W. Chan, S. Chi, K. Cin, J. Istanto, M. Nagami, J. Sew, T. Suthiwan, & I. Walker (Eds.), *Proceedings of CLaSIC 2010* (pp. 721–737). National University of Singapore, Centre for Language Studies.

Sciamarelli, M. (2017). Should language teachers avoid global issues when teaching? British Council.

Scrivener, J. (2012). *Classroom management techniques*. Cambridge University Press.

SECTION III
Teaching English language skills and components in new circumstances

8
TEACHING LISTENING IN NEW CIRCUMSTANCES

Joseph Siegel

Introduction

Language has been learned through listening for generations. Proficient listening provides access to information, linguistic development, and interactive opportunities. Listening is the first of the four main language skills (listening, speaking, reading, and writing) to development for first language (L1) learners, as the positive influences of hearing parents' voices while in the womb transition to early forms of input such as "baby talk" (Lightbown & Spada, 2021). As a child grows, interlocutors (e.g., parents, siblings, caregivers, and teachers) continue to accommodate or adjust the level, rate, and/or complexity of their speech to approximate the child's level of listening comprehension until they have developed sufficient listening abilities. The amount and type of input in the L1 are generally much greater than the aural input second language (L2) learners are exposed to, meaning that conditions for L2 listening development are much more limited than in the L1.

Because of these distinctions between L1 and L2 listening development, explicit attention in L2 classrooms has been devoted to L2 listening skills. Various broad approaches to L2 teaching and learning have made explicit efforts to account for how listening proficiency (a) develops in its own right and (b) integrates with other language skills and (c) functions in communication more generally. Whereas in the early days of widespread institutional L2 learning, often characterized by the Grammar-Translation method in which learners focused only on grammar, reading, and writing, oral and aural components gradually began to receive more attention (Richards &

Rodgers, 2014). The Audio-Lingual method, for instance, involved frequent spoken repetition of speech that learners heard; in other words, students did lots of "listen and repeat" drilling that was initiated with listening, albeit at a rather superficial level, since the act of repeating does not ensure comprehension or the ability to construct an original, meaningful response (Rilling, 2018). Starting around the 1970s, more interactive and meaning-based approaches such as Communicative Language Teaching (CLT) in general (e.g., Hedge, 2000; Loumbourdi, 2018; Siegel, 2022) and manifestations thereof (e.g., Task-Based Language Teaching) have recognized the need for active and adept listeners who can comprehend various types of messages delivered by different speakers in a variety of contexts.

Not only have views of listening changed, but materials and tools for teaching L2 listening have continued to develop, presenting teachers and learners with a range of options. In the past, materials were often scripted, lacking linguistic phenomena common to spontaneous speech; that is, recorded L2 materials were stilted, and features such as blending words, changes in the rate of speech, a range of accents, false starts, and hesitations were absent, leading to an inauthentic listening experience. In response to this undesirable situation, materials now typically acknowledge the reality of the listening act and include such natural features. The internet has, of course, immensely amplified the quantity, quality, and variety of content available. Textbooks used to be accompanied by tapes or CDs for listening practice. Teachers were the ones who controlled these resources, pushing "play" and "stop" on a single machine, meaning that the entire class had a singularly controlled listening experience. L2 listening in the classroom was performed in lockstep, not accounting for the various needs and levels of the individuals of which the group was comprised.

In more recent times, textbook publishers often deliver listening content online (e.g., via learning platforms), and since students sometimes have their own computer or tablet and headphones, they can be more in control of their own listening experience (e.g., deciding when to play, pause, rewind, and relisten). These digital tools have impacted how L2 listening is learned and taught in the L2 classroom. They have expanded the amount and range of exposure to spoken L2 for learners in classrooms, but there are also immense opportunities for extramural L2 listening development, both student-initiated and teacher-assigned. Teaching via distance (e.g., via Microsoft Teams, Skype, Zoom, etc.) further presents new opportunities and challenges in relation to L2 listening development, as these platforms demand a re-evaluation of how traditional ideas and practices for L2 listening may transfer into new classroom formats.

Given both the crucial role of L2 listening development in the overall L2 acquisition process and the many traditions associated with teaching listening in the L2 classroom, this chapter focuses on how aspects of traditional L2 listening instruction can merge with new teaching and learning circumstances. The chapter begins by describing previous views of the role of the learner in L2 listening development before briefly reviewing traditional, core concepts in listening, some that apply to listening universally and others that are more relevant for L2 listening development specifically. These concepts are then integrated into subsequent sections intended to draw comparisons between traditional practices for L2 listening development and the new circumstances that some teachers and students now operate in. Topics include listening materials, multimodality, models of L2 listening instruction, and classroom activities. Throughout the chapter, various related aspects that may impact and be impacted by teaching listening in new circumstances are discussed.

Past views and trends

New circumstances in relation to the teaching of L2 listening relate in large part to the growing accessibility of digital tools and the endless content that can be delivered via these devices. In particular, listening materials (either those explicitly intended for the learning of L2 listening or authentic materials (AM) designed originally for L1 users but sometimes incorporated by L2 teachers) have become more readily available than in the past. Moreover, since many students have access to laptops, tablets, and/or smartphones (either issued by schools or students' personal devices), a range of teaching activities and formats can be arranged for L2 listening that were simply not possible under previous circumstances (Jones, 2018).

Expectations on students and teachers with regard to L2 listening have also been evolving. Whereas listening is sometimes positioned as a purely receptive skill in which listeners are passive and only react to incoming input (e.g., Mendelsohn, 1994), more recent understanding and conceptualizations of the skill demonstrate a more active role for the listener. Based on participatory notions and shared responsibility in communication, listeners are expected to co-construct meaning along with speakers. Listeners are expected to, for example, draw on relevant background and generic knowledge, monitor their comprehension, ask for clarification or reformulation if necessary, and provide feedback to the speaker (e.g., confirming understanding and/or indicating non-understanding). Furthermore, debates about whether listening was being taught or merely tested in L2 classrooms have been raised in recent decades. Commentators (e.g., Field, 2008; Siegel, 2014) pointed out that a tenuous emphasis on the "comprehension approach" and "listen-answer-check" cycles lacked developmental focus and positioned learners only as test-takers who aurally scanned input for correct answers to multiple choice questions. Listeners are now expected to play active roles in preparing for, monitoring, interacting, and reflecting on their own listening performance (Graham & Santos, 2015; Siegel, 2015; Vandergrift & Goh, 2012).

Core concepts

While pedagogic circumstances surrounding listening have rapidly developed, the essential operations that occur when listening remain constant. Regardless of what materials students listen to, what activities they are expected to undertake, or whether they are in face-to-face or online environments, the listening process, at least in the purely aural sense, remains the same. One prominent framework used to illustrate the listening process is Clark and Clark's (1977), which involves a three-set process: (1) perception of individual phonemes; (2) parsing the speech stream into meaningful chunks (e.g., words, phrases, etc.); and (3) utilization, or relating what is heard to one's previous knowledge of topic, context, speaker, etc. Field (2008) promotes decoding the speech stream and meaning-building, which approximate Clark and Clark's (1977) conceptualization.

Top-down and bottom-up listening processes are generally the most common theoretical view of listening as expressed in L2 listening literature & (e.g., Lynch & Mendelsohn, 2013). Top-down processing involves what the listener brings to the listening event, including expectations, background knowledge, and previous experiences. Bottom-up processing, on the other hand, consists of the listener's cognitive engagement with the actual acoustic input, processing incoming speech, and parsing it into meaningful chunks. These various notions of how listening operates are relevant to teaching the skill since conscious attention to incoming speech is essential regardless of subject or delivery system.

People have always listened to numerous different text types: conversations, music, stories, speeches, etc. While there are some common skills for each of these different types of listening, each respective genre of listening also demands some distinctive skills. Listening events are either one- or two-way, depending on whether the listener has the option to interrupt the speaker to ask for clarification, slower speed, or additional information. Speeches, formal presentations, lectures, TV and radio programmes, and podcasts are examples of the former, while conversations, group discussions, and spoken interactive online dialogues are examples of the latter. This distinction is evident in the Common European Framework for Reference for Language (CEFR). On that influential steering document, the general skill of listening is further subdivided into specific components, such as understanding as members of a live audience, understanding announcements and instructions, and understanding conversations between other people (Council of Europe, 2020, pp. 48–52). With the advent of multimodality and the expanding functionality of digital tools, messages can be delivered and/or supported via a number of simultaneous paths; for example, some distinctions between simply listening to a textbook audio text and viewing a short video meant for L1 users online are evident. The former relies solely on processing the acoustic signal while the latter involves that acoustic signal supplemented with visuals, animation, images, the speaker's body language and facial expressions, etc. CEFR also accounts for multimodality and its influence on listening in its sub-skill "audio-visual comprehension" (Council of Europe, 2020, p. 52).

In his seminal paper on L2 listening, Richards (1983) indicated this distinction by outlining micro-skills for both conversation (i.e., two-way) and lecture (i.e., one-way) listening skills. In the roughly 40 years since these lists were created, the types of one-way listening events have certainly expanded beyond the traditional notion of "lecture", but the distinction between one- and two-way listening remains an important one for the field. The sophistication of listening events has also increased. Listeners these days often want and are sometimes expected to comprehend a variety of accents delivered at varying rates of speed and with sometimes diverse intonation patterns. The content of listening texts is no longer limited to simple conversations about everyday topics or basic transactional dialogues for travel; increasingly, L2 users also need to gain content knowledge (e.g., EMI, CLIL) accessed via listening.

Current trends

Materials for teaching L2 listening

There is no shortage of materials for teachers and students to use for L2 listening development, and this supply only continues to grow. Traditionally, textbook publishers have typically released audio/visual materials that accompany their textbooks (e.g., that align with certain unit themes, written activities in text- and/or workbooks, etc.). While such materials used to be marked as rather inauthentic in that they lacked features of spontaneous and natural speech production, materials and scriptwriters now aim to have their listening texts more closely replicate real-world speech (e.g., with hesitations, interruptions, two speakers talking simultaneously, etc.). In addition to scripted materials that have been created with the expressed intention of listening development for L2 learners, AM are readily available online (e.g., podcasts, videos, music, etc.). AM "were not written to serve as practice grounds or hunting grounds for language learners. They were written to convey information, transmit ideas, express opinions and feelings" between L1 users (McGrath, 2002, p. 107). Even so, many teachers and students find AM appealing for several reasons, among them: (a) the up-to-date nature of the content, (b) the motivation that comes from engaging with challenging material and topics, and (c) the flexibility for students and teachers to select materials of interest to any group or individual. These benefits are often lacking in listening texts commercially produced for L2 learning.

Given the range of options available, the teacher is no longer solely responsible for selecting the texts that are used for L2 listening practice. With the aforementioned texts that accompany textbooks, it was the materials writers who produced the texts and the teachers (or head teachers or administrators) who selected the textbooks. Students and teachers may have had little power to influence the texts that they were given. They could not make decisions related to, for example, topic, accent, rate of speech, utterance length, number of turns, length of text, etc. that all impact L2 listening development. With the plethora of options available online, however, teachers can now easily supplement or replace textbook listening material that suits their students' needs and/or interests better. Furthermore, students can suggest content to teachers and/or select from the wide variety of texts available.

Such options lead to more student-centred approaches in L2 listening development, more autonomous learning, and extensive listening, a type of listening practice originally applied to reading (i.e., extensive reading) that has been adopted for listening as well. Essentially, students self-select listening materials at or near their present level of comprehension (i.e., where they can understand a majority of the text without the need for repetition, dictionaries, etc.). They listen to ample amounts of content for enjoyment and without rigid tasks attached to the content (Renandya & Farrell, 2011); commentators have argued, however, that extensive listening alone may be insufficient for L2 listening development and that it should be used in conjunction with teacher input and more structured practice (e.g., Siegel, 2011). Students can complete this type of listening independently, either in or out of class, and then collaborate on different tasks, a type of learning situation that is markedly distinct from having the teacher select and being in control of listening texts with all students listening to the same text in lockstep. Materials and logistical options now offer a much more individualized L2 listening experience, assuming the teacher takes advantage of such options.

Online materials offer unlimited opportunities for students to be exposed to various accents and dialects, rates of speech, and registers (i.e., levels of formality) in listening texts, well beyond what any single commercially-published material could provide. Moreover, listening texts can be selected with particular goals and interests in mind (e.g., for test-preparation, for career training, and for English for academic purposes and English for specific purposes courses). As such, teachers can incorporate a much broader listening experience for their students by locating and using a variety of one- and two-way listening texts as relevant to a given course or topic. Since, as mentioned earlier, each listening event requires certain sub-skills and strategies, teachers can expand the listening repertoires of their students beyond the traditional "listen-to-answer-test-questions" perspective and align listening practice with more real-world activities such as giving recounts, stating opinions and impressions, and summarizing.

Multimodality and L2 listening

One often-overlooked area in the L2 listening experience is the impact that multimodality has on understanding. In years past, L2 listening often meant a focus on the sounds produced from a tape or CD player; that is, listeners operated as eavesdroppers who only had access to the acoustic sounds from which to make meaning. Visual and physical signals that usually accompany listening in authentic situations (i.e., apart from phone calls) were largely absent. In classrooms, both L2 and otherwise, multimodality has always been involved, as aspects such as eye contact, facial expression, gesture, movement, writing on the blackboard, etc. all help to support communication. These more basic multimodal streams provide information to the listener that aids them in accurately interpreting messages; in other words, they provide content and contextual clues to spoken texts (e.g., Koumi, 2006; Wagner, 2018). Such information helps learners activate their existing pragmatic and contextual knowledge (e.g., Wagner, 2008; Wang, 2021) and to form more accurate hypotheses and inferences about meaning (Cross, 2011; Gruba, 2004). Images, writing, and symbols in written material also support listening; for example, textbooks may display pictures of two speakers so that students can envision the speakers as they listen to a conversation.

In an era where mere audio signals are being replaced with video materials, additional multimodal signals are being sent to help listeners. The visual information presented in videos can include speakers and their relevant characteristics (e.g., presumbed gender, age, socio-economic status, cultural background, etc.); context as established by the setting and background seen in videos; and attitudes as expressed via body language and facial expressions. Koumi (2006), for example, discusses how different forms of multimodal input (e.g., animated diagrams, 3D objects, and films) can elicit various approaches to comprehension. L2 listeners can take advantage of such information by processing it along with the acoustic output, and doing so (i.e., processing information that comes from multiple paths of delivery) requires updated skills beyond just perceiving phonemes and parsing the speech stream. Listeners now need to have the concentration to simultaneously account for information coming in various forms and which may have different levels of importance and relevance for deciphering an intended message.

Teachers need to account for multimodal processing on top of the focus on L2 input. Since taxonomies of listening skills and strategies (e.g., Richards, 1983; Vandergrift, 1999) have been the basis for L2 listening instruction and materials but were generated before the role of multimodality in comprehension gained fuller understanding, new skills are certainly in demand. In addition, this range of information input options can be used to cater to different learning styles and preferences (e.g., Fleming, 1995). However, as Dörnyei and Ryan (2019) argue, learners should not only receive input through their preferred sensory channels but instead be exposed to all types of input in order to expand their comprehension skills and engage with the range of listening experiences they will likely encounter in and out of the classroom. In any case, listening skills in this new era should be viewed more holistically than in the past, as materials, teachers, and listening goals acknowledge the significant contributions made by multimodal channels to the listening experience.

Models for L2 listening instruction

Several broad models for the teaching of L2 listening exist, and these can all be built upon in order to account for L2 listening development within new circumstances. Among these established pedagogic views are the pre-listening, while-listening and post-listening sequence, the teaching of listening sub-skills, and listening strategy instruction.

The three-step sequence (i.e., pre-, while-, and post-listening segments) allows teachers to engage various aspects of the listening process (i.e., both bottom-up and top-down processes) within the same lesson. As Hedge (2000) points out, the pre-listening stage allows listeners to "contextualize the text … [and] appreciate the setting" (p. 249). By, for example, brainstorming, looking at pictures, and reflecting on similar previous listening experiences with the topic, listeners can develop hypotheses, make predictions, and apply their background knowledge (i.e., top-down aspects). The while-listening stage engages listeners with the actual acoustic input, as they perform tasks ranging from matching pictures to answering questions to identifying generic patterns and so on. The post-listening stage allows for reactions to and discussions of the text content and for reflection on listening performance. Teachers and/or students may wish to relisten to confirm understanding and/or to identify and focus on portions of a text that caused confusion. When difficult instances are identified, targeted practice for the challenging sound/word combinations can be used to enhance bottom-up processing (Field, 2008; Siegel & Siegel, 2015). Teachers should importantly keep focus on the while-listening aspect and ensure that it receives a significant amount of attention. In the past, this three-stage approach has been used in an unbalanced fashion, with disproportionate attention given to the pre- and/or post-listening stages and insufficient attention to the actual processing of input.

Within this broadly-application three-stage sequence, teachers and listening textbooks often focus on discrete sub-skills for listening. These include, for instance, listening for gist, listening for details, distinguishing fact from opinion, understanding the speaker's attitude, and recognizing reduced forms in speech (Richards, 1983). The teaching of L2 listening can include focusing on any one or a combination of these subsections depending on the topic and text being used. Given the range of multimodal delivery and logistical options for listening practice outlined above, the notion of sub-skills for listening remains relevant but additional skills that incorporate multimodality as well as individual and collaborative listening situations need to be acknowledged. For example, listening and understanding a news report that is accompanied by graphics and/or charts involves comparing the acoustic signal to the visual presentation of information (e.g., to confirm that the same idea is being expressed via both channels of input). As a second example, understanding the speaker's attitude can typically be done by accounting for intonation, volume, and facial expression, but these three factors may not be as clear or accessible in online communication as they are during in-person interactions. As such, listeners in this new era need to flexibly attend to the stronger signals that are available to them and not rely solely on those that are typically available face-to-face.

Depending on whether it is a one- or two-way event, the listener may avail themselves of certain types of listening strategies. Based on the work on language learning strategies in general (e.g., O'Malley & Chamot, 1990; Oxford, 1990, 2011, 2017; Rubin, 1975) and taxonomies of listening skills in particular (e.g., Richards, 1983; Vandergrift, 1999), proponents of listening strategy instruction and training have argued for explicit attention to different types of strategies for various listening events. Listening strategies provide another framework for organizing and conducting the teaching of L2 listening. Many of these pedagogic perspectives on listening strategies (e.g., Graham & Santos, 2015; Siegel, 2013, 2015; Vandergrift & Goh, 2012) are based on the ideas of metacognitive, cognitive, and socio-affective strategies.

Metacognitive strategies, as applied to L2 listening, include planning for, monitoring comprehension levels during, and reflecting on performance after each listening event (Vandergrift & Goh, 2012). Cognitive strategies involve interaction with and the processing of the actual acoustic input; for example, visualizing, attending to intonation, parsing the speech stream, comparing the input to predictions, noticing organizational and transitional signals, and recognizing key words are included in this category. Socio-affective strategies are of two types: one draws on the interactive nature of two-way listening in that the listener can ask for repetition and/or clarification, confirm their understanding, etc. while the other relates to the regulating of emotions, such as remaining calm even when uncertain, building self-confidence, and reducing listening anxiety. Affective strategies are relevant to L2 listening particularly in high-stakes events where listeners get only one chance to listen and can be especially applicable to online listening, which can create a sense of isolation. These and other types of listening strategies have been organized into several teaching cycles in order to operationalize theoretical concepts into classroom practice (e.g., Graham & Santos, 2015; Siegel, 2013, 2015; Vandergrift & Goh, 2012).

Listening strategies certainly remain important when teaching listening in new circumstances; however, as with listening sub-skills, they need to be augmented to accommodate listening done online. For instance, metacognitive strategies for maintaining attention and avoiding distraction when listening online are crucial, given the potential attraction of surfing the net or performing other online tasks when, ideally, 100% attention would be on the set listening task. Cognitive strategies for online listening might involve digital (as opposed to longhand) notetaking, processing and attending to information from multiple simultaneous streams, and fact-checking to ensure information heard online can be corroborated (e.g., being source-critical). With the available functionality of online platforms such as Microsoft Teams and Zoom, listeners can ask for help or repetition not only with their voices but also via the chat (either to the group or to individuals) and the "raise hand" icon. Emotional aspects of listening might be compounded due to potential cognitive overload since online listening involves not only L2 listening but also digital skills and multitasking in the online environment. As such, teachers need to consider the additional and augmented strategies that online listening entails in comparison to listening done in-person, both in the one- and two-way varieties.

These pedagogic views on the organizing and delivery of L2 listening instruction (i.e., the three-stage approach, sub-skills, and strategies) have been and will continue to be relevant and practical for classroom teaching. As demonstrated by the discussion in this section, their basic principles can be helpful for teaching L2 listening in new circumstances but some adaptations and additions are needed to account for listening in diverse ways for different purposes and in various environments.

Classroom activities for L2 listening

Broader models for L2 listening instructions manifest themselves in discrete classroom activities that involve learners engaging with listening texts in various ways. Traditionally, the listening practice has been limited to teacher-controlled and test-like situations in which students listen merely for the purpose of completing comprehension questions (e.g., matching, multiple choice, and gap-fill). Dubbed the "comprehension approach" by Field (2008), this type of activity is more test-replication or preparation than listening development and has limited value for listening in authentic situations. That is, the skills and strategies for performing well on a listening test may not transfer directly to higher L2 listening proficiency in practice.

Teachers have several options to address bottom-up and top-down aspects of listening, which can be arranged using the three stages of pre-, while- and post-listening. Exercises for stimulating top-down processing include key-word brainstorming, considering the genre of the upcoming listening text, activating background knowledge of both content and context, and making predictions about what will be heard. Activities such as dictation, which focuses on bottom-up aspects, provide visible evidence of students' perception and parsing abilities and can be used to stimulate pair collaboration, although this may be more complicated in online teaching. Other activities that focus on decoding the speech stream involve pair listen and repeat, focusing on blended sounds, and listening out for differences (e.g., in grammar) between similar sentences or stories (Siegel & Siegel, 2015). All of these activities lend themselves to the physical classroom. They can, however, also be implemented in online environments, albeit with potentially more clarity of instructions and time for setting up collaborative interactions (e.g., using breakout rooms, making pairs with consideration for L2 proficiency, etc.).

In the past, listening was often conceived as an individual activity; in other words, students completed sets of comprehension questions on their own, followed by the teacher reading out the correct answers. Little developmental attention was paid to which incorrect answers students might have chosen and where in the process of listening to the text they may have misunderstood. Instead, correct answers meant good listeners and wrong answers meant weaker listeners. The class then moved on to the next text or activity. With more user-friendly delivery systems for L2 listening materials, teachers and/or students can much more easily rewind and pinpoint places in a text that caused listening problems. If troubling sound combinations are identified, teachers can replay and later create specific remedial practice activities that focus on the trouble spots. This sequence can also be used by individual students who might, for example, be listening to different texts in a computer lab or on separate tablets. They have choices to replay certain sections of the text based on individual needs, thereby increasing learner autonomy and highlighting the importance of metacognitive awareness. Not surprisingly, multiple listenings, either to parts of or entire texts, lead to greater comprehension and reduced listening anxiety.

When teaching is conducted by distance or in a hybrid format, at least some listening practice needs to be completed within the online platform. Teachers can take advantage of the accessibility of digital tools for listening by assigning a single text or a range of texts for students to listen to during the online class within a set time limit. In this set-up, students listen on their own and therefore can control the pace at which they work (i.e., whether they listen straight through, pause briefly to reflect before continuing, or do multiple listenings). Such control used to be the domain only of the teacher. Now, students can be more in control of their own listening. Activities such as jigsaw listening, in which students listen to different parts of the same text or different texts on the same topic and then form groups to discuss what they heard, can be arranged online using breakout room features. While more traditional comprehension-type activities may be necessary at times (e.g., such as for needs analysis, assessment, streaming, etc.), these can be supplemented with listening activities that more closely simulate real-world situations, including listening and summarizing, listening and offering an opinion, and listening to locate supporting or contradictory information. These activities are possible in the physical classroom but may work better online given that clear information gaps can be created in the online environment, thereby generating authentic communicative situations.

Future adaptations

The teaching of L2 listening in new circumstances offers exciting possibilities, namely those provided by online environments and the multitude of listening texts and class formulations they offer. Interactive online environments like *Second Life*, *Zoom*, and *Microsoft Teams* allow for new and varied types of listening experiences beyond those typically experienced in the traditional classroom. For example, the listening experience can be augmented in these environments by chat boxes, emojis, and digital gestures, and they offer a range of plenary, small group, and one-to-one listening opportunities. Teachers and students can decide among these different class formations, which can help provide privacy when desired as well as create information gaps that can be used to create authentic listening purposes and the need for negotiation of meaning. In addition to these structural options for listening development, content on the internet continues to expand and provides a vast variety of listening texts, ranging from traditional one-way lectures and news reports to more interactive podcasts and interviews to persuasive promotional materials generated both commercially and by individuals. Meanwhile, the core operations of listening remain the same whether in physical classes or online. Listeners always need to develop proficiency in perceiving sounds, parsing the speech stream, and drawing on their previous experience to make sense of incoming input. A combination of bottom-up and top-down processes needs attention in order to foster a holistic proficiency in L2 listening. To support listening comprehension, the impact of multimodality needs to be accounted for in both listening practice and assessment. Listening, broadly defined, is not only about the aural signal that reaches the ear but also about combining the aural signal with other avenues of input, such as images, gestures, movements, and facial expressions, along with special positioning, to help support message delivery and interpretation. Already-established models of listening instruction like top-down and bottom-up processing, a metacognitive perspective, and listening strategies can be applied to online contexts, although with adaptations to acknowledge differences between physical and virtual educational environments. This will help to take advantage of opportunities offered by digital tools like *Zoom* and *Teams*, which are used in one-on-one or class teaching. In short, previous pedagogic and research work on L2 listening development in classroom settings (as discussed earlier in the chapter) has much to offer the continued teaching of this crucial skill in new circumstances.

References

Clark, H., & Clark, E. (1977). *Psychology and language: An introduction to psycholinguistics*. Harcourt Brace Jovanovich.

Council of Europe. (2020). *Common European framework of reference for languages: Learning, teaching and assessment. Companion volume with new descriptors*. https://rm.coe.int/common-european-framework-of-reference-for-languages-learning-teaching/16809ea0d4

Cross, J. (2011). Comprehending news videotexts: The influence of the visual content. *Language Learning & Technology*, 15(2), 44–68. http://dx.doi.org/10125/44251

Dörnyei, Z., & Ryan, S. (2019). *The psychology of the language learner revisited*. Routledge.

Field, J. (2008). *Listening in the language classroom*. Cambridge University Press.

Fleming, N. D. (1995). I'm different; not dumb: Modes of presentation (VARK) in the tertiary classroom. In A. Zelmer (Ed.), *Research and Development in Higher Education, Proceedings of the 1995 Annual Conference of the Higher Education* and *Research Development Society of Australasia (HERDSA)*, HERDSA, 18, pp. 308–313.

Graham, S., & Santos, D. (2015). *Strategies for second language listening*. Palgrave.

Gruba, P. (2004). Understanding digitized second language videotext. *Computer Assisted Language Learning*, 17(1), 51–82. https://doi.org/10.1076/call.17.1.51.29710

Hedge, T. (2000). *Teaching and learning in the English classroom*. Oxford University Press.

Jones, R. (2018). Learning through technology. In A. Burns & J. Richards (Eds.), *The Cambridge guide to learning English as a second language* (pp. 319–326). Cambridge University Press.

Koumi, J. (2006). *Designing video and multimedia for open and flexible learning*. Routledge.

Lightbown, P., & Spada, N. (2021). *How languages are learned*. Cambridge University Press.

Loumbourdi, L. (2018). Communicative language teaching. In J. I. (Ed.), *The TESOL encyclopedia of English language teaching*. John Wiley & Sons, Inc. 10.1002/9781118784235.eelt0167

Lynch, T., & Mendelsohn, D. (2013). Listening. In *An introduction to applied linguistics* (2nd ed.) (pp. 190–206). Routledge.

McGrath, I. (2002). *Materials evaluation and design for language teaching*. Edinburgh University Press.

Mendelsohn, D. (1994). *Learning to listen: A strategy-based approach for the second language learner*. Dominie Press.

O'Malley, J., & Chamot, A. (1990). *Learning strategies in second language acquisition*. Cambridge University Press.

Oxford, R. (1990). *Language learning strategies: What every teacher should know*. Heinle & Heinle.

Oxford, R. (2011). *Teaching and researching language learning strategies* (1st ed.). Pearson Education.

Oxford, R. (2017). *Teaching and researching language learning strategies* (2nd ed.). Routledge.

Renandya, W. A., & Farrell, T. S. C. (2011). 'Teacher, the tape is too fast!' extensive listening in ELT. *ELT Journal*, 65(1), 52–59. https://doi.org/10.1093/elt/ccq015

Richards, J. C. (1983). Listening comprehension: Approach, design, procedure. *TESOL Quarterly*, 17(12), 219–240. https://doi.org/10.2307/3586651

Richards, J., & Rodgers, T. (2014). *Approaches and methods in language teaching* (3rd ed.). Cambridge University Press.

Rilling, S. (2018). Audio-lingual method. In J. Liontas (Ed.). *The TESOL encyclopedia for English language teaching*. Wiley & Sons. 10.1002/9781118784235.eelt0157

Rubin, J. (1975). What the "good language learner" can teach us. *TESOL Quarterly*, 9(1), 41–51. https://doi.org/10.2307/3586011

Siegel, J. (2011). Thoughts on L2 listening pedagogy. *ELT Journal*, 65(3), 318–321. https://doi.org/10.1093/elt/ccr029

Siegel, J. (2013). Methodological ingenuity for second language listening. In J. Schwieter (Ed.), *Studies and global perspectives of second language teaching and learning* (pp. 113–139). Information Age Publishing.

Siegel, J. (2014). Advice in listening instruction: Degrees of transferability. *International Journal of Innovation in ELT and Research*, 3(2), 121–138.

Siegel, J. (2015). *Exploring listening strategy instruction through action research.* Palgrave.

Siegel, J. (2022). *Teaching English in Secondary School: A handbook for teachers.* Studentlitteratur.

Siegel, J., & Siegel, A. (2015). Getting to the bottom of L2 listening instruction: Making a case for bottom-up activities. *Studies in Second Language Learning and Teaching, 5*(4), 637–662. https://www.ceeol.com/search/article-detail?id=330127

Vandergrift, L. (1999). Facilitating second language listening comprehension: Acquiring successful strategies. *ELT Journal, 53*(3), 168–176. https://doi.org/10.1093/elt/53.3.168

Vandergrift, L., & Goh, C. (2012). *Teaching and learning second language listening: Metacognition in action.* Routledge.

Wagner, E. (2008). Video listening tests: What are they measuring? *Language Assessment Quarterly, 5*(3), 218–243. https://doi.org/10.1080/15434300802213015

Wagner, E. (2018). A comparison of L2 listening performance on tests with scripted or authenticated spoken texts. In G. Ockey, & E. Wagner (Eds.), *Assessing L2 listening: Moving towards authenticity* (pp. 29–43). John Benjamins.

Wang, L. (2021). *An exploration of the effect of visuals on students' l2 listening test-taking processes* (Publication No. 28416022). [Doctoral dissertation, Temple University].

9
TEACHING READING

Peter Watkins

The past

Reading plays a ubiquitous part in the lives of many people. Among other things, we use reading to communicate with friends and family via short text messages, entertain ourselves through reading a story, and learn new information, such as when we study at school. For many people, even those who would not identify as avid readers, reading is everywhere. Whether we enjoy reading or not, reading is undoubtedly an enormously important skill to master and is linked to both our life chances and our well-being (Hilhorst et al., 2018). When we think about learning languages other than our own first language (L1), reading takes on a further role because it is potentially a rich source of input, or exposure, to the target language, something which is seen as essential in learning a second language (L2) (Ortega, 2009).

Unlike listening, reading is not a naturally acquired skill. It has to be deliberately learned through guidance from those who have already learned and are skilled in the practice. This often starts with parents/caregivers, first of all, reading to their children with both looking at the text and pictures in a book and then supporting their children's efforts to decode those same familiar texts. Like the other language skills—speaking, listening, and writing—reading is made up of a bundle of subskills, and these are often categorized as being part of lower-level processing or higher-level processing skills.

Lower-level and higher-level processing

Lower-level processing skills include the instant, accurate decoding of words (particularly high-frequency words), and a large vocabulary is crucial to developing good reading comprehension (Nation & Coady, 1988). Readers also use grammar (or syntactic) knowledge to break the text into meaningful units, and efficient readers are also likely to have an awareness of discourse organization and so are able to anticipate the turns a text may take. These structural patterns will obviously vary with text type, and so learners need to become familiar with a range of different texts because knowledge of discourse patterns is linked with improved comprehension (Wolfe, 2005). In addition, as readers read, so they need to build up the main ideas of the text and continually add new information and ideas into the mental representation they hold.

Higher-level processing skills include making inferences and noticing less obvious messages contained within the text. We also need to link new information to our background knowledge and beliefs, and this facilitates critical reading. We have to use metacognitive skills to monitor our understanding and, where necessary, adopt strategies to repair any breakdowns in our understanding.

Reading comprehension

As noted above, as we read, we extract the main ideas of the text and fit them into our developing model of understanding. The reader's understanding is made up of two strands, termed a text model and a situational model of comprehension (Grabe, 2009; Grabe & Stoller, 2018). The text model is essentially our efforts to recreate what we believe to be the author's intended meaning. However, reading is an interactive, not a passive, skill, and we do not stop at creating a text model of understanding. We also develop a situational model of understanding whereby we question the text and take a stance, asking ourselves if we agree with the author's arguments and how those arguments fit with our own beliefs and values.

Of course, some texts lend themselves more obviously to a situational model of processing than others. If we consider the reading of an opinion column in a newspaper, we can immediately see the need to employ a situational model of comprehension as we filter the information from the text through our own beliefs and also our attitudes towards the topic, writer, and publication. We interpret the text, and analyze the text critically, in light of our existing beliefs.

However, in other circumstances, the role of the situational model is less prominent. If we read the instructions for how to take a particular medicine on the side of a bottle, we will trust the source and simply try to accurately interpret the writer's message, although even here, we will be checking for plausibility. If the instruction says, 'Take 20 tablets twice a day', we may question whether that can really be the case and wonder whether there is an error in the instructions.

First language reading and second language reading

Reading in a first and second language have much in common, but there are also some obvious differences, the most prominent of which is vocabulary size. Typically, when we start to read in our L1, we have already built up considerable lexical knowledge. For example, most estimates suggest that a six-year-old will know between 5000 and 7000 words in their L1 (Graves, 2016). A child will also be building implicit knowledge of how words combine. However, L2 learners often begin reading without much understanding of L2 vocabulary and grammar, and the absence of that knowledge can severely hamper successful L2 reading. There is consistent research evidence that there is a strong relationship between vocabulary knowledge and L2 reading ability (Carver, 2003; Verhoeven, 2000), making lexical knowledge indispensable to developing L2 reading skills.

There is also a potential difference in terms of motivation. In most L1 contexts, learning to read is a social expectation, a stated goal of education policy, and is key to life chances. These factors increase the motivation to learn to read. L2 readers, on the other hand, may see less reason to read and may perhaps be demotivated by the text types with which they are presented in classrooms, particularly where they are accompanied by anxiety-raising comprehension tests.

However, the L2 reader also has some advantages over the L1 reader, not least in that they can draw on L1 knowledge, and where the L1 and L2 are close, the reader may recognize cognate words, or find breaking the sentence into meaningful units easier because the syntactic patterns encountered are familiar. This advantage will diminish considerably where there is more distance between languages, and where a new script has to be learned, there will be additional difficulties in processing (Jiang et al., 2020). An L2 reader who has already learned to read in their L1 will also have potential access to the reading strategies that they have already developed. However, much caution is required around this assumption. There is very strong evidence that L1 skills and strategies can only be applied to L2 reading when a 'language threshold' is met (Alderson et al., 2015; Jeon

& Yamashita, 2014). In other words, the L2 reader must know sufficient L2 vocabulary and grammar to be able to process the text comfortably before being able to access their L1 skills and strategies. Whether a particular learner crosses such a threshold will depend on the text that they are reading and its degree of difficulty relative to the L2 knowledge of the reader.

Scripted vs authentic material

One of the more obvious questions that we should ask about reading instruction is 'what texts should our learners read?' and this leads to a discussion of authentic material. Typically, authentic material is defined as that which 'was not originally produced for teaching purposes, such as a newspaper article or television advertisement' (Watkins, 2014, p. 163). However, such definitions fail to capture the complexity of authentic material in that they do not take into account the ways in which texts may be adapted to a greater or lesser extent. Clearly, there is a continuum from the entirely authentic on the one hand to the entirely scripted on the other.

Early advocates of Communicative Language Teaching recommended the use of authentic material. Allwright (1976) stated, 'Use no materials, published or unpublished, actually conceived or designed as materials for language teaching' (cited in Allwright & Hanks, 2009, pp. 46–7). Such advice was given on the basis that authentic materials represented the texts that learners would have to deal with outside the classroom and would therefore be both better preparation for 'the real world' and more motivating. However, the reality is that teachers often have to use either heavily adapted or scripted texts when teaching reading because it is hard to find authentic reading materials that are appropriate in terms of length and complexity for low-level learners. Also, as Macaro (2003) has pointed out, there is actually little research on whether learners care a great deal about the authenticity of texts. Instead, teachers should focus on whether the texts they use have at least some features of the text types that their learners will engage with outside the classroom, and less about whether those features have been included through the use of authentic texts or clever scripting (Watkins, 2017). One other key consideration when selecting texts for learners is that they should be intrinsically interesting to the learners, although this is often a challenge as in some contexts the texts used may be prescribed by some higher authority, such as an education ministry.

Having reviewed some of the major issues in reading itself, we will now turn our attention to how it is changing and also how it is typically taught.

Current trends

How reading has changed

What we read and how we access texts have changed dramatically since around the turn of the century, with us increasingly accessing texts from a screen of some description. Some texts we read may be a simple PDF or Word document, but we are also likely to access multimedia texts, hyperlinked texts, and texts that have new organizational structures as compared to those encountered through most of the 20th century. These new text types include things such as websites, with their highly non-linear structure, achieved through a variety of tabs and options, and also short text messages where the reader is not just a reader but also a co-creator of the emerging discourse. This means that in addition to traditional reading skills, we also need to apply new reading skills in the 21st century. For example, we need to be able to search for texts, select the most appropriate results from an enormous number of possibilities, and be ever more critical in our reading, as the internet's capacity for self-publication has removed some of the traditional filters of verification and reliability.

One interesting line of enquiry that has emerged in this regard is whether traditional printed texts and on-screen texts are equally easy to understand. Virginia Clinton (2019) reviewed 33 studies. She found that there was no difference in the speed of reading and also found no difference in comprehension when reading works of fiction. However, she found an advantage for paper over screens when considering informational texts. She also found that readers typically were able to apply more metacognitive skills and strategies when reading from paper, concluding, 'Readers may be more efficient and aware of their performance when reading from paper compared to screens'.

Clinton's review echoes that of Delgado et al. (2018), in which 54 studies were reviewed. Again, a key finding was that there was improved comprehension with paper and, as with Clinton's finding, the benefit was only seen with informational texts (not narrative ones). Delgado et al.'s review also suggested that readers were overconfident when reading online (so again, an issue with less good metacognitive skills being applied, as identified by Clinton). The review also showed that study time allocation became more erratic in online reading environments.

These research reviews have great importance for the teaching of reading in both L1 and L2 contexts. Clearly, the trend towards screen reading is not going to be reversed, with many texts only available as screen versions. This suggests a need to reconsider the reading curricula we provide so that we can build the skills essential to reading successfully in the 21st century.

This will be discussed in the 'Future adaptations' section below. However, before looking ahead to the future, we will discuss the way in which reading is typically currently taught in L2 classrooms.

The pattern of reading lessons

Reading lessons in ELT coursebooks, across publishers, and across proficiency levels tend to follow a remarkably similar pattern. Hugely successful coursebooks such as the *Headway* series (for example, Soars et al., 2018), the *Keynote* series (for example, Dummet et al., 2015), and the *Cutting Edge* series (for example, Cunningham et al., 2013) all follow the same essential reading lesson pattern. In a typical reading lesson, they will:

1 Build interest in the topic of the text
2 Pre-teach some key vocabulary that appears in the text
3 Set a reading task that can be done quickly and does not require detailed understanding
4 Set a reading task that requires more detailed understanding and uses questions that have a clear, unambiguous single correct answer
5 Set up a discussion centring around the topic of the text, or some other extension activity, that does not require a detailed discussion (and therefore understanding) of the text itself

Moreover, this lesson format has remained unchallenged over a number of years. If we compare the editions of *Headway* and *Cutting Edge* referred to above with their earlier editions (Cunningham et al., 2001; Soars & Soars, 1996), we see that although the texts have been updated, the approach to reading lessons and the teaching of reading remain unaltered.

When we look across publications, we may find some variations to this basic pattern—the pre-teaching of vocabulary may be omitted, or a language focus may be added, for example—but the basic pattern can be identified in the large majority of teaching materials.

There are several strengths to the model, not least the familiarity for both teachers and learners. Teachers know the pattern well, and hopefully, this reduces the time required for planning their reading lessons, time that could be used to better effect elsewhere, perhaps. Learners can feel confident that there will be adequate preparation for the text they have to read. There is a chance to check and build background knowledge at the first stage, and this is important because comprehension is achieved by integrating the information identified in the text with our existing knowledge (Koda, 2007) and as Grabe (2009, p. 74) comments, 'There is no debate that readers with considerably more background knowledge on a topic read a text differently and more efficiently'. This suggests that time spent building background knowledge will support comprehension.

Comprehension is also supported through the second stage—pre-teaching vocabulary. Simply put, learners need to know, at least receptively, the words in the text in order to be able to understand the text. For fluent, uninterrupted reading, this means knowing 98–99% of the words contained in the text (Nation, 2006). Clearly, the pre-teaching of vocabulary is a sensible strategy designed to increase the proportion of recognized words and so support comprehension and also guard against learners becoming demotivated and frustrated if they cannot read the text reasonably fluently. Some materials may also provide brief glossaries of keywords so that learners can quickly locate the meaning of unknown items. While often necessary, the pre-teaching of vocabulary does not mirror reading in situations outside the classroom. If I read a newspaper story, I am not pre-taught several vocabulary items before starting, and learners will, at some point, have to cope without this support.

Generally, teachers focus learners on the questions set at stages three and four above, before learners are expected to read. This is an acknowledgement that reading tends to be goal oriented (we read for a purpose), and so learners should be aware of the information they are looking for before attempting to read the text. If questions are set after reading, there is a chance that recall is assessed, rather than comprehension. The final extension activity (stage 5) may give learners the opportunity to draw on information they have taken from the text, but often this is not a prerequisite of the task. In fact, rather than pushing learners to go back to the text to justify opinions and so on, it often appears that the activity is more a consideration of lesson organization and the need to provide learners with something energizing and interactive, having completed the usually solitary, and slower paced reading activity that has gone before.

Criticisms of the model

While this reading lesson format has served learners and teachers reasonably well over a considerable length of time, there are criticisms that can be made of it. The first and perhaps most important criticism is the extent to which it teaches reading at all. It is true that regular reading practice is likely to lead to improvement in reading, but this model does little to 'teach' reading explicitly. The questions set at stages 3 and 4 (above) typically have a single correct answer and act as a comprehension test. Learners may find it reassuring and even motivating to know that they have answered the questions correctly; however, if they answer incorrectly, there is little to build the skills they need to do better in the future. And if getting something right is motivating, we must surely accept the corollary that getting something wrong is demotivating. The model of reading instruction adopted in course materials is very product focused (*did the learners identify the correct answer?*) rather than supporting learners in the process of L2 reading and helping them to improve.

A further problem is that the need to create questions that have a single indisputably correct answer may lead to materials writers focusing on what can be easily tested, rather than using the questions to focus learners on the most important parts of the text. When used well, questions can support reading by directing the learner to those key points, but questions that push the reader to focus on an inconsequential detail rather than the substantial messages of the text may get in the way of overall comprehension.

The answering of questions that have a single correct answer may present learners with a cognitive challenge, as they locate the relevant section of the text and then closely read it to arrive at the correct answer. However, they rarely provide opportunities for learners to engage affectively with the text, and providing opportunities for such affective engagement has consistently been called for in the literature on principled materials evaluations (for example, Tomlinson, 1998, 2010) primarily because it helps to maintain motivation for the reading task.

A further difficulty with the current model is the fairly uniform nature of the texts that are selected. The length of texts in published materials tends to be quite short and quite challenging for the target level. In other words, in the vast majority of ELT classrooms, the focus is on what is termed 'intensive' reading—the reading of relatively short, relatively difficult texts for detailed understanding. This contrasts with 'extensive reading', which focuses on the use of relatively longer, easier texts and a belief, or at least hope, that learners will read for pleasure.

The texts used in typical teaching materials also often represent a restricted range of genres which do not always reflect the sort of texts that learners engage with outside the classroom. One such example is the kind of 'written conversation' that we create while using messaging apps. Even where such texts are reproduced in course materials, it is hard to create an authentic role for the reader, which, as mentioned above, would typically include co-creating the text that they are reading as they contribute messages, as well as receive them. Similarly, traditional approaches to the teaching of reading in L2 classes have struggled to accommodate multimedia texts and new text organizational principles, such as those underpinning website design.

The argument here is not that current practices should be rejected completely and replaced. Instead, it is about how we can create more complete and better-balanced L2 reading programmes that genuinely serve the developing needs of our learners as we progress through the 21st century.

Future adaptations

In this section, we will look at how the teaching of reading could be adapted to take into account both research evidence and the changing nature of reading, as discussed above. As we saw, the basic structure of reading lessons, as represented by coursebook material, has remained pretty fixed for a number of years, so it is worth looking at how we might be able to provide a more balanced reading syllabus in order to improve the experience of learners both in the classroom and when they read outside the classroom. We will focus on two areas of potential change in particular. Later we will address the need to focus on reading fluency, as well as reading accuracy, but first, we will look at the need to develop online reading skills.

Online reading

Our learners will read more and more from screens as we move forward, and texts will become further and further removed from the traditional print appearance of the 20th century. Co-creation of texts using short messages, navigating websites, and multimedia texts are already the norm in our lives, and we need to bring these into the classroom and help our learners prepare for their challenges. For example, short messages have reduced context, and judging the tone of exchanges can be a challenge leading to potential misunderstandings, particularly in an L2.

21st-century readers have an almost limitless selection of texts available to them, but this also brings with it the challenge of selecting the most appropriate ones for our reading purpose. Navigating websites can be difficult, and even more so in an L2. The sheer amount of information may prove daunting, and readers have to constantly evaluate whether a link is worth clicking on, and when they do, they need to quickly evaluate if the text that appears is meeting their goals. That is to say, are they finding the information they require? Whenever a link is followed, the reading of the original text is interrupted, and this may negatively impact efforts to build a coherent understanding of it. Hyperlinks, graphics, and other multimedia input can potentially support reading, but they can also make it harder to focus attention.

While readers in the 21st century need all the skills readers have always needed, it follows that our learners may also need focused practice in new areas, such as:

- selecting the most appropriate responses to a search based on their goals
- deciding which hyperlinks to follow, and judging whether the link is useful
- recognizing the tone of conversational, reduced context messages

In addition, research evidence (see above) suggests that when reading from a screen, we may have less awareness of our own performance and degree of comprehension. This would suggest that our learners would benefit from being taught:

- specific metacognitive strategies to monitor reading performance

While the need to read critically has always been important, it seems reasonable to assume that the internet makes critical reading ever more important. It seems axiomatic that we must all be able to differentiate relatively impartial news reporting from that which presents the arguments from just one perspective, or that we can recognize facts from lies. However, research suggests that this is difficult even in our L1 (Domonoske, 2016), so our learners need practice, and one element of an updated reading syllabus might be

- identifying the true and trustworthy from the untrue and fabricated

Overall, it seems likely that reading from screens and online will become the norm in most classrooms as we move forward and also that we need to ask whether traditional reading curricula provide learners with the support that they most need.

Developing reading fluency

As we observed above, most reading lessons focus on testing the accuracy of the learners' understanding of a text. However, there is a consensus within research that developing reading fluency is also hugely important (e.g., Geva & Ramírez, 2015; Grabe & Stoller, 2018). Accuracy and fluency are clearly related. If reading is inaccurate, it may well impact reading fluency because the reader will need to go back and reread. However, the balance in most course materials, and therefore presumably most classrooms, favours accuracy to the almost total exclusion of fluency.

The development of fluency can be targeted in several specific ways in the classroom, and none of these need to be intimidating for teachers because they are very simple to put into practice. Particularly at low proficiency levels, reading fluency will be supported by simple teaching strategies such as:

- putting a focus on vocabulary building
- putting a focus on the instant recognition of words and phrases, particularly frequent words

There are many possible activities to achieve these goals, such as having learners race against each other to recognize previously taught items. The rereading of texts may also improve reading fluency, with gains seen in new reading texts as well as the ones being reread (Kuhn & Stahl, 2003). However, teachers need to develop a repertoire of classroom tasks that require their learners to reread the texts that they have previously seen without this appearing to be no more than repetition. Useful activities include making minor alterations to a previously read text and asking learners to find the changes, or asking learners to use previously read texts to create quizzes for other members of the class, thereby having to reread the texts used (Watkins, 2017). In brief, we can say that learners need to:

- read a lot of texts, including rereading texts

The critique of the standard lesson format for teaching reading drew attention to the fact that the majority of classroom time is devoted to intensive reading. However, there is considerable research into extensive reading, and a strong case for its wider use can be made. Extensive reading refers to the reading of large volumes of text that is relatively easy for the reader to comprehend, and to this extent, it is another key way in which reading fluency may be improved.

Research shows that extensive reading leads to improvements in reading rate and comprehension (Jeon & Day, 2016; Nakanishi, 2015) and also to vocabulary growth (Jeon & Day, 2016; Suk, 2016). We could further hypothesize that the encountering of words and phrases in context, as happens in extensive reading, does not just improve the quantity of words known but also improves the depth of knowledge held about each word, in terms of, for example, stylistic restrictions of use and common collocational patterns. There is evidence that extensive reading also supports the development of writing skills (Mermelstein, 2015; Park, 2016) and can also help with grammar acquisition (Lee et al., 2015). Finally, Day and Bamford (1998) claim that extensive reading may be more motivating than traditional intensive reading, which is most associated with classroom practice. This could be accounted for by several things, not least the degree of autonomy usually associated with extensive reading and also the reduced assessment of reading comprehension.

Summing up the evidence that supports extensive reading, Hedgcock and Ferris (2009, p. 208) are categorical in their judgement:

"Rarely in language education do we find a teaching approach [extensive reading] that is so universally hailed as beneficial, important, and necessary ... yet is so underutilized and even ignored in curricula, course/lesson design, and materials development."

The reasons why extensive reading remains underutilized are varied. One such problem is probably around the financial cost of setting up the programmes. Advocates of extensive reading suggest that a wide range of texts be made available so that learners can choose those that intrinsically interest them. These texts generally have to be graded in some way (to take account of the fact that reading in these programmes should be relatively easy), and so there is a cost involved in providing appropriate extensive reading material. Going forward, this particular problem may be eased by the use of online material made available for free. For example, www.readtheory.org currently provides such a service.

Extensive reading is a very learner-centred form of learning and teaching, and so academic cultures in which traditional teacher-fronted pedagogy is prized may not find it appealing. Also, in many classrooms around the world, curricula are already very full and so it can be difficult to find the time to implement new processes. These objections need not mean that an extensive reading programme cannot be created. Extensive reading usually happens outside class time and so requires only limited classroom time to set up. In some teaching contexts, extensive reading materials are available, but teachers report very limited take-up. There are various possible reasons for this, and one interesting area of future research may be to investigate the extent to which learners are aware of the benefits of extensive reading (outlined above) and whether they may be more inclined to engage with the process if they were. Perhaps the assumption that 'reading is its own reward' needs to be revisited and more measures to promote extrinsic motivation put in place. There may be a case to go further than this. As Belletti Figueira Mulling and Watkins (2022, p. 49) observe:

"... learners must be informed of the affordances of the material delivered and guided on how to learn best. It is not sufficient to deliver a set of self-access reading material (no matter how good they are in terms of content appeal, level adequacy) if these are not accompanied by learner training and ongoing support on how to use the resources."

This suggests that learners will benefit from:

- having a large selection of graded materials available
- being aware of the potential benefits of extensive reading
- being made aware of the expectations associated with the extensive reading programme (for example, the amount of time that should be spent)
- training in the strategies to use to benefit from the reading experience

Summing up

Reading has changed hugely since around the end of the 20th century, both in terms of what we read and the ways in which we access reading texts. This has brought with it the need to develop additional reading skills that were either not required in traditional print mediums, or at least were required to a much lesser extent.

However, there is little evidence that our learners are getting adequate preparation and support to develop the skills that they need to become proficient readers in a second language. Given how central reading in English is to many people, the status quo needs to be challenged. For example, as English medium instruction proliferates across many education systems, a lack of reading ability in English, where learning to read is replaced by reading to learn, will have a negative impact on life chances as it compromises success in other school subjects.

We need to ensure that adequate time is dedicated to developing reading skills both in the classroom and outside. We need to increase the exposure to online texts in the classroom and ensure that learners have both strong traditional reading skills (for example, the instant decoding of words and matching those to lexical knowledge) and also are systematically developing the new skills required for online reading.

We need to reconsider the balance between the traditional focus on reading accuracy and incorporating some reading fluency activities. We need to re-examine the balance we provide between intensive reading and extensive reading.

These are some of the key ways in which we can respond to the new circumstances of reading in the 21st century.

References

Alderson, J., Haapakangas, E. L., Huhta, A., Nieminen, L., & Ullakonoja, R. (2015). *The diagnosis of reading in a second and foreign language*. Routledge.

Allwright, D., & Hanks, J. (2009). *The developing language teacher*. Palgrave.

Belletti Figueira Mulling, A., & Watkins, P. (2022). Reading in self-access material: What can we learn from self-Instructed learners and their reported experience?

The Reading Matrix, 22(1), 37–55. https://www.readingmatrix.com/files/27-ajpptanm.pdf

Carver, R. (2003). The highly lawful relationships among pseudoword decoding, word identification, spelling, listening, and reading. *Scientific Studies of Reading*, 7, 127–154. https://doi.org/10.1207/S1532799XSSR0702_2

Clinton, V. (2019). Reading from paper compared to screens: A systematic review and meta-analysis. *Journal of Research in Reading*, 42(2), 288–325. https://onlinelibrary.wiley.com/doi/full/10.1111/1467-9817.12269

Cunningham, S., Moor, P., & Comyns Carr, J. (2001). *Cutting edge pre-intermediate*. Pearson.

Cunningham, S., Moor, P., & Crace, A. (2013). *Cutting edge pre-intermediate* (3rd ed.). Pearson.

Day, R., & Bamford, J. (1998). Extensive reading in the second language classroom. *RELC Journal*, 29(2), 187–191. doi: 10.1177/003368829802900211.

Delgado, P., Vargas, C., Ackermann, R., & Ladislao, S. (2018). Don't throw away your printed books: A meta-analysis on the effects of reading media on reading comprehension. *Educational Research Review*, 25, 23–38. https://www.sciencedirect.com/science/article/pii/S1747938X18300101

Domonoske, C. (2016). Students have 'dismaying' inability to tell fake news from real, study finds. *NPR Newsletter*. https://www.npr.org/sections/thetwoway/2016/11/23/503129818/study-finds-students-have-dismaying-inability-to-tell-fake-news-from-real?t=1568135940172

Dummet, P., Stephenson, H., & Lansford, L. (2015). *Keynote intermediate*. National Geographic.

Geva, E., & Ramírez, G. (2015). *Focus on reading*. Oxford University Press.

Grabe, W. (2009). *Reading in a second language: Moving from theory to practice*. Cambridge University Press.

Grabe, W., & Stoller, F. (2018). How reading comprehension works. In J. Newton, D. Ferris, C. M. Goh, W. Grabe, F. Stoller, & L. Vandergrift (Eds.), *Teaching English to second language learners in academic contexts* (pp. 7–27). Routledge.

Graves, M. F. (2016). *The vocabulary book: Learning and instruction* (2nd ed.). Teachers College Press.

Hedgcock, J., & Ferris, D. (2009). *Teaching readers of English: Students texts and contexts*. Routledge.

Hilhorst, S., Lockey, A., & Speight, T. (2018). A society of readers. https://demos.co.uk/wp-content/uploads/2018/12/A-Society-of-Readers-Formatted-1.pdf

Jeon, E. Y., & Day, R. R. (2016). The effectiveness of ER on reading proficiency: A meta-analysis. *Reading in a Foreign Language*, 28(2), 246–265. https://files.eric.ed.gov/fulltext/EJ1117026.pdf

Jeon, E. H., & Yamashita, J. (2014). L2 reading and its correlates: A meta-analysis, *Language Learning*, 64, 160–212. https://doi.org/10.1111/lang.12034

Jiang, X., Grabe, W., & Carrell, P. (2020). Reading. In N. Schmitt and M. Rodgers (Eds.) *An introduction to applied linguistics* (3rd ed.). Routledge.

Koda, K. (2007). Reading and language learning: Crosslinguistic constraints on second language reading development. In K. Koda (Ed.), *Reading and language learning*. Special issue of *Language Learning*, 57, 1–44. 10.1111/0023-8333.101997010-i1

Kuhn, M., & Stahl, S. (2003). Fluency: A review of developmental and remedial practices. *Journal of Educational Psychology*, 95, 3–21. https://doi.org/10.1037/0022-0663.95.1.3

Lee, J., Schallert, D., & Kim, E. (2015). Effects of extensive reading and translation activities on grammar knowledge and attitudes for EFL adolescents. *System*, 52, 38–50. https://doi.org/10.1016/j.system.2015.04.016

Macaro, E. (2003). *Teaching and learning a second language : A guide to recent research and its applications.* London and New York: Continuum..
Mermelstein, A. D. (2015). Improving EFL learners' writing through enhanced extensive reading. *Reading in a Foreign Language, 27*(2), 182–198. https://files.eric.ed.gov/fulltext/EJ1078420.pdf
Nakanishi, T. (2015). A meta-analysis of extensive reading research. *TESOL Quarterly, 49*(1), 6–37. https://doi.org/10.1002/tesq.157
Nation, I. S. P. (2006). How large a vocabulary is needed for reading and listening? *Canadian Modern Languages Review, 63,* 59–82. 10.1353/cml.2006.0049
Nation, I. S. P., & Coady, J. (1988). Reading and vocabulary. In R. Carter & M. McCarthy (Eds.), *Vocabulary and language teaching* (pp. 97–110). Longman.
Ortega, L. (2009). *Understanding second language acquisition.* Hodder Education.
Park, J. (2016). Integrating reading and writing through extensive reading. *ELT Journal, 70*(3), 287–295. 10.1093/elt/ccv049.
Soars, L., & Soars, J. (1996). *New headway intermediate.* Oxford University Press.
Soars, L., Soars, J., & Hancock, P. (2018). *Headway intermediate* (5th ed.). Oxford University Press.
Suk, N. (2016). The effects of extensive reading on reading comprehension, reading rate, and vocabulary acquisition. *Reading Research Quarterly, 52*(1), 73–89. https://doi.org/10.1002/rrq.152
Tomlinson, B. (1998). Introduction. In B. Tomlinson (Ed.), *Materials development in language teaching* (pp. 1–24). Cambridge University Press.
Tomlinson, B. (2010). Principles and effective materials developing. In N. Harwood (Ed.), *English Language teaching materials: Theory and practice* (pp. 81–108). Cambridge University Press.
Verhoeven, L. (2000). Components of early second language reading and spelling. *Scientific Studies of Reading, 4,* 313–330. https://doi.org/10.1207/S1532799XSSR0404_4
Watkins, P. (2014). *Learning to teach English* (2nd ed.). Delta Publishing.
Watkins, P. (2017). *Teaching and developing reading skills.* Cambridge University Press.
Wolfe, M. B. W. (2005). Memory for narrative and expository text: Independent influences of semantic associations and text organization. *Journal of Experimental Psychology: Learning, Memory, & Cognition, 31,* 359–364. https://doi.org/10.1037/0278-7393.31.2.359

10
CHALLENGES AND OPPORTUNITIES IN TEACHING SPEAKING

John Trent

Introduction

Attaining a high level of competency in speaking is a key learning goal of many students of English as a second or foreign language (Richards, 2009). Indeed, competency in an additional language beyond one's mother tongue is often associated with speaking that language (Thornbury, 2012). Yet achieving such competency is a complex undertaking that demands knowledge and application of a broad range of skills. Fluency, for instance, requires not only the ability to conceptualize, formulate, and articulate speech but that these processes are largely automated. In addition, there is a need for speakers to manage turn-taking and to be cognizant of the paralinguistic features of spoken interaction. Skillfulness in speaking is also often associated with working quickly, carrying out tasks using minimal resources, detecting and rejecting errors, planning ahead, and performing well in adverse conditions (Thornbury, 2005).

In the face of greater accountability, scrutiny, and bureaucracy, teaching has become an increasingly complex undertaking around the globe (Day & Gu, 2010; Trent, 2012). Recent global events, in particular the global pandemic resulting from the COVID-19 virus, have added considerable uncertainty to this already complex task. One source of this uncertainty in terms of the teaching of speaking is the rapidly changing way speaking is taught and learnt as lessons shift from in-person to remote contexts. This chapter discusses some of the implications for teaching speaking in this uncertain educational environment and considers several principles that could guide teachers and their students as they investigate, plan, and take part in

DOI: 10.4324/9781003361701-14

different forms of speaking episodes and opportunities. The chapter begins, however, by examining what is meant by speaking before moving on to review several issues that have traditionally been regarded as central to the teaching of spoken language skills in second language learning contexts.

Past approaches to teaching speaking

This section examines the issues of what speaking is and explores several key issues in the teaching and learning of speaking, including the challenges of communication, achieving fluency, the reluctance of some students to speak in a second/additional language, how errors in speaking are addressed, and speaking beyond the classroom.

What is speaking?

Speaking, Bailey (2005) argues, 'consists of producing systematic verbal utterances to convey meaning' (p. 2). As Richards (2015) points out, the status of English as an international language has resulted in a growing recognition of the need for fluency in the spoken language for business, social, political, and educational purposes. Yet achieving this goal is complex. For example, while a person may be able to function adequately in one situation, such as in an educational context, this does not necessarily imply that these skills are transferable to other situations, such as employment. The challenges inherent in the teaching and learning of the spoken language are underscored by the fact that speaking is interactive and spontaneous, requiring the producing, receiving, and processing of information.

Adding to this complexity, in terms of both teaching and learning, are the different forms that communicative competence can adopt. Linguistic competence, for example, refers to mastery of the sounds, words, and grammatical patterns of spoken English. By the 1970s, this form of competence came to be viewed as one component of the broader concept of communicative competence, which enables 'the speaker to know how to say what to whom, when' (Nunan, 1999, p. 226). This form of competence includes sociocultural competence or the ability how to communicate politely and appropriately beyond the classroom. Another form of competence is strategic competence, which requires speakers to be aware of their own strengths and limitations in using the spoken language and to be able to access the means for making oneself understood with words or through non-verbal means (Bleistein et al., 2013). Finally, discourse competence refers to how phrases and sentences are tied together in ways that others will be able to understand the meaning. This form of competence is commonly thought of in terms of cohesion – the grammatical relations between the various components of a sentence – and coherence, which refers to the construction of texts.

Issues in teaching speaking

The goal of teaching speaking is, according to Bleistein et al. (2013), 'for students to be able to speak English in real situations' (p. 27). Designing and implementing classroom activities that achieve this goal can be challenging. This section explores several issues that teachers and their students may confront in moving towards this goal, including getting lost in communication, attaining fluency, reticence in speaking, the presence of different learning styles, providing feedback to students, and the use of technology in teaching speaking.

Getting lost in communication

At their heart, speaking activities must require that students communicate. As Ur (2012) puts it, one of the main goals of any speaking activity is to ensure that 'the students should actually talk a lot' (p. 117). Yet, as Bleistein et al. (2013) note, some classroom speaking activities can easily be completed by students working alone. Information gap activities can address this limitation by necessitating actual communication between students. Bailey (2003), for instance, argues that appropriately designed activities, such as information gap jigsaw and role play, in which one person has information that others lack require learners to use the target language, can ensure that learners use the target language to share information.

In summary, preparing students for communicative experiences outside of the classroom could be guided by the principle of 'get(ing) them lost in communication and unaware of the classroom' (Bleistein et al., 2013, p. 29). Opinion gaps, discussion activities, and projects can all be used for this purpose. Essential to the success of such speaking activities is the immersion of students in the activity.

Towards fluency

Fluency, according to Brumfit (1984), refers to 'natural language use, whether or not it results in native-speaker-like comprehension or production' (cited in Thornbury, 2012, p. 202). Attaining such fluency underpins many classroom activities, particularly those focusing on informal conversational interaction (Ur, 2012). If fluency is the aim of classroom instruction, then students should be provided with ample opportunities to acquire the skills essential to manage interactive talk (Thornbury, 2012). However, a possible challenge to this aim emerges if accuracy dominates fluency. As Bleistein et al. (2013) point out, 'getting stuck in the accuracy (or mechanical) stage is all too easy' (p. 30). Suggestions for addressing this issue include moving form-focused activities towards real-world communication and making drills and practices as interactive as possible. In terms of interaction, Ur (2012) recommends the use of group work as a means of increasing the amount of learner talk which can also encourage participation from learners who may be unwilling to speak in front of the entire class.

Student reticence

Language classroom anxiety – 'the situationally triggered anxiousness that learners experience when they try to interact in the target language during lessons' (Bailey, 2005, p. 163) – is one of the most significant challenges confronting language teachers, with a variety of cultural, linguistic, and psychological factors thought to account for this anxiety (Nunan, 1999).

In a detailed study of English language teachers and their students in Hong Kong, Tsui (cited in Nunan, 1999) identified several factors underpinning the reluctance of the latter to speak in the classroom. These include a fear of making mistakes, teachers' aversion to silence in the classroom, and an allocation of turns within the classroom that favoured more capable students. This study identified a range of strategies to overcome the reluctance of some students to speak, such as increased wait-time and improved questioning techniques on the part of teachers. Willingness to accept a variety of answers and incorporate peer support and group work into speaking activities were also thought to be of value in addressing student reticence (Bailey, 2005). Finally, Nazari and Allahyar (2012) argue that teachers should position their students as co-participants in classroom activities, allowing them to initiate conversations and play an active role in the co-construction of knowledge in the classroom.

Learning styles

Another issue confronting teachers in their teaching of speaking is the fact that classrooms are populated by learners with very different styles of learning. While several different learning styles have been identified, according to Bailey (2005) it is differences between reflective and impulsive learners that teachers of speaking need to be particularly cognizant of within the classroom. While the former prefers to consider carefully their answers prior to speaking, the latter are more impulsive, willing to take the risk of possibly making errors. Two issues arise when considering this reflective-impulsive dimension. First, teachers should not judge mistakes too harshly and potentially risk silencing the impulsive learner. Second, teachers need to display patience with reflective learners who might require additional time before they speak and who, in the meantime, may still be actively engaged in the lesson (Bailey, 2005, pp. 170–171).

Dealing with errors

As Bailey (2005) points out, student errors in speaking can create a 'dual dilemma' (p. 172) for teachers in that they must confront several questions. For example, when an error is made, should the teacher respond to the error? If a response is forthcoming, who should make it? How should the response be made? When should the response be made? There may in fact be legitimate reasons why a teacher may answer the first question in the negative; that is, no teacher response is given when an error is made. One of the possible reasons might be not wishing to discourage learner participation in speaking activities. As to the question of who should correct an error, if a response is to be made, Bailey (2005) suggests that 'students may learn more if they themselves correct problems in speech' (p. 173). Learners working to correct their own errors may be more memorable, leading to actual learning, as opposed to having the correct form given to them by the teacher. Involving learners in the correction of errors could also take the form of peer correction. Learners working together to identify and correct errors can be less threatening than correction by teachers. However, if these strategies are unsuccessful, correction by the teacher is likely to be necessary. Indeed, some research suggests that correction by the teacher, who is seen as the source of knowledge and authority, is preferred by many students (Ganji, 2009).

Speaking beyond the classroom

The issues discussed in this chapter have, thus far, assumed that teaching and learning the spoken language takes place within a classroom. However, as Richards (2015) argues, technology, the media, the internet, and the use of English in virtual social networks now provide a greater range of opportunities for authentic language use, including spoken language, than can be found within most classrooms.

Chat rooms, for instance, can represent one means for learners to engage in real-time oral communication with other learners as well as first-language users. Indeed, some learners may find such experiences less stressful than being required to speak in front of their teacher and peers within the classroom, potentially leading to 'more successful comprehension as well as a greater quantity of target language production than classroom-based communication' (Richards, 2015, p. 7). These opportunities could also contain the potential for learners to reimagine themselves as multilingual learners and users of the English language (Lam, 2006). Chat rooms, by allowing learners to construct and develop new virtual identities, can transcend classroom-based issues, such as the need to preserve face and reticence to speak, leading not only to learners engaging in a greater quantity of spoken communication but also in speech that is more fluent and less hesitant (Richards, 2015). Other examples include the use of online social media language learning websites in which a learner can be partnered either with other speakers in a form of language exchange (Kozar, 2015) or take lessons from teachers (Beatty, 2015), as well as through the use of online computer games (Kuure, 2011). Finally, opportunities to acquire and practise spoken language skills beyond the classroom are not necessarily dependent on access to information and communication technologies, as Kerekes' (2015) recollection of using songs and lyrics for language learning demonstrates.

Recently, some of the ideas and themes discussed above have been challenged and disrupted by rapidly changing world events, including the global pandemic caused by the COVID-19 virus. This has resulted in widespread, rapid, and profound changes in language instructions and learning, including the move to learning online. Against this background, new questions, challenges, and opportunities emerge for teaching speaking. For example, what is implied by the move from traditional in-person, on-campus learning to remote contexts? How can teachers motivate students to speak and overcome learner reticence? The following section considers ways in which language teachers might address these challenges by exploring alternative possibilities for teaching speaking.

Present trends of teaching speaking

This section discusses emerging challenges and opportunities in teaching speaking in a second/additional language. Moorhouse and Kohnke (2021) point out that the COVID-19 induced global pandemic 'has led to huge challenges for language teachers and learners' (p. 2). At the forefront of these is the move from in-person teaching to synchronous and asynchronous online teaching. Moorhouse and Kohnke's (2021) review of literature documenting language teachers' responses to the pandemic reveals that while language teachers have moved swiftly to online learning environments, many found reconceptualizing language in this form to be challenging.

Moorhouse and Kohnke (2021) note that while interaction between learners and teachers is crucial to language learning, its nature and form take on very different characteristics online. This observation, which could be extended to include interaction between the learners themselves, has implications for the nature and effect of classroom oral interaction in general and the teaching of speaking in particular. To date, however, the evidence presents a mixed picture. On the one hand, synchronous online language lessons might reduce student anxiety, with more reticent students potentially more willing to contribute compared to in-person lessons (Kamal et al., 2021). On the other hand, reports suggest that the quantity and quality of interactions are inferior to those achieved during in-person classes. Online interactions have been characterized as being more formal and offering fewer opportunities for private turns and informal discussion, with the result that student engagement in lessons is reduced (Moser et al., 2021). A study of teacher anxiety over livestream teaching amongst 12 high school English language teachers in mainland China by Liu et al. (2022) found 10 of the participants to be anxious about handling teacher-student communication and interaction in an online teaching environment. Some teachers, for example, reported feeling alienated from students and doubted if learning in this environment was effective in improving students' English language skills.

Relatively few studies, however, have investigated how specific language skills are being taught and learnt during the pandemic (Moorhouse & Kohnke, 2021). In one of the rare reports on the contemporary teaching of speaking skills, Cowie (2021) describes the use of Flipgrid with undergraduate English language learners at a university in Japan. In this example, learners were able to create short videos in which, working collaboratively, they created their own script, rehearsed, and eventually performed and uploaded the video. Students were able to receive comments from the teacher as well as produce additional videos to comment on the performances of other students. Several dimensions are evident in this type of activity. First, learners are able to exercise agency as they engage in social interaction to collaboratively negotiate the production of the video. Autonomous learning is also encouraged as the students make decisions about the video content and the video production process. This also allows scope not only for teacher feedback but also peer review in which students play a leading role in helping each other to learn and achieve their goals. Moreover, if videos play an active part in students' lives outside the classroom, such activities are likely to be both motivating and enjoyable.

This review of recent literature suggests that the pandemic has created both challenges and opportunities for teaching speaking. The following section suggests additional ways in which the dimensions discussed above, namely agency, autonomous learning, peer and teacher feedback, motivation, and enjoyment, can be harnessed to guide the design and implementation of speaking activities in and beyond the classroom.

Future directions of teaching speaking

The process of integrating in-class and out-of-class teaching and learning opportunities could begin with the selection of spoken materials and activities. Allowing students to select their own speaking materials and share these with the class can support learner agency, motivation, and autonomous learning. As Reinders (2011) points out, 'part of the development towards autonomy involves learners having the awareness and ability to locate the right resources for their learning needs' (p. 180). In addition, any teacher-selected materials should pay attention to activities that students enjoy. Teachers could, for instance, survey students and then collaborate with them to design and implement speaking activities. This form of teacher-student interaction would be underpinned by the goal of maximizing participation by students at all stages of the activity, from conception, planning, and materials development to implementation, feedback, and reflection.

While fostering participation and autonomy on the part of learners in relation to their engagement with the spoken language are the goals, the role of the teacher is likely to remain critical to their achievement. Therefore, project-based work, carried out by students individually or in small groups, that provides opportunities to acquire and develop spoken language skills can begin with structured, in-class opportunities to discuss, plan, and gather resources necessary for their project supported by the teacher where necessary. Next, students could move from this structured, supported phase of the project to taking responsibility for working collaboratively out-of-class to complete the project. Finally, an opportunity should be provided for students to self-reflect on if, and how, their spoken language skills have been enhanced through such project work could be used to highlight the value of this type of student-driven project to learners.

Possible introductory activities that could serve as a demonstration for students include 'news report or talk show', in which students work in groups to write scripts, take on a variety of roles, such as sports, weather, or finance reporter, and produce news reports or talk shows they are familiar with from television. 'Re-enacting' is a similar possible demonstration activity in which students work in small groups to reproduce scenes from contemporary movies, possibly altering the storylines and endings. Recreating contemporary movie videos that emphasize target grammatical structures and/or vocabulary could also be useful.

Following this introductory demonstration episode, it will be important to embed student ownership as a key component of learning by ensuring that all subsequent activities are led and directed by the learners themselves. Therefore, subsequent planning, design, and implementation of speaking activities should rest largely with the learners. For example, learners could engage in small group activities that require them to draw upon resources from their own individual social contexts to construct speaking episodes for themselves and their classmates. Resources for these activities could be drawn from sources such as the learners' experiences with digital gaming (Chik, 2015) and social media tools (do Carmo Righini, 2015).

This learner-led approach to the teaching and learning of speaking might assist some to overcome their reticence and anxiety by empowering them to take on new learner identities. The type of learner ownership, involvement, and direction described here could also assist in moving students from self-identifying, as well as being identified by others, as passive receivers of speaking opportunities to creators of speaking opportunities. If conducted in small groups with other learners, such student-directed selection, design, and implementation of speaking activities can lead to the formation of peer communities, which have been found to play an important role in supporting, reassuring, and encouraging students during online learning experiences as well as providing opportunities for additional incidental spoken interaction through discussion and debate (Farrell & Brunton, 2020). Speaking experiences of this type are consistent with recent calls for a usage-based approach to language acquisition in which learners begin by memorizing prototypical constructions using activities such as scripting, rehearsing, and performing dialogues and then move into activities that require them to recall and apply these constructions while engaged in meaningful communication (Richardson & Thornbury, 2016).

Success in student-teacher joint ventures such as these can empower students by allowing them to appreciate the leading role they can potentially fulfil in their own learning. Encouraging students to independently explore other opportunities for speaking beyond the classroom results in the personalization of spoken language episodes and supports the development of greater autonomy in their language learning journey.

At different stages of this collaborative enterprise, teachers can find opportunities to engage in spoken interaction with individual students outside the classroom. This individual, personalized communication between teachers and their students in out-of-class settings is likely to be more informal than might be the case within the classroom, potentially reducing power imbalances by creating a more equal relationship between the teacher and students and therefore helping the teacher to further address issues of student reticence and anxiety when speaking.

Being underpinned by the aim of providing learners with opportunities to make more choices and decisions, and in doing so take greater control over their engagement in spoken interaction, these suggestions for learner involvement in classroom speaking opportunities could also help them acquire and develop new transferable skills. These skills include peer collaboration and teamwork, both of which are essential in spoken interaction as learners function in the world beyond that of the classroom.

Challenges ahead

The challenges of creating effective interactive speaking activities of the type described above remain considerable. First, it is crucial to ensure a relaxed atmosphere is established, one in which students believe they are supported by the teacher and by peers and accept the significance of the speaking activity will be crucial components in preparing students for the activity. Creating a positive emotional climate, therefore, is imperative in teaching speaking. Another challenge will be to ensure student commitment to learning over extended time periods; initial enthusiasm for new and different modes of learning will need to be sustained and enhanced over longer time periods. Thus, activity design will need to consider ways in which students can be encouraged and supported to draw upon their own background knowledge and experiences as one way of giving greater responsibility to students. This can potentially maintain their motivation throughout an entire speaking course, for example.

Other factors that underpin effective speaking activities will continue to be relevant to the adaptions discussed in the previous section. In particular, the role of the teacher in integrating in-class and out-of-class teaching and learning opportunities will be critical to the success of the suggestions described above. For example, teachers must ensure that all learners do have sufficient talk time, which can be more challenging when attempting such integration. As learners take on the important role of materials and activities designers, teacher guidance is necessary to ensure tasks are comprehensible to all learners. How teachers monitor student activity and progress will also need to be considered, including providing corrective feedback.

If these challenges can be met, the benefits of integrating in-class and out-of-class teaching and learning opportunities can be substantial. For instance, shifting students to the centre of the design and implementation of speaking activities in the way suggested can provide them with practice in developing a range of generic skills, such as teamwork, collaboration, and organization. In the process of practicing these skills, incidental opportunities for speaking practice in the target language arise. By encouraging student leadership in this way, such skills – teamwork, communication, and collaboration – become the foundation of positioning students as the developers of their own and others' speaking skills.

In summary, the most significant challenge and opportunity for teachers of speaking in the future could be to shift from providing speaking opportunities to students to creating the potential for students to construct their own opportunities for learning to speak. The activities described above, which draw on students' input to the design and implementation of opportunities for speaking in the target language, can enhance their experiences of language learning more generally and in doing so potentially improve their retention in language learning programmes.

Conclusion

Looking to the future, it is unclear how rapidly changing circumstances will shape the teaching and learning of spoken English as a second or additional language. However, it is apparent that the type of changes brought about by, for instance, the global pandemic present particular challenges for the teaching of speaking. One reason for this is that in-person interaction and communication between teacher and students, and amongst students themselves, has traditionally been the norm in teaching and learning the spoken language. Nevertheless, this chapter has pointed to research suggesting that recent migration from traditional in-person classroom experiences to remote contexts also presents teachers of speaking and their students with new teaching and learning opportunities. Against this background of change and uncertainty, the need to maximize the benefits to learners from their engagement in spoken activities and experiences will continue to be paramount. To achieve this, this chapter has argued that teachers and their learners should be willing and able to explore and take on new roles in the teaching and learning process, with particular emphasis on the potential these roles will present for connecting classroom-based teaching of speaking with out-of-class speaking opportunities.

References

Bailey, K. (2003). Speaking. In D. Nunan (Ed.), *Practical English language teaching* (pp. 47–65). McGraw Hill.
Bailey, K. (2005). *Speaking*. McGraw Hill.
Beatty, K. (2015). Essentially social: Online language learning with social networks. In D. Nunan & J. Richards (Eds.), *Language learning beyond the classroom* (pp. 95–104). Routledge.
Bleistein, T., Smith, M., & Lewis, M. (2013). *Teaching speaking*. TESOL International Association.
Brumfit, C. (1984). *Individual freedom in language teaching*. Oxford University Press.
Chik, A. (2015). "I didn't know how to talk basketball before playing NBA 2K10": Using digital games for out-of-class language learning. In D. Nunan & J. Richards (Eds.), *Language learning beyond the classroom* (pp. 75–84). Routledge.

Cowie, N. (2021). The development of an ecology of resources for online English as a foreign language (EFL) teacher in a Japanese university during the COVID-19 pandemic. *International Journal of Educational Research and Innovation, 15*, 419–430. https://dx.doi.org/10.46661/ijeri.5356

Day, C., & Gu, Q. (2010). *The new lives of teachers*. Routledge.

do Carmo Righini, M. (2015). The use of social media resources in advanced level classes. In D. Nunan & J. Richards (Eds.), *Language learning beyond the classroom* (pp. 85–94). Routledge.

Farrell, O., & Brunton, J. (2020). A balancing act: A window into online student engagement experiences, *International Journal of Educational Technology in Higher Education, 17*, 25. https://doi.org/10.1186/s41239-020-00199-x

Ganji, M. (2009). Teacher-correction, peer-correction and self-correction: Their impacts on Iranian students' IELTS essay writing performance. *Journal of ASIA TEFL, 6*(1), 117–139.

Kamal, M., Zubanova, S., & Isaeva, A., et al. (2021). Distance learning impact on the English language teaching during COVID-19. *Education and Information Technologies, 26*, 7307–7319. https://doi.org/10.1007/s10639-021-10588-y

Kozar, O. (2015). Language exchange websites for independent learning. In D. Nunan & J. Richards (Eds.), *Language learning beyond the classroom* (pp. 105–114). Routledge.

Kerekes, E. (2015). Using songs and lyrics in out-of-class learning. In D. Nunan & J. Richards (Eds.), *Language learning beyond the classroom* (pp. 33–42). Routledge.

Kuure, L. (2011). Places for learning: Technology-mediated language learning practices beyond the classroom. In P. Benson & H. Reinders (Eds.), *Beyond the language classroom* (pp. 35–46). Palgrave.

Lam, W. S. E. (2006). Re-envisioning language, literacy, and the immigrant subject in new mediascapes. *Pedagogies: An International Journal, 1*(3), 171–195. https://doi.org/10.1207/s15544818ped0103_2

Liu, H., Yan, C., & Fu, J. (2022). Exploring livestream English teaching anxiety in the Chinese context, *Teaching and Teacher Education, 111*, Article 103620. https://doi.org/10.1016/j.tate.2021.103620

Moorhouse, B., & Kohnke, L. (2021). Responses of the English-language-teaching community to the COVID-19 pandemic. *RELC Journal, 52*(3), 359–378. 10.1177/00336882211053052.

Moser, K., Wei, T., & Brenner, D. (2021). Remote teaching during COVID-19: Implications from a national survey of language educators. *System, 97*, Article 102431. https://doi.org/10.1016/j.system.2020.102431

Nazari, A., & Allahyar, N. (2012). Increasing willingness to communicate among English as a foreign language (EFL) students: Effective teaching strategies. *Investigations in University Teaching and Learning, 8*, 18–29.

Nunan, D. (1999). *Second language teaching & learning*. Heinle & Heinle.

Reinders, H. (2011). Materials development for learning beyond the classroom. In P. Benson & H. Reinders (Eds.), *Beyond the language classroom* (pp. 175–189). Palgrave.

Richards, J. (2009). *Teaching listening and speaking: From theory to practice*. SEAMEO Regional Language Centre.

Richards, J. (2015). *Key issues in language teaching*. Cambridge University Press.

Richards, J. (2015). The changing face of language learning: Learning beyond the classroom. *RELC Journal, 46*(1), 5–22. https://doi.org/10.1177/0033688214561621

Richardson, S., & Thornbury, S. (2016). *What's new in ELT besides technology?* Part of the Cambridge Papers in ELT series. Cambridge University Press.
Thornbury, S. (2005). *How to teach speaking.* Longman.
Thornbury, S. (2012). Speaking instruction. In A. Burns & J. Richards (Eds.), *The Cambridge guide to pedagogy and practice in second language teaching* (pp. 198–206). Cambridge University Press.
Trent, J. (2012). The internationalization of tertiary education in Asia: Language, identity and conflict. *Journal of Research in International Education, 11*(4), 50–69. https://doi.org/10.1177/1475240911434339
Ur, P. (2012). *A course in English language teaching.* Cambridge University Press.

11
L2 WRITING PEDAGOGY
Responding to emerging needs and emergencies

Ismaeil Fazel

Introduction

In the latter half of the twentieth century, it became increasingly evident that writers who write in English as a second or an additional language (L2 writers, as a shorthand) face unique needs and challenges distinct from their Anglophone (L1, henceforth) counterparts (Matsuda et al., 2003). Against this backdrop, the interdisciplinary field of second language writing (L2 writing) emerged at the intersection of the two parent fields of Composition and Rhetoric, focused on teaching writing to Anglophone English speakers (L1), and Applied Linguistics/TESOL, dedicated to assisting English as a second language (L2) writer (Silva & Leki, 2004). Despite being a relatively young and nascent field, L2 writing has witnessed a remarkable evolution and has grown to become a recognised and vibrant discipline in its own right – one which is now believed to have indeed "come of age" (Leki et al., 2008, p. 1). Since its inception over half a century ago, L2 writing has arguably come a long way, as evidenced by the launch of its flagship journal (*Journal of Second Language Writing*) in 1992, which further affirmed its disciplinary identity.

Following this brief introductory background, a synthetic (conceptual) overview of the field will be provided. Subsequently, an empirical (bibliometric) overview of the recent developments and trends in the field (2020 to date) will be presented. The chapter will close by speculating on future directions and providing recommendations for researchers and practitioners in L2 writing. By and large, the developments in the field can be categorised into (1) the past trends (i.e., the formative influences and historical shifts

DOI: 10.4324/9781003361701-15

that have shaped the field, (2) the present trends (i.e., the current and recent developments and pedagogies in the field), and (3) the future trends, as will be explained in what follows.

The past trends

As with any other dynamic field of education, L2 writing instruction has been influenced by shifting theoretical perspectives and zeitgeists of different eras as well as by new needs and exigencies of L2 writers that have emerged from time to time. For the purposes of this chapter, in what follows, I will provide a developmental overview of the field of L2 writing pedagogy. The developmental history of the field can be broadly divided into three distinct historical phases with shifting emphases, namely, product-focused, process-focused, and post-process era, which will be succinctly reviewed in what follows. A comprehensive historical recounting of the field is beyond the scope of the chapter, though. (See Ferris & Hedgcock, 2023 for a comprehensive review of the field.). However, a brief overview of these approaches is presented here.

The product-oriented approach, known for its heavy focus on text as the final product of the composition process, is deemed to be the most prototypical and traditional approach to teaching L2 writing. The product approach emanated from composition pedagogy prevalent in American schools, colleges, and universities around the 1960s. In essence, this approach primarily emphasises the final written product above all else, with little consideration given to the process of writing itself. In this traditional instructional framework, students were typically introduced to literary samples and then required to follow a set of prescriptive and formulaic rhetorical rules to produce a variety of school-related genres such as exposition, comparison, and contrast, process analysis, argumentation, among others, which may not accurately reflect the diverse range of academic and non-academic genres that students are exposed to in their daily or academic lives outside of English classes (Caplan & Johns, 2019; Hyland, 2004, 2013, 2019). Apart from this lack of authenticity, critics further argue that this approach can lead to a narrow focus on grammar and correctness, rather than promoting creativity and critical thinking (Matsuda, 2003; Tardy, 2016). Additionally, the product-oriented approach may not allow for sufficient scaffolding and support for language learners who may conceivably need guidance in the process to fully develop their writing skills (Campbell & Latimer, 2012; Caplan & Johns, 2019; Ferris & Hayes, 2019). That said, this conventional text-focused approach continues to be a heavy influence on the teaching of L2 writing even to this day.

In light of the aforementioned critiques, the product-oriented approach with its predominant focus on text gradually gave way to what became known as the process approach. It is worthwhile to note that the shift in paradigm from the product-oriented to process-focused approach was in large measure influenced by the increasing consideration of the psychological dimensions of writing, due to the emergence and rise of psychological and cognitive theories of learning prevailing at that time (Hyland, 2022). As a seminal pedagogical paradigm originating in L1 writing and composition pedagogy around the 1970s–1980s, the process approach views the writer as a generator of ideas. Pioneering studies on L1 students indicated that composing is not a straightforward, linear process, but rather an iterative cycle whereby ideas are generated, developed, and refined. Writing, in this perspective, entailed a recursive process where "writers go back in order to move forward" (Zamel, 1982, p. 197). Research in this vein demonstrated that L2 writers, much akin to their L1 counterparts, also go through similar recursive and cognitive processes in the stages of text construction (Manchón, 2011; Olson & Land, 2007). In this instructional approach, L2 student writers are directed to engage in a sequence of stages – pre-writing, drafting, and revising – leading up to the construction of the final product through a series of writing drafts (Stapleton 2010; Zamel, 1982). By emphasising the process (i.e., planning, drafting, sharing, revising, and editing), students are presumed to have more opportunities to reflect critically on their own work and develop their writing skills. Whilst the focus in the product approach was on the final product (text and its quality), the process approach placed the emphasis on "the development of individual writers as they produce texts" (Ferris & Hedgcock, 2023, p. 80). In other words, in the process approach, what L2 writers learn through engagement in the process of writing is actually considered to be of more importance than what they produce (i.e., the final text). However, there are also some inherent potential challenges associated with the process-based approach. One of the crucial challenges is that the process model can be labour-intensive and time-consuming for instructors. Supporting the needs of individual L2 writers with multi-drafts and ample feedback can demand significant resources that may be challenging for writing instructors to provide. The process approach, while having its distinct merits, required a careful balance of resources and support from instructors to maximise its benefits for L2 writers.

Over time, the process approach came under criticism on various grounds. Critics (e.g., Atkinson, 2003; Atkinson & Connor, 2008; Stapleton, 2002) have argued that the predominant emphasis of process-oriented pedagogy on the procedural stages of text production, together with the premium placed upon the notion of personal voice, might be culturally unfamiliar to some L2 (multilingual) writers particularly those in non-western contexts, as many process-focused models may "draw heavily on inaccessible cultural knowledge" (Hyland, 2003, p. 21). The process approach was also critiqued for its heavy focus on the individual writer, which could potentially "disempower teachers and cast them in the role of well-meaning bystanders" (Hyland, 2003, p. 19).

One of the main criticisms of process approach is that it ignores the (social) contexts in which texts are produced. Against this backdrop, writing and composition started to be increasingly seen as being a socially-mediated, literacy practice, involving not only the individual writer – which was the chief focus of the process pedagogy – but also the audience and the broader social context surrounding the writing, which marked the beginning of a new post-process era in L2 writing (Bazerman, 1988; Gee, 2014; Hyland, 2004, 2019). The post-process perspective to L2 writing pedagogy, in essence, seeks to "highlight the rich, multifocal nature of the field" and to "go beyond now-traditional views of L2 writing research and teaching" (Atkinson, 2003, p. 12).

Before proceeding to the more recent developmental trends in the field, it is worthwhile mentioning that these formative perspectival paradigms have substantially contributed to the conceptual and pedagogical evolution of L2 writing praxis as it is today, and they continue to influence the field. In fact, some elements of the aforementioned approaches are still being used judiciously and eclectically, or in combination, by many L2 writing practitioners, material developers, and scholars.

The present trends

Since the turn of the century, different informative pedagogical movements and developments have come to the fore, which are worth touching upon here, given their ongoing and formative impact on the field. These novel pedagogical approaches include genre-based approaches, translingualism, and technology-enhanced L2 writing instruction, including collaborative writing and multimodal composition, among others, which will be concisely explained in the ensuing paragraphs.

Genre-based instruction, which has gained increasing traction in the field in the past decade or so, is premised on the view that writing is not just about language, but also involves social, cultural, and communicative practices. The notion of genre has been variously defined as "a class of communicative events that share some set of communicative purposes" (Swales, 1990, p. 58), or "configurations of meaning that are recurrently phased together to enact social practices" (Martin, 2002, p. 269). It has also been conceptualised as "abstract, socially recognized ways of using language"

(Hyland, 2007, p. 149). Three foundational pedagogies subsumed under the genre-based approach include the Systemic-Functional Linguistics (SFL), also known as the Sydney School genre approach, English for Specific Purposes (ESP) genre approach, and Rhetorical Genre Studies (RGS) approach. (For a full discussion and overview, see Paltridge, 2014; Tardy, 2016, 2017.) Although genre-based pedagogies differ widely (Hyon, 1996), most genre methods see writing as both linguistic (akin to product approaches) and socially-based context-specific.

Yet another recent trend that has come to the spotlight of the L2 writing community in the past couple of decades is the translingual approach or translingualism, also known as translanguaging and translingual pedagogy. A translingual approach, in essence, problematises monolingualism and promotes multilingualism (Silva & Wang, 2021). It has been characterised by its proponents as "a new paradigm" that "sees difference in language not as a barrier to overcome or as a problem to manage, but as a resource for producing meaning in writing, speaking, reading, and listening" (Horner et al., 2011, p. 303). Translingualism is mainly predicated on the view that language difference is seen as a resource, not a deficit, for meaning making and that language is performative and constantly in contact with different semiotic resources, creating new meanings (e.g., Canagarajah, 2013; Horner et al., 2011). Central to the translingual approach is the notion of code-meshing or code-mixing (Canagarajah, 2013), conceptualised as the ability of multilingual writers to combine two or more linguistic registers in a single act of speaking or writing, which is deemed as an advantage of "multilingual writing" (Kobayashi & Rinnert, 2023, p. 207). That said, the translingual approach has also faced criticism mainly due to its presumed lack of pedagogical practicality and viability (Atkinson et al., 2015; Gevers, 2018; Matsuda, 2013, 2014; Schreiber & Watson, 2018).

Another burgeoning trend in L2 writing research and practice is the use of technology in L2 writing pedagogy and assessment. The advent of the internet and advancements in digital technology heralded the beginning of a new era in communication. The digital revolution, otherwise known as the "digital turn" (Kergel et al., 2017), gave rise to new communication needs and challenges for L2 writers, which needed to be catered to by L2 writing pedagogy (Li, 2021). The development of digital technologies introduced novel forms of electronic and multimodal reading and writing, such as emails, blogs, and wikis, among others, or "digital genres" (Belcher, 2023, p. 33).

The emergence of new means and modes of digital communication also expanded the conceptualisation of literacy beyond the ability to read and write. In today's digital era, literacy goes far beyond the ability to read and write. "Literacies" are seen as social practices that are multiple, multimodal, and dynamic (Chen, 2013). Subsumed under the notion of literacies are digital literacies, which entail "reading and writing on electronic devices and the Internet" (Ware et al., 2016, p. 307). Digital literacies involve "using language in combination with other semiotic resources for communication, entering into relationships with new kinds of audiences, and constructing new kinds of identities" (Hafner, 2013, p. 830).

The digital turn has also ushered in a wealth of novel pedagogical technologies and affordances that can be harnessed for teaching purposes in L2 writing (Qin & Stapleton, 2022). Salient among these innovative pedagogies are digital collaborative writing (Storch, 2013, 2022), multimodal composition (Zhang et al., 2021), and data-driven learning (DDL) using technology-mediated corpora (Cotos et al., 2017). Digital technology has also revolutionised feedback and assessment practices, bringing to the fore possibilities such as automated writing feedback (Li et al., 2017; Zhang, 2020), and multimodal feedback, utilising affordances of audio and visual modes (e.g., screencast feedback, voice feedback, and commenting), as reported in emerging studies (e.g., Cunningham, 2019).

The appeals and arguments for the increasing use of technology in L2 writing pedagogy are compelling and grounded in research (e.g., Elola & Oskoz, 2017; Hafner & Ho, 2020; Warschauer, 2017). Nonetheless, a few caveats are in order here. First, technological affordances are not equally distributed in all contexts around the world, which constrains a thorough implementation of technology-infused L2 writing instruction in some contexts. Second, L2 writing teachers are not equally prepared or adept at using new technologies, and quite conceivably have differential levels of technological knowledge and expertise, which has important implications for L2 writing teacher education.

The selective overview presented above laid out a synoptic overview of the evolutionary trajectory of second language writing (mainly prior and up to 2020). Overall, the field has increasingly witnessed a gradual broadening of its scope to include sociocultural and contextual factors bearing upon L2 writing. This movement, often called "social turn", is predicated on "a deep appreciation for the social, and often political, context in which L2 writers must learn and live" (Polio & Williams, 2011, p. 501). The next section will highlight the developments in the field, particularly focusing on the scholarship that has emerged in the past three years (2020 to present).

Traditionally, the L2 writing scholarship has focused on three major inter-related focal themes, namely, L2 writers, their writing (text and text production process, including response to student writing), and writing instruction (Hyland, 2006; Matsuda et al., 2003). The salient trends and themes in L2 writing scholarship have been identified in recent seminal review studies on L2 writing (e.g., Riazi et al., 2018; Sun & Lan, 2023). Riazi et al. (2018) conducted a comprehensive synthesis of empirical research published in *JSLW* between 1992 and 2016. The dominant topics they reported were feedback, writing instruction, language and literacy development, assessment, and composing processes.

In a similar vein, more recently, Sun and Lan (2023), in a bibliometric study, provided an overview of the dominant research trends in L2 writing scholarship published between 2000 and 2020 across various scholarly journals. They found that certain topics, such as collaborative writing, peer feedback, syntactic complexity, and writing in EFL contexts, have been subject to increasing interest in the past two decades.

To my knowledge, there has not yet been any trend analysis of L2 writing scholarship covering the period from 2020 onwards. The unexpected advent of the COVID-19 global pandemic in early 2020 and the ensuing disruptions to traditional face-to-face education are argued to have ushered in a paradigm shift in all domains of education (Fayed & Cummings, 2021) and, by extension, in English language education and L2 writing pedagogy.

It was, therefore, of interest to see if the trends in the field had undergone any significant shifts in response to the recent pandemic. As such, in order to identify the most recent trends and adaptations that have emerged in the field (L2 writing) from 2020 onwards, a bibliometric analysis of the literature (2020–2023) was undertaken. Bibliometric research is new to Applied Linguistics (Chong & Plonsky, 2023), yet its use seems to be on the rise, as indicated by the increasing number of publications in this vein (e.g., Aryadoust & Ang, 2021; Hyland & Jiang, 2019).

For the purposes of this chapter, first, a comprehensive search was conducted on Web of Science (WOS) Core Collection, the most commonly used database for bibliometric research, to find publications in English relevant to L2 writing published between 2020 (January 1st) and 2023 (May 1st). The search was conducted with common keywords revolving around L2 writing – including "L2 writing", "second language writing"," EAL writing", "ESL writing", "EFL writing", and "bi/multilingual writing". The keywords were truncated and combined using Boolean search protocols to conduct search strings in titles, keywords, and abstracts of publications, which initially yielded 1021 records.

For the purposes of this analysis, only publications in the Web of Science categories of Linguistics, Language Linguistics, and Education Educational Research were included, which left 901 publications. Then, items such as book reviews, editorials, and review articles were excluded. Only full-length articles (empirical and otherwise) were selected, leaving 733 articles for analysis. Subsequently, the corresponding data, that is, the bibliographic information (title, authors, institutions, year of publication, journal name, abstracts, keywords, subjects, disciplines, references, etc.), of all 733 items were downloaded into RIS formatted files for further bibliometric analyses.

The bibliographic data from the relevant publications (*n* = 733) were then subjected to analysis using VOS viewer software (Van Eck & Waltman, 2010), a Java-based bibliometric visualisation software package. The package was developed by Leiden University in the Netherlands for constructing and visualising bibliometric networks, including bibliographic coupling, co-citation, and keyword co-occurrence. Using the bibliographic information from the 733 published articles, a bibliometric analysis was conducted using VOS viewer software version 1.6.18, focusing on keyword co-occurrence networks to identify and map out the influential thematic trends in the literature. In bibliometrics, keyword co-occurrence analysis is often used to analyse the strength of links between different co-occurring keywords in a large corpus of records, which yields a big-picture view of prominent research patterns in disciplines.

The keyword co-occurrence in the VOS viewer was set at a minimum of 20 co-occurrences. Out of the total of 2575 keywords identified, 33 key terms meeting the aforementioned threshold of having co-occurred at least 20 times in the corpus were selected and utilised to generate visualised networks based on keyword co-occurrences, which will be presented and explained below.

First, to attain a holistic overview of the emerging trends in the field, a visualised density analysis of the data (i.e., 733 publications) is presented in Figure 11.1. It is worth pointing out that the thermographic patches in

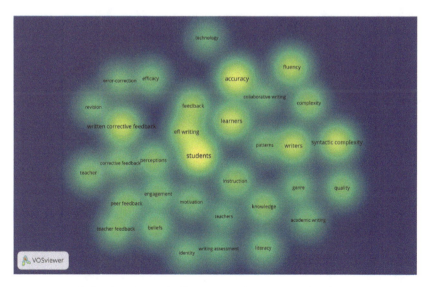

FIGURE 11.1 A density view of salient research topics in the data (2020–2023) (*n* = 733)

Figure 11.1 indicate the numerical density of papers published on a given research topic. That is to say, the larger the number of publications in a certain area, the more glowing the colour of the related thermographic patch.

As shown in the figure, research topics that have been receiving considerable scholarly attention in the recent (2020–2023) scholarly literature include three key topics: (a) L2 writers – "students", and its variants "learners" and "writers", (b) L2 writing – particularly writing in "EFL" contexts, and measures of writing quality ("accuracy", "complexity", and "fluency"), and (c) feedback – "written corrective feedback" and "feedback".

Moreover, a term co-occurrence analysis (network analysis) was conducted (see Figure 11.2), which depicts the most prominent topic clusters in the recent literature on L2 writing (2020–2023). In general, the smaller the distance between two terms, the larger the number of co-occurrences of the terms. The size of each circle represents the frequency of a given keyword, with a larger circle indicating that the keyword appears more frequently.

As displayed in Figure 11.2, the recent scholarly literature under study has formed three discernible clusters, with significant correlations between the keywords within each cluster. The three clusters represent certain focal topics that have received particular attention in the recent literature,

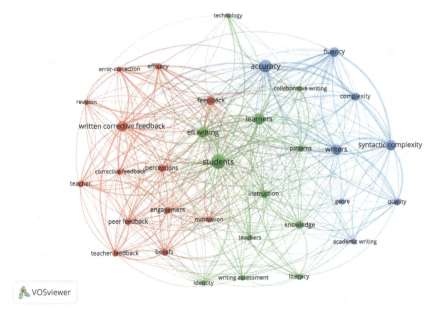

FIGURE 11.2 Keywords co-occurrence network analysis of studies 2020–2023 ($n = 733$)

namely, (1) students (L2 writers), and their writing, with an ancillary focus on L2 writing teachers, (2) student-produced writing and its quality indices, and (3) feedback (response to student writing), affective aspects of L2 writing, and L2 writing teachers, as explained below:

- Cluster 1 (Green) demonstrates a predominant focus on "students" (i.e., learners or L2 writers) and student writing, particularly writing in EFL settings, collaborative writing with the aid of technology, and (rhetorical) patterns in student writing.

  There is also an ancillary yet important focus on L2 writing teachers, their instructional knowledge and assessment literacy, as well as their professional identity.
- Cluster 2 (Blue) entails a chief focus on L2 writing quality, which is often indexed by complexity, accuracy, and fluency (CAF) in academic writing genres (Housen & Kuiken, 2009; Michel, 2017).
- Cluster 3 (Red) mainly denotes the prominence of response to student writing (feedback and its varied forms). Over half of the nodes in this cluster – including "written corrective feedback", "feedback", "peer feedback", "teacher feedback", "corrective feedback", "error-correction", and "revision" – revolve around the notion of feedback. The cluster also features a focus on the effective dimensions of L2 writing (beliefs, perceptions, efficacy, motivation, and engagement), which are gaining more currency of late. Furthermore, there is a recurrence of the term "teacher", as with Cluster 1 (Green), which suggests its ancillary, yet seemingly increasing, prominence in the recent body of literature.

It is also important to note that, in the network analysis depicted above, certain topics occur in more than one cluster, an indication of their particular salience. The terms "students" and "learners" (in Cluster Green) and "writers" (in Cluster Blue), as well as the key terms "teacher" (in Cluster Blue) and "teachers" (in Cluster Green), appear in two clusters. The salient keywords and their respective occurrences, as well as their respective total link strengths, are given in Table 11.1, which helps with interpreting Figure 11.

Overall, based on the findings, a few key observations stand out. It appears that the traditional focus in the field on L2 writers and their writing continues to persist and will quite conceivably flourish further. The finding showing the prominence of collaborative writing and the use of technology in writing resonates with similar findings reported by Sun and Lan (2023). Also of note is the rising interest in measures of writing quality (i.e., complexity, accuracy, and fluency), which in part agrees with the finding by Sun and Lan (2023), showing an increase in complexity-related research. The

TABLE 11.1 Salient Keywords as well as Their Respective Occurrences and Total Link Strengths in the Corpus (2020–2023)

Cluster	Keyword	Occurrences	Total link strength
Cluster 1 (Green)	students	116	408
	learners	74	307
	EFL writing	63	175
	instruction	43	183
	knowledge	40	139
	literacy	29	90
	patterns	28	109
	identity	23	60
	collaborative writing	22	91
	teachers	21	79
	writing assessment	21	64
	technology	20	60
Cluster 2 (Blue)	accuracy	94	430
	syntactic complexity	69	309
	writers	66	280
	fluency	59	299
	complexity	41	158
	quality	35	158
	genre	28	72
	academic writing	26	78
Cluster 3 (Red)	written corrective feedback	69	242
	feedback	48	145
	perceptions	39	141
	beliefs	35	126
	peer feedback	33	119
	teacher	32	108
	engagement	31	111
	teacher feedback	31	121
	efficacy	30	140
	corrective feedback	28	112
	motivation	28	95
	error-correction	23	115
	revision	23	97

dominant focus on student-produced text and its attributes hearkens back to the traditional product-focused orientation in L2 writing, as mentioned in the overview of the historical paradigms. That said, the current text-oriented orientations tend to focus on authentic genres, which distinguishes them from the traditional product approach, which was critiqued for its inauthenticity.

The finding showing the prominence of feedback-related research is also akin to similar findings reported in previous review studies (e.g., Pelaez-Morales, 2017; Riazi et al., 2018; Sun & Lan, 2023). The focus on feedback and revisions is reminiscent of the process-focused approach, where the emphasis was laid on the composition stages and revision processes. A key point differentiating the current focus on feedback from the traditional process approach is the emphasis of the former on the social aspects of writing, as evinced in practices such as peer feedback; the traditional process approach had a heavy cognitive focus, as noted in the first part of the chapter. The findings further indicate burgeoning attention to research in non-ESL settings, particularly in "EFL" contexts, which supports similar findings reported by Riazi et al. (2018) and Sun and Lan (2023).

Particularly worth noting is that the topic of "L2 writing teachers" has been garnering burgeoning interest, which has been long called for by scholars in the L2 writing community (e.g., Casanave, 2009; Hirvela & Belcher, 2007, 2022). The critical importance of attention to the expertise and practices of teachers was further highlighted by the exigencies arising during the recent pandemic, which placed teachers in a uniquely crucial yet challenging position, where they had to adaptively fulfil multiple roles at the same time. The sudden transition to remote teaching challenged educators, including language and L2 writing teachers, to adapt their teaching practices to the virtual mode. They additionally had to repurpose their educational materials, resources, and activities to fit the purposes of remote instruction. Not only did they have to plan, devise, and deliver content lessons in a new digital mode – with whatever digital competence knowledge, and skills they possessed – but they were also often obligated to serve as instructional designers (Pedrotti et al., 2021) and curriculum developers (Tarrayo & Anudin, 2023) all at the same time, with little, if any, assistance from educational technology experts and institutional centres for teaching and learning.

Pedagogical exigencies arising in the pandemic times brought to the fore the need for adaptability and flexibility by teachers in response to evolving circumstances. Of relevance here is the notion of "adaptive expertise" (Hirvela, 2020), which refers to teachers' ability to "identify instructional roadblocks, then generate successful responses" (Hayden et al., 2013, p. 395). Future research should cast more light on the under-explored yet crucial topic of L2 writing teachers, which can have important implications for L2 writing teacher training and professional development. The success or lack thereof in any teaching and learning process is in large part predicated on the expertise and competence of teachers, who are at the helm of teaching and learning design and delivery. It is clearly important to equip L2 writing teachers with the requisite sensibilities to enable and empower them to adaptively and dynamically navigate their pedagogy and respond to new and emerging exigencies and circumstances that may arise in the future. Of late, the topic of L2 writing teacher expertise has been gaining burgeoning interest in the L2 writing scholarly community (e.g., Burns, 2022; Cumming, 2022; Lee & Yuan, 2021; Matsuda & Xu, 2022). It is promising to see growing interest in the expertise and praxis of L2 writing teachers, which has important implications for L2 writing teacher education and professional training. Scholarship in this important area needs to expand in scope to include new sensibilities and competencies, including pedagogical digital literacy, that are required for adaptively responding to new and evolving circumstances in the L2 writing landscape. The increasing, though long overdue, attention to L2 writing teacher preparation and training is arguably of the essence, given the key role played by L2 writing teachers in the design and delivery of L2 writing instruction, particularly paramount in today's rapidly changing world, which is characterised by rapidly progressing technological advancements and breakthroughs, as will be further discussed in the ensuing section.

Future trends

In light of the preceding review of recent emerging themes, it can be reasonably speculated that certain focal themes will continue to stand out in L2 writing scholarship. In general, it appears that the conventional focus of the field on L2 writers and their writing practices will remain in the limelight of the field in the near foreseeable future. Particularly, areas such as multimodal writing and automated (technology-mediated) written feedback will continue to receive scholarly attention, given the growing trend of digitalisation of writing spaces. In addition, the topic of L2 writing teacher education will conceivably continue to receive sustained scholarly attention in the field.

Apart from the aforementioned areas, a crucial and controversial topic that is bound to gain burgeoning traction in the L2 writing community is the advent and ubiquitous access to generative Artificial Intelligence (AI) technologies, most notably Generative Pre-trained Transformer (ChatGPT) released on November 30th of 2022, which has drawn unprecedented attention both within and beyond academia. While some have embraced and highlighted the potential and promise of AI in education (e.g., Halaweh, 2023; Zhu et al., 2023), critics have brought to the fore the ethical concerns, most notably issues surrounding academic integrity and plagiarism (e.g., Eke, 2023; Stokel-Walker, 2023). When it comes to L2 writing instruction, AI tools lend themselves well to being used in the writing process. AI affordances can, for example, be utilised in the pre-writing stage to generate and organise ideas or search for relevant information. L2 writers would also conceivably benefit from interacting with AI-enabled writing tools, such as ChatGPT. These AI tools can also be tapped by L2 writers to receive instant feedback on their drafts, which can enrich their learning experience. Clearly, though, there is a need for L2 writing teachers to cultivate students' critical digital literacy skills (Buckingham, 2015), while scaffolding their appropriate use of AI to facilitate their learning. It is also important to set clear and explicit guidelines for the responsible and ethical use of AI to preclude, or at least minimise the possibility of, potential misuses. Overall, newly emerging AI technologies like ChatGPT can potentially serve as a valuable instructional tool in L2 writing pedagogy.

Judicious and effective integration of AI tools, such as ChatGPT, arguably demands critical cognisance of the affordances and constraints of AI technologies, which highlights the importance of teachers' pedagogical expertise and competence when utilising AI tools, with implications for teacher training in this regard (Celik, 2023; Jeon & Lee, 2023). It is incumbent upon institutions and professional associations to design and deliver tailored training and professional development programmes for L2 writing practitioners, such that they can become "critical users of technology" (Mina, 2019, p. 1) to enable and empower them to aptly harness the affordances of technology prudently, adaptively, and judiciously in their instructional practice, as part of their professional repertoire.

On the research front, most publications in this vein have been non-empirical and mainly in the form of commentaries drawing chiefly on personal observations or anecdotal experiences. It is also of note that these publications, empirical and otherwise, have overwhelmingly appeared in sciences, particularly in medicine and health-related disciplines. Empirical research in this vein is beginning to emerge in the general field of language education (e.g., Jeon & Lee, 2023). This far, to my knowledge, there has not been any published research exploring the impact of AI tools and technologies in L2 writing classrooms, which points to a clear void in the relevant scholarship, which has implications for policy and practice. There is arguably an urgent and pressing need to have substantive and systematic research into the affordances and constraints of newly emerging AI-assisted writing technologies. Findings emerging from such empirical investigation can be potentially conducive to the development of an evidence-based framework delineating a set of recommended best practices to guide the appropriate application of AI in L2 writing instruction.

References

Aryadoust, V., & Ang, B. H. (2021). Exploring the frontiers of eye tracking research in language studies: A novel co-citation scientometric review. *Computer Assisted Language Learning*, *34*(7), 898–933. https://doi.org/10.1080/09588221.2019.1647251

Atkinson, D. (2003). L2 writing in the post-process era: Introduction. *Journal of Second Language Writing*, 12, 3–15. https://doi.org/10.1016/S1060-3743(02)00123-6

Atkinson, D., & Connor, U. (2008). Multilingual writing development. In C. Bazerman (Ed.), *Handbook of research on writing: History, society, school, individual, text* (pp. 515–532). Routledge.

Atkinson, D., Crusan, D., Matsuda, P. K., Ortmeier-Hooper, C., Rucker, T., Simpson, S., & Tardy, C. (2015). Clarifying the relationship between L2 writing and trans-lingual writing: An open letter to writing studies editors and organization leaders. *College English*, 77(4), 383–386. http://www.jstor.org/stable/24240054

Bazerman, C. (1988). *Shaping written knowledge: The genre and activity of the experimental article in science*. University of Wisconsin Press.

Belcher, D. (2023). Digital genres: What they are, what they do, and why we need to better understand them. *English for Specific Purposes*, 70, 33–43. https://doi.org/10.1016/j.esp.2022.11.003

Buckingham, D. (2015). Defining digital literacy-what do young people need to know about digital media? *Nordic Journal of Digital Literacy*, 10, 21–35. https://doi.org/10.18261/ISSN1891-943X-2015-Jubileumsnummer-03

Burns, A. (2022). Emergence in teacher writing expertise: Teachers be(com)ing expert. *Journal of Second Language Writing*, 58, 100938. https://doi.org/10.1016/j.jslw.2022.100938

Campbell, K. H., & Latimer, K. (2012). *Beyond the five-paragraph essay*. Stenhouse.

Canagarajah, A. S. (Ed.). (2013). *Literacy as translingual practice: Between communities and classrooms*. Routledge.

Caplan, N. A., & Johns, A. M. (Eds.). (2019). *Changing practices for the L2 writing classroom: Moving beyond the five-paragraph essay*. University of Michigan Press.

Casanave, C. P. (2009). Training for writing or training for reality? Challenges facing EFL writing teachers and students in language teacher education programs. In R. M. Manchón (Ed.), *Writing in foreign language contexts: Learning, teaching, and research* (pp. 256–277). Multilingual Matters.

Celik, I. (2023). Towards intelligent-TPACK: An empirical study on teachers' professional knowledge to ethically integrate artificial intelligence (AI)-based tools into education. *Computers in Human Behavior*, 138, 107468. https://doi.org/10.1016/j.chb.2022.107468

Chen, H. I. (2013). Identity practices of multilingual writers in social networking spaces. *Language Learning & Technology*, 17(2), 143–170.

Chong, S. W., & Plonsky, L. (2023). A typology of secondary research in applied linguistics. *Applied Linguistics Review*. https://doi.org/10.1515/applirev-2022-0189

Cotos, E., Link, S., & Huffman, S. (2017). Effects of DDL technology on genre learning. *Language Learning & Technology*, 21(3), 104–130.

Cumming, A. (2022). Modeling expertise as variable options. *Journal of Second Language Writing*, 58, 100937. https://doi.org/10.1016/j.jslw.2022.100937

Cunningham, K. J. (2019). Student perceptions and use of technology-mediated text and screencast feedback in ESL writing. *Computers and Composition*, 52, 222–241. http://dx.doi.org/10.1016/j.compcom.2019.02.003

Eke, D. O. (2023). ChatGPT and the rise of generative AI: Threat to academic integrity? *Journal of Responsible Technology*, 13, 100060. https://doi.org/10.1016/j.jrt.2023.100060

Elola, I., & Oskoz, A. (2017). Writing with 21st century social tools in the L2 classroom: New literacies, genres, and writing practices. *Journal of Second Language Writing*, 26, 52–60. https://doi.org/10.1016/j.jslw.2017.04.002

Fayed, I., & Cummings, J. (Eds.) (2021). *Teaching in the post COVID-19 era*. Springer.
Ferris, D. R., & Hayes, H. (2019). Transferable principles and processes in undergraduate writing. In N. A. Caplan, & A. M. Johns (Eds.), *Changing practices for the L2 writing classroom: Moving beyond the five-paragraph essay* (pp. 116–132). University of Michigan Press.
Ferris, D. R., & Hedgcock, J. S. (2023). *Teaching L2 composition: Purpose, process, and practice* (4th ed.). Routledge.
Gee, J. P. (2014). *An introduction to discourse analysis: Theory and method* (4th ed.). Routledge.
Gevers, J. (2018). Translingualism revisited: Language difference and hybridity in L2 writing. *Journal of Second Language Writing*, 40, 73–83. http://dx.doi.org/10.1016/j.jslw.2018.04.003
Hafner, C. A. (2013). Digital composition in a second or foreign language. *TESOL Quarterly*, 47(4), 830–834. http://dx.doi.org/10.1002/tesq.135
Hafner, C. A., & Ho, W. Y. J. (2020). Assessing digital multimodal composing in second language writing: Towards a process-based model. *Journal of Second Language Writing*, 47, 100710. http://dx.doi.org/10.1016/j.jslw.2020.100710
Halaweh, M. (2023). ChatGPT in education: Strategies for responsible implementation. *Contemporary Educational Technology*, 15(2), ep421. https://doi.org/10.30935/cedtech/13036
Hayden, H. E., Rundell, T. D., & Smyntek-Gworek, S. (2013). Adaptive expertise: A view from the top and the ascent. *Teaching Education*, 24(4), 395–414. http://dx.doi.org/10.1080/10476210.2012.724054
Hirvela, A. (2020). Exploring second language writing teacher education: The role of adaptive expertise. In L. Seloni & S. H. Lee (Eds.), *Second language writing instruction in global contexts: English language teacher development* (pp. 13–30). Multilingual Matters.
Hirvela, A., & Belcher, D. (2007). Writing scholars as writing teacher educators: Exploring writing teacher education. *Journal of Second Language Writing*, 16, 125–128. http://dx.doi.org/10.1016/j.jslw.2007.08.001
Hirvela, A., & Belcher, D. (2022). Expertise in L2 writing instruction: The road less travelled. *Journal of Second Language Writing*, 58, 100936. http://dx.doi.org/10.1016/j.jslw.2022.100936
Horner, B., Lu, M.-Z., Royster, J. J., & Trimbur, J. (2011). Language difference in writing: Toward a translingual approach. *College English*, 73(3), 303–321. http://www.jstor.org/stable/25790477
Housen, A., & Kuiken, F. (2009). Complexity, accuracy, and fluency in second language acquisition. *Applied Linguistics*, 30(4), 461–473. http://dx.doi.org/10.1093/applin/amp048
Hyland, K. (2003). Genre-based pedagogies: A social response to process. *Journal of Second Language Writing*, 12, 17–29. http://dx.doi.org/10.1016/S1060-3743(02)00124-8
Hyland, K. (2004). *Genre and second language writing*. University of Michigan Press.
Hyland, K. (2006). *English for academic purposes: An advanced resource book*. Routledge.
Hyland, K. (2007). Genre pedagogy: Language, literacy and L2 writing instruction. *Journal of Second Language Writing*, 16(3), 148–164. http://dx.doi.org/10.1016/j.jslw.2007.07.005
Hyland, K. (2013). *Genre and second language writing* (2nd ed.). University of Michigan Press.
Hyland, K. (2019). *Second language writing* (2nd ed.). Cambridge University Press.

Hyland, K. (2022). *Teaching and researching writing* (4th ed.). Routledge.
Hyland, K., & Jiang, F. (2019). Points of reference: Changing patterns of academic citation. *Applied Linguistics*, *40*(1), 64–85. http://dx.doi.org/10.1093/applin/amx012
Hyon, S. (1996). Genre in three traditions: Implications for ESL. *TESOL Quarterly*, *30*, 693–722. http://dx.doi.org/10.2307/3587930
Jeon, J., & Lee, S. (2023). Large language models in education: A focus on the complementary relationship between human teachers and ChatGPT. *Education and Information Technologies*, 1–20. https://doi.org/10.1007/s10639-023-11834-1
Kergel, D., Heidkamp, B., Telléus, P. K., Rachwal, T., & Nowakowski, S. (Eds.). (2017). *The digital turn in higher education: International perspectives on learning and teaching in a changing world*. Springer.
Kobayashi, H., & Rinnert, C. (2023). L1/L2/L3 writers' advantages: Text and process. In H. Kobayashi & C. Rinnert (Eds.), *Developing multilingual writing: Agency, audience, identity* (pp. 207–237). Springer.
Lee, I., & Yuan, R. E. (2021). Understanding L2 writing teacher expertise. *Journal of Second Language Writing*, *52*, 1–12. https://doi.org/10.1016/j.jslw.2020.100755
Leki, I., Cumming, A., & Silva, T. (2008). *A synthesis of research on second language writing in English*. Routledge.
Li, M. (2021). *Researching and teaching second language writing in the digital age*. Palgrave Macmillan.
Li, Z., Dursun, A., & Hegelheimer, V. (2017). Technology and L2 writing. In C. A. Chapelle & S. Sauro (Eds.), *The handbook of technology and second language teaching and learning* (pp. 77–92). Wiley-Blackwell. https://doi.org/10.1002/9781118914069
Manchón, R. M. (Ed.). (2011). *Learning-to-write and writing-to-learn in an additional language*. John Benjamins.
Martin, J. R. (2002). A universe of meaning: How many practices? In A. M. Johns (Ed.), *Genre in the classroom: Multiple perspectives* (pp. 269–283). Lawrence Erlbaum.
Matsuda, P. K. (2003). Second language writing in the twentieth century: A situated historical perspective. In B. Kroll (Ed.), *Exploring the dynamics of second language writing* (pp. 15–34). Cambridge University Press.
Matsuda, P. K. (2013). It's the wild West out there: A new linguistic frontier in U.S. college composition. In A. S. Canagarajah (Ed.), *Literacy as translingual practice: Between communities and classrooms* (pp. 128–138). Routledge.
Matsuda, P. K. (2014). The lure of translingual writing. *PMLA*, *129*(3), 478–483. http://dx.doi.org/10.1632/pmla.2014.129.3.478
Matsuda, P. K., Canagarajah, A. S., Harklau, L., Hyland, K., & Warschauer, M. (2003). Changing currents in second language writing research: A colloquium. *Journal of Second Language Writing*, *12*(2), 151–179. http://dx.doi.org/10.1016/S1060-3743(03)00016-X
Matsuda, P. K., & Xu, F. (2022). Expertise in second language writing instruction. *Journal of Second Language Writing*, *58*, 100935. https://doi.org/10.1016/j.jslw.2022.100935
Michel, M. (2017). Complexity, accuracy and fluency (CAF). In S. Loewen & M. Sato (Eds.), *The Routledge handbook of instructed second language acquisition* (pp. 50–68). Routledge.
Mina, L. W. (2019). Analyzing and theorizing writing teachers' approaches to using new media technologies. *Computers and Composition*, *52*, 1–16. http://dx.doi.org/10.1016/j.compcom.2019.01.002

Olson, C. B., & Land, R. (2007). A cognitive strategies approach to reading and writing instruction for English language learners in secondary school. *Research in the Teaching of English, 41*, 269–303. http://www.jstor.org/stable/40171732

Paltridge, B. (2014). Genre and second-language academic writing. *Language Teaching, 47*(3), 303–318. https://doi.org/10.1017/S0261444814000068

Pedrotti, G., Sporn, Z., & Capitani, L. (2021). Navigating the shift from language instructor to instructional designer: How foreign language pedagogy can adapt in the age of e-learning. In I. Fayed & J. Cummings (Eds.), *Teaching in the post-COVID-19 era* (pp. 415–423). Springer.

Pelaez-Morales, C. (2017). Short communication: L2 writing scholarship in JSLW: An updated report of research published between 1992-2015. *Journal of Second Language Writing, 38*, 9–19. https://doi.org/10.1016/j.jslw.2017.09.001

Polio, C., & Williams, J. (2011). Teaching and testing writing. In M. H. Long & C. J. Doughty (Eds.), *Handbook of language teaching* (pp. 486–517). Blackwell.

Qin, J., & Stapleton, P. (Eds.). (2022). *Technology in second language writing: Advances in composing, translation, writing pedagogy and data-driven learning*. Taylor & Francis.

Riazi, M., Shi, L., & Haggerty, J. (2018). Analysis of the empirical research in the journal of second language writing at its 25th year (1992–2016). *Journal of Second Language Writing, 41*, 41–54. https://doi.org/10.1016/j.jslw.2018.07.002

Schreiber, B. R., & Watson, M. (2018). Translingualism ≠ code-meshing: A response to Gevers' "Translingualism revisited" (2018). *Journal of Second Language Writing, 42*, 94–97. https://doi.org/10.1016/j.jslw.2018.10.007

Silva, T., & Leki, I. (2004). Family matters: The influence of applied linguistics and composition studies on second language writing studies: Past, present, and future. *Modern Language Journal, 88*(1), 1–13. https://doi.org/10.1111/j.0026-7902.2004.00215.x

Silva, T., & Wang, Z. (Eds.). (2021). *Reconciling translingualism and second language writing*. Routledge.

Stapleton, P. (2002). Critiquing voice as a viable pedagogical tool in L2 writing: Returning the spotlight to ideas. *Journal of Second Language Writing, 11*, 177–190. https://doi.org/10.1016/S1060-3743(02)00070-X

Stapleton, P. (2010). Writing in an electronic age: A case study of L2 composing processes. *Journal of English for Academic Purposes, 9*(4), 295–307. https://doi.org/10.1016/j.jeap.2010.10.002

Stokel-Walker, C. (2023). ChatGPT listed as author on research papers: Many scientists disapprove. *Nature, 613*(7945), 620–621. https://www.nature.com/articles/D41586-023-00107-z

Storch, N. (2013). *Collaborative writing in L2 classrooms*. Multilingual Matters.

Storch, N. (2022). Theoretical perspectives on writing, corrective feedback and language learning in collaborative writing conditions and collaborative processing of WCF. In R. M. Manchón & C. Polio (Eds.), *Handbook of second language acquisition and writing* (pp. 22–33). Routledge.

Sun, Y., & Lan, G. (2023). A bibliometric analysis on L2 writing in the first 20 years of the 21st century: Research impacts and research trends. *Journal of Second Language Writing, 59*, 100963. https://doi.org/10.1016/j.jslw.2023.100963

Swales, J. M. (1990). *Genre analysis: English in academic and research settings*. Cambridge University Press.

Tardy, C. M. (2016). *Beyond convention: Genre innovation in academic writing*. University of Michigan Press.

Tardy, C. M. (2017). The challenge of genre in the academic writing classroom: Implications for L2 writing teacher education. In J. Bitchener, N. Storch, & R. Wette (Eds.), *Teaching writing for academic purposes to multilingual students: Instructional approaches* (pp. 69–83). Routledge.

Tarrayo, V. N., & Anudin, A. G. (2023). Materials development in flexible learning amid the pandemic: Perspectives from English language teachers in a Philippine state university. *Innovation in Language Learning and Teaching, 17*(1), 102–113. https://doi.org/10.1080/17501229.2021.1939703

Van Eck, N., & Waltman, L. (2010). Software survey: VOSviewer, a computer program for bibliometric mapping. *Scientometrics, 84*(2), 523–538. https://doi.org/10.1007/s11192-009-0146-3

Ware, P., Kern, R., & Warschauer, M. (2016). 14. The development of digital literacies. In R. M. Manchón & P. K. Matsuda (Eds.), *Handbook of second and foreign language writing* (pp. 307–328). De Gruyter Mouton.

Warschauer, M. (2017). The pitfalls and potential of multimodal composing. *Journal of Second Language Writing, 38*, 86–87. https://doi.org/10.1016/j.jslw.2017.10.005

Zamel, V. (1982). Writing: The process of discovering meaning. *TESOL Quarterly, 16*, 195–209. https://doi.org/10.2307/3586792

Zhang, Z. (2020). Engaging with automated writing evaluation (AWE) feedback on L2 writing: Student perceptions and revisions. *Assessing Writing, 43*, 100439. https://doi.org/10.1016/j.asw.2019.100439

Zhang, M., Akoto, M., & Li, M. (2021). Digital multimodal composing in postsecondary L2 settings: A review of the empirical landscape. *Computer Assisted Language Learning, 36*(4), 694–721. https://doi.org/10.1080/09588221.2021.1942068

Zhu, C., Sun, M., Luo, J., Li, T., & Wang, M. (2023). How to harness the potential of ChatGPT in education? *Knowledge Management & E-Learning, 15*(2), 133–152. https://doi.org/10.34105/j.kmel.2023.15.008

12
ADAPTABLE TEACHING OF GRAMMAR, VOCABULARY, AND PRONUNCIATION

Enhancing fluency and engagement through online apps

Xinrong He and Barry Lee Reynolds

Background

English has become a lingua franca for international communication (Baker, 2009). It provides English as a second/foreign language (ESL/EFL) learners with access to a wealth of information and resources that increase their job prospects and opportunities for cultural exchange. This has led many governments to make English a mandatory subject in their education curriculums and to offer professional development for language teachers. Universities also frequently offer English-medium instruction courses to improve the English proficiency of students and staff to create an internationalized environment (Macaro et al., 2018; Reynolds & Yu, 2016). However, despite these efforts, many ESL/EFL learners still face challenges in achieving effective and fluent communication in English.

Vocabulary, grammar, and pronunciation are three key components of language proficiency. Limited vocabulary size results in learners failing to find the words to express their thoughts and ideas. A solid understanding of grammar, including sentence structure, verb tense, and parts of speech, is crucial for producing intelligible sentences. Good pronunciation, which includes proper sounds, intonation, stress patterns, and rhythm, is vital for being understood by listeners. Many researchers and practitioners view the acquisition of these three components from a wide range of perspectives, such as the "input hypothesis" (Krashen, 1985) and "output hypothesis" (Swain, 2005), intentional learning and incidental learning (Hulstijn, 2013), and the more recent informal digital language learning (Lee, 2019;

Lee 2019). This indicates that the learning of the three components is complicated and multifaced.

Considering the cost-benefit principle of language learning, "the best return is gained from learning the most frequent items first" (Nation, 2013, p. 11). This requires language learners to focus on the most frequent and useful items (i.e., words, sounds, grammar) as they contain greater learning value. It is important for English teachers to identify what are the high-frequency words and grammar as well as be equipped with knowledge of the problematic sounds of targeted learners so that specific instruction and practice can be provided for these items.

High-frequency vocabulary, grammar, and problematic sounds

To apply the cost-benefit principle of language learning, teachers need to be informed about the most frequent and useful language items, including high-frequency vocabulary, grammar, and sounds. High-frequency vocabulary refers to words and phrases that people frequently use in different contexts. According to Schmitt and Schmitt (2014), English vocabulary can be classified into three levels based on their frequency of use: high, mid, and low. High-frequency words are the commonly used words in English and make up the majority of the language. Research by Nation (2013) has shown that these high-frequency words account for approximately 80% of all written English and almost 90% of all spoken English. This means that if ESL/EFL learners can master the most frequently used words in English, they will be able to understand and communicate effectively in most everyday situations. To get their hands on these high-frequency words, teachers could refer to the General Service List of English Words created by Michael West. This classic list can also be found on Paul Nation's personal website under the "Vocabulary Resources Booklet" section.

In terms of frequency, just like with vocabulary, there are certain grammatical features that are much more commonly used than others (Nation, 2013). In fact, the distribution of grammar is like vocabulary, where there are a few very high-frequency items and a much larger number of low-frequency items. High-frequency grammar refers to features of the language that occur very frequently in both spoken and written discourse, and they typically have simpler and shorter structures. For example, the simple present tense and simple past tense are very commonly used in English, and they have relatively straightforward structures (e.g., "I walk" or "I walked"). These structures are so commonly used that they become almost automatic for native speakers, and they require very little conscious effort to produce or understand. In contrast, the low-frequency grammar is those structures that are used less frequently and have more complex structures.

These might include things like the conditional mood, passive voice, or various forms of the perfect tense (Nation, 2013). While these structures are still important for conveying certain kinds of meaning, they require more effort and attention to produce and understand, and they are less likely to appear in everyday speech and writing.

When it comes to learning pronunciation, the most frequent and useful items could refer to the problematic sounds of a targeted learner population. Many learners struggle with specific sounds that are problematic for them, especially those that "do not exist in their first language" (Nation, 2013, p. 86). These sounds can cause confusion for the listener, making it difficult for them to understand what the learner is saying. For example, a Chinese speaker may have difficulty with the English "th" sound, which does not exist in Mandarin Chinese. The "th" sound is produced by placing the tongue between the teeth and blowing air out, as in the word "think" or "bath". This sound can be challenging for Mandarin Chinese learners to master, as it requires a different placement of the tongue and lips than they are used to. It is also common for learners to make mistakes with sounds that are present in both their first language and the foreign language they are learning. This can happen when the sound is used in a different position in a word or is not pronounced in the same way in the foreign language. For example, the Mandarin Chinese learner may struggle with English stress patterns, which are used to distinguish words that are otherwise spelled identically. In Mandarin Chinese, stress is not used in this way, so the learner may have difficulty distinguishing between different stress patterns and using them correctly in conversation.

There seem to be two extremes in current language courses. One focuses on the formal instruction of language features offering students limited chances to use what they have learned. This is because focused attention to language features can positively contribute to language learning (Ellis, 2005, 2006). This approach involves training strategies such as utilizing word cards, translation exercises, learning grammar through substitution tables, memorizing exemplary sentences, and pronunciation drills. But this approach does not provide opportunities for learners to practice using language in real-world communication.

The other extreme, instead, focuses on communication. Based on the "output hypothesis" (Swain, 2005), supporters believe that engaging in meaningful interaction could promote language acquisition through production. This method incorporates the three components of language acquisition implicitly within reading and listening practices. They entail activities such as graded reading, listening to English-language music and watching films, and engaging in extensive listening practice. This kind of course provides learners with an abundance of opportunities to receive and produce messages; however, sufficient comprehensible input from both reading and listening is also critical for language learning (Krashen, 1985; Nation, 2007; Newton 2009). Therefore, the best strategy might be the combination of the two extremes to design a more balanced language course (Nation, 2007).

The discussion on whether to focus on the "form" or "meaning" of these language components in instruction remains unsettled. According to Schmidt (1994), learning cannot occur without conscious attention to a language's structure and grammar. However, there are differing opinions on how much emphasis should be placed on form-focused instruction. Some researchers argue that learners should primarily focus on meaning; for example, Long (1996) suggests that acquisition is most effective when learners are actively engaged in decoding and encoding messages within the context of genuine communication. In other words, the ideal conditions for acquisition occur when learners are immersed in real-world situations where they are motivated to understand and use the language to communicate effectively.

Even classroom English teachers aware of these issues struggle with how to increase their learners' independent learning of these components. Learner autonomy plays a critical role in the language learning process (Little, 2007), especially in an era of new technology where ESL/EFL learners have a multitude of input sources at their fingertips. With the widespread availability of the internet and digital devices such as laptops, smartphones, and tablets, students can now access a multitude of digital resources to enhance their English language skills (e.g., Chang & Hsu, 2011; Stockwell, 2010). Many online platforms have been created and used for ESL/EFL teaching and learning, such as *IdiomsTube* (https://www.idiomstube.com) and *English Central* (www.englishcentral.com), offering a wealth of materials, such as audio and video lessons, quizzes, and interactive games, allowing learners to actively engage with the language in a fun and interactive way outside of the classroom. This interactive repetitive exposure to language input and opportunities for language output enhance learners' language fluency and motivate language learning autonomy. Therefore, these and resources like them offer language teachers opportunities to integrate these online applications into their language instruction in class and further encourage learners to engage with them out-of-class.

Current trends

The current trend of language teaching emphasizes that teachers should know how to teach these items through a well-balanced language course (Nation & Yamamoto, 2012). An explanation of how to construct a well-balanced course of vocabulary, grammar, and pronunciation will be presented in this section.

Four strands principle: How to design a well-balanced course

Nation (2013, p. 8) suggests that "a well-balanced language course should consist of four roughly equal strands–meaning-focused input, meaning-focused output, language-focused learning, and fluency development". And each of these strands should get an equal amount of time in the total course. The detailed explanation of each strand is as follows:

Meaning-focused input: Emphasizes acquiring knowledge through the methods of listening and reading. The learners' primary focus should be understanding the content they are reading or listening to.
Meaning-focused output: Emphasizes acquiring knowledge through speaking and writing. The learners' attention should be focused on communicating messages to others.
Language-focused learning: Corresponds most closely to traditional teaching, as it highlights deliberate attention to language features.
Fluency development: The last strand aims at helping students maximize the utilization of their existing knowledge of the language.

To effectively implement the four strands principle, a "teacher needs to know a range of useful activities in each strand and know how to use them effectively" (Nation, 2013, p. 10). This means if teachers want to apply the four strands principle to guide the instruction of high-frequency words, grammar, and sounds, they need to learn how to distinguish each strand and provide correspondent activities for it.

In the meaning-focused input strand, teachers can take several approaches to provide and organize large amounts of comprehensible input of target language components through both listening and reading (Nation, 2013). One effective activity for this strand is extensive reading. This activity could expose learners to target high-frequency vocabulary in meaningful contexts, and it can help them build their vocabulary and improve their reading comprehension skills. Another useful activity is reading aloud. Teachers can read a storybook, newspaper article, or a chapter from a novel to the learners. This provides a model for pronunciation for learners to correct and improve their pronunciation errors, and it can also help learners develop their listening skills.

Besides receiving meaning-focused input from teachers, classmates could also provide input. For example, teachers can assign topics for learners to conduct research on and students can prepare a talk or presentation. During the presentation, the rest of the class can listen and take notes and then ask questions or give feedback to the presenter. This kind of activity enables learners to play multiple roles, e.g., both language learners and users, in a learning environment. As Reynolds and Yu (2020, p. 17) highlight, "the more frequently students [play the] role of users of English, the more fluency gains they achieve". To further boost learning through comprehensible input, teachers can add a deliberate learning element. For example, when doing extensive reading, teachers can highlight high-frequency words and ask learners to use them in sentences. During presentations, teachers can ask learners to use a certain high-frequency grammar structure.

To support learners' engagement in the meaning-focused output strand, there are several strategies that teachers can employ. One strategy is to encourage learners to produce spoken and written output in a variety of appropriate genres. This can include activities such as writing emails, reports, and essays, as well as participating in discussions, debates, and presentations. By engaging in these activities, learners can practice using language in different contexts and become more comfortable expressing themselves in different formats. Matching writing and speaking tasks to learners' needs is essential for effectively encouraging learners to engage in meaning-focused output activities. Teachers should identify areas where learners need to improve and design tasks that target those specific aspects. For example, if learners are struggling with high-frequency grammar, teachers could design tasks that require learners to work with those specific troublesome grammatical structures.

Language-focused learning emphasizes the explicit teaching of specific language features, so teachers should help learners deliberately learn high-frequency words, grammar, and problematic sounds through a range of form-focused activities. For example, pronunciation practice can help learners improve their ability to produce and distinguish between sounds in the target language. Substitution tables and drills can help learners practice using high-frequency grammar structures and sentence patterns in context. Vocabulary learning from word cards can help learners increase their knowledge of the most frequently used words in the language (Nation, 2007, 2013). However, it is not just the activity type that is important for language-focused learning and instruction. Feedback is an essential component for second language acquisition (Li, 2010), as it allows learners to identify areas where they need to improve and make necessary adjustments to their language use (see Chapter 6 of this volume). Teachers should provide feedback on written work as well as on spoken language in class.

In the fluency development strand, teachers should provide fluency development activities in each of the four skills: listening, speaking, reading, and writing (Nation, 2007, 2013). This approach is based on the idea that language learners need opportunities to practice using the language in a meaningful and communicative way, in order to become more confident and fluent speakers of the language. There are lots of activities that can help learners to practice using the language in a natural and spontaneous way. For example, speed-reading can be helpful for improving fluency because it requires learners to process the language more quickly and accurately. Similarly, repeated reading involves reading the same text multiple times and this can help learners to improve their reading fluency and accuracy. By reading the same text multiple times, learners can become more familiar with the language, which can help them to read more quickly and accurately. Some examples of other fluency development activities include 4/3/2 activities, regular ten-minute writing programs, and listening to stories (Nation, 2007, 2013).

Additionally, it is crucial for teachers to explain to their students how important it is to balance their engagement in different types of language learning activities. Learners can benefit greatly from applying the four strands principle when assuming responsibility for their own learning while embarking on self-directed language learning (Nation & Yamamoto, 2012). This is very important for the development of language learner autonomy.

Enhance fluency by engaging with online platforms

With the development of technology, more and more digital tools are used to help learners develop language proficiency. There are different aspects of proficiency, e.g., accuracy, complexity, or fluency involved in language learning (Skehan, 1998, 2009), and these aspects are interdependent. Here, the term "fluency" in language learning refers to the ability to efficiently comprehend and produce language with a reasonable rate. If language components cannot be recognized or produced in a timely manner that allows for real-world communication, then the direct instruction or learning of these components is not valuable. For instance, Grabe and Stoller (2002) found when the speed of vocabulary recognition is too slow, it becomes difficult to understand the flow of text, and reading becomes a boring process of decoding words.

To improve language fluency, a large amount of input and output is critical (Ellis, 2005; Nation, 2007). However, the limited learning time inside the class is not enough for providing sufficient input and output. Therefore, learners need to take part in out-of-class language learning activities to receive additional input as well as engaging in language use that requires language production (Tam & Reynolds, 2022). Before the emergence of Web 2.0, there was a limited number of channels for engaging in out-of-class language learning. However, with the development of digital technology, learners can use diverse devices, such as mobile phones or computers, to access a large number of online learning materials outside of the classroom. This kind of learning often takes place without explicit attention to language items. Based on whether there is deliberate attention to specific language items, researchers have classified language learning into incidental learning and intentional learning (Hulstijn, 2003).

Research suggests that both intentional and incidental methods can effectively aid in the development of fluency in language components. Intentional learning refers to a deliberate effort to memorize various language components, e.g., word form, meaning and sounds, or grammatical rules through repetition (Hulstijn, 2003). On the other hand, incidental learning refers to "the learning that occurs as a result of using language with no particular intention to learn a particular linguistic element" (Schmitt, 2010, p. 98), e.g., through passive exposure from listening or reading (Hulstijn, 2013).

Although some studies show that intentional learning is more effective than incidental learning, both contribute to a learner's mastery of a language. Incidental learning is still of value because explicit learning cannot account for the language knowledge that learners need to master to become fluent users (Pellicer-Sánchez, 2015). Take vocabulary learning for example; there is a lexical barrier between native and non-native English speakers. Nation (2013) reported that native English speakers have an average vocabulary size of 22,000 to 32,000 words, while advanced second language learners typically have a receptive vocabulary size of around 11,000 words. Due to time constraints, it is impossible for L2 learners to acquire such a large number of words through intentional learning alone, and many words need to be attained incidentally. Direct instruction of vocabulary cannot account for all the words acquired by a learner whether it is in their first or second language.

The quantity of exposures that learners receive is a significant concern in relation to incidental learning. Repeated exposure to target language items is crucial for their acquisition. If learners want to learn to read, write, or speak, they need to do lots of corresponding practice. Webb (2007) investigated how repetition affected the acquisition of ten dimensions of vocabulary knowledge. His examination of exposure to one, three, seven, and ten encounters with targeted words suggests increasing the number of exposures could lead to improvements in all dimensions of vocabulary knowledge. Rebuschat and Williams (2011) found that incidental repeated exposure to grammar resulted in the improvement of grammatical performance. However, teachers should ensure not only quantity of repeated exposure but also quality of repetition.

Online applications provide an important route for learners to improve their language proficiency through repeated and varied exposures to language input. For example, *YouTube* (www.youtube.com) is a very popular online platform which contains a limitless number of English videos on different topics with automated subtitles or captions. The use of *YouTube* aligns with Nation's (2007) four-strand principle, and it not only enables learners to be exposed to comprehensible input but also provides opportunities to engage in language-focused items. Dual-coding theory (Paivio, 1979) suggests that learners acquire vocabulary knowledge more effectively through dual rather than single code. Subtitled or captioned videos found on *YouTube* combine the audio and captions/subtitles to enhance the comprehensibility of the input (Kanellopoulou et al., 2019), leading to positive effects on second language acquisition. For example, Reynolds et al. (2022) reported that watching captioned or subtitled videos, irrespective of the video type, could exert a positive influence on the acquisition of vocabulary. Watching captioned videos can also draw learners' attention to the subtitles (Winke et al., 2013), allowing them to make connections between word form and pronunciation and establishing a form-meaning link for unfamiliar words (Montero Ferez et al., 2015). This is beneficial for the acquisition of vocabulary as well as pronunciation skills. However, learners may need guidance from teachers on how to select the most appropriate videos for viewing. Many new programs are being developed that "piggyback" on the affordance of the videos that *YouTube* provides.

An example is the platform *IdiomsTube*, which aims at facilitating the informal learning of formulaic expressions (FEs) from *YouTube* videos (Lin, 2021). The term "formulaic expression" refers to a wide range of word combinations that have become established in language, such as idioms, conversational phrases, proverbs, binomials, and collocations (Wray, 2005). These formulaic expressions are very common in daily communication, and they are essential for developing English proficiency. *IdiomsTube* enables learners to receive extensive comprehensible exposures to formulaic expressions from tailored online YouTube videos followed by specialized and autogenerated practice tasks.

Different learners may have different attitudes, motivations, or preferences for out-of-class learning, and their proficiency levels also vary (Wong, 2012). Ellis (2005) suggests that second language learning could be more successful if the instruction is matched to students' particular aptitude for learning and the students are motivated. Compared with *YouTube*, *IdiomsTube* could automatically analyze the difficulty level of videos and then recommend videos that match the proficiency levels and interests of learners. Besides, *IdiomsTube* could provide learners with enjoyable and effective FE learning experiences with different personalized and adaptive FE practicing tasks, such as filling in the blanks, spelling, and pronunciation, supported by the learner's profile database which contains their preference for videos. By using *IdiomsTube*, learners could receive ample comprehensible inputs of FEs as well as conduct diverse output practices. This also resonates with Nation's four-strand principle. Meanwhile, repeated exposure to the spelling and pronunciation of high-frequency formulaic expressions is helpful for their acquisition and fluency development as well.

Some online applications also provide well-designed interactive courses which enhance the development of fluency. For example, *English Central* is a video website that provides learners with interactive video courses, and its three-part approach "watch, learn, speak" is deliberately designed to result in language proficiency development. *English Central* courses include developing fluency in listening, speaking, reading, and writing which is required by the fluency development strand (Nation, 2007). In the "watch" part, learners view segmented videos where each word is clickable from a large storage of videos based on learners' interests. Learners can click on any word to check its pronunciation and meaning. This part is a preparation step for later fluency activities as the fluency strand only exists when there is no unfamiliar language or large unfamiliar content. The "learn" part involves replacing specific vocabulary words with blanks in a cloze exercise designed to evaluate a learner's listening and spelling abilities. Learners watch a video while filling in missing words, then study the spelling, meaning, pronunciation, part of speech, and usage of these words in the sentences from the videos. In the "speak" part, learners listen to a line of audio from a video and then repeat it, receiving feedback on pronunciation and fluency, resulting in learners' development of intelligible fluent English. Through the three-part learning process, learners receive repeated exposure to words, pronunciation, and grammar, leading to the learning of these components.

Besides, the three-part approach of *English Central* consistently focuses on assisting learners to receive and convey messages and not just the direct learning of new language items. Learners are helped to utilize their existing knowledge in practicing all four language skills. Reynolds and Yu (2016) found that the administrative staff who participated in an English for Specific Purposes course increased their willingness to use English when communicating with international students in a Taiwanese University after their practice on the *English Central* website. These administrative staff were more comfortable with English speaking and listening after engaging in the online platform. *English Central*'s three-part process provided the learners with opportunities to enhance their proficiency outside the classes.

There are lots of online applications that learners could utilize outside the classroom. The platforms discussed in this chapter are just three examples. Repetition-based online applications such as these enable learners to develop language proficiency through out-of-class informal learning methods. Thus, it is necessary for teachers to be knowledgeable of them, recognize their importance, and encourage students' engagement in their use.

Future adaption

With the development of technology, using digital tools to assist language learning out-of-class has become increasingly popular. Lee (2019) defines this method of English learning as informal digital learning of English (IDLE). In fact, IDLE is just one of the many important subfields of informal language learning, which together play a crucial role in second language acquisition. Besides enhancing fluency, engaging in informal language learning can result in a multitude of benefits.

Informal language learning can supplement formal language learning programs, providing learners with additional opportunities to practice, and reinforce the language skills they are learning in class. For example, the cultivation of cross-cultural communication skills is generally ignored or receives less attention in traditional class settings (Sun, 2015). However, cross-cultural communication is becoming increasingly important in an era of globalization. By engaging with informal language materials that are easily accessible through online applications, learners can learn about customs, traditions, ways of thinking, and communication styles that are unique to the cultures of the English language. This kind of cultural exposure can help learners better understand the nuances of language that are often lost in traditional language learning settings.

Informal language learning could also increase the accessibility and convenience of learners to receive exposure to authentic language use that they are interested in. There is a large amount of informal language learning resources, which are often readily available and easily accessible, making it easier for learners to practice their language skills whenever and wherever they choose. Whereas, decades ago, out-of-class informal English learning activities for most English as a second language learners were often limited to hearing English songs or watching films and TV series, now, with the development of technology, i.e., Web 2.0, learners can gain access to various English learning materials via the applications on their digital devices. Through exposure to this input, learners can gain an understanding of the language as it is spoken and used by proficient speakers of English, including colloquial expressions, idioms, and slang, which can help learners understand and use the language more effectively in real-life situations (Liontas, 2015; Rogers, 2018). Most importantly, these materials are not assigned by teachers who may not be able to consider the interests and needs of all students in formal instruction settings. Informal language learning allows learners to choose the language materials and topics that interest them the most, which makes the learning experience more personalized and relevant to their individual needs and goals. This can make language learning more enjoyable and engaging and also motivate learners to continue learning the language and make progress in their language learning journey.

Learning a new language can be a challenging and intimidating experience, particularly for those who are not accustomed to speaking it on a regular basis. One of the key benefits of informal language learning is that it provides a safe and supportive environment for learners to practice and make mistakes (Chakowa, 2018). Unlike a formal classroom setting, where learners may feel pressured to perform and may be subject to correction and criticism, informal language learning takes place outside of a formal classroom setting, allowing learners to take risks and make errors without fear of judgment or failure. This can be a valuable opportunity for learners to build confidence in their language abilities and to develop a more positive attitude toward language learning. Confidence is an important factor for effective communication, and it closely relates to the learner's willingness to communicate (MacIntyre & Gardner, 1994). When learners feel comfortable and at ease using the language, they are more likely to express themselves clearly and effectively (Yashima, 2002). In addition, learners who are more confident in their language skills are likely to be more motivated to continue learning and practicing the language, which can lead to further improvements in their abilities.

Overall, while informal English learning is very beneficial for second language acquisition, it is important to note that it may not provide the same level of structure and teacher guidance as formal classes, and learners may need to be self-motivated and disciplined in order to make progress. Given these challenges, we have the following suggestions for teachers.

First of all, *emphasize the accuracy and quality of exposure content*. The current era is marked by an unprecedented surge in the volume of new information available on the Internet. This content is highly diverse, encompassing a broad spectrum of genres that range from formal to informal. This diversity offers students an extensive range of options to choose from when seeking to expand their knowledge base. Nonetheless, research suggests that having an excessive number of options can have negative consequences, including hindering the learning process and overwhelming learners. As noted by Iyengar and Lepper (2000) and Vohs et al. (2008), such an overwhelming volume of information can impose a heightened cognitive load on learners, which can result in difficulties in effectively processing and retaining information. Therefore, it is very important for teachers to encourage learners to focus on accuracy and quality of online information by providing recommendations for reliable sources and by helping learners develop critical thinking skills to evaluate the information they find. Teachers should consider learners' interests and needs when recommending sources or applications. This involves taking an interest in the extracurricular activities of learners and possibly educating themselves about what students find engaging and valuable.

Second, *foster motivation and engagement*. Informal language learning requires a high degree of self-motivation and discipline. Without intrinsic motivation and support, learners may struggle to stay motivated and committed to their language learning goals (Guilloteaux & Dornyei, 2008). Teachers can help learners stay motivated and engaged by creating a positive learning environment, such as building a community, and encouraging peer-to-peer interaction and collaboration, such as group projects, language exchanges, or language clubs. This can help learners feel connected and supported and also provide them with opportunities to practice their language skills.

Third, *provide feedback and encourage self-reflection*. Feedback is crucial for language learners to improve their skills (Caruso et al., 2019). In an informal setting, learners may not have access to feedback from teachers, which can make it difficult for them to identify and correct mistakes. The self-directed nature of informal language learning may also pose comprehension difficulties, particularly with regard to complex grammar rules and linguistic subtleties. Therefore, teachers can give learners feedback on their language skills by reviewing their work and offering suggestions for improvement. This can help learners identify and correct their mistakes. Besides, teachers can encourage learners to reflect on their language learning progress, identify areas they need to improve, and set realistic goals.

References

Baker, W. (2009). The cultures of English as a lingua franca. *TESOL Quarterly*, *43*(4), 567–592. https://doi.org/10.1002/j.1545-7249.2009.tb00187.x

Caruso, M., Fraschini, N., & Kuuse, S. (2019). Online tools for feedback engagement in second language learning. *International Journal of Computer-Assisted Language Learning and Teaching*, *9*(1), 58–78. https://doi.org/10.4018/ijcallt.2019010104

Chakowa, J. (2018). Enhancing beginners' second language learning through an informal online environment. *Journal of Educators Online*, *15*(1). https://doi.org/10.9743/jeo2018.15.1.7

Chang, C.-K., & Hsu, C.-K. (2011). A mobile-assisted synchronously collaborative translation–annotation system for English as a foreign language (EFL) reading comprehension. *Computer Assisted Language Learning*, *24*(2), 155–180. https://doi.org/10.1080/09588221.2010.536952

Ellis, R. (2005). Principles of instructed language learning. *System*, *33*(2), 209–224. https://doi.org/10.1016/j.system.2004.12.006

Ellis, R. (2006). Researching the effects of form-focussed instruction on L2 acquisition. *AILA Review*, *19*, 18–41. https://doi.org/10.1075/aila.19.04ell

Grabe, W., & Stoller, F. L. (2002). *Teaching and researching reading*. Routledge.

Guilloteaux, M. J., & Dornyei, Z. (2008). Motivating language learners: A classroom-oriented investigation of the effects of motivational strategies on student motivation. *TESOL Quarterly*, *42*(1), 55–77. https://doi.org/10.1002/j.1545-7249.2008.tb00207.x

Hulstijn, J. H. (2003). Incidental and intentional learning. In C. J. Doughty & M. H. Long (Eds.), *The handbook of second language acquisition* (pp. 349–381). Blackwell Publishing Ltd. https://doi.org/10.1002/9780470756492.ch12

Hulstijn, J. H. (2013). Incidental learning in second language acquisition. In C. A. Chapelle (Ed.), *The encyclopedia of applied linguistics* (Vol. 5, pp. 2632–2640). Wiley-Blackwell. https://doi.org/10.1002/9781405198431.wbeal0530

Iyengar, S. S., & Lepper, M. R. (2000). When choice is demotivating: Can one desire too much of a good thing. *Journal of Personality and Social Psychology*, *79*(6), 995–1006. https://doi.org/10.1037//0022-3514.79.6.995

Kanellopoulou, C., Kermanidis, K., & Giannakoulopoulos, A. (2019). The dual-coding and multimedia learning theories: Film subtitles as a vocabulary teaching tool. *Education Sciences*, *9*(3), 210. https://doi.org/10.3390/educsci9030210

Krashen, S.D. (1980) Relating theory and practice in adult second language acquisition. In S.W. Felix (ed.) *Second Language Development: Trends and Issues*. Tubingen : Gunter Warr, 185–20. https://doi.org/10.1016/0346-251X(80)90035-4

Krashen, S.D. (1985). *The Input Hypothesis: Issue and Implications*. Longman

Lee, J. S. (2017). Informal digital learning of English and second language vocabulary outcomes: Can quantity conquer quality? *British Journal of Educational Technology*, *50*(2), 767–778. https://doi.org/10.1111/bjet.12599

Lee, J. S. (2019). Quantity and diversity of informal digital learning of English. *Language Learning & Technology*, *23*(1), 114–126. https://doi.org/10125/44675

Li, S. (2010). The effectiveness of corrective feedback in SLA: A meta-analysis. *Language Learning*, *60*(2), 309–365. https://doi.org/10.1111/j.1467-9922.2010.00561.x

Lin, P. (2021). Developing an intelligent tool for computer-assisted formulaic language learning from YouTube videos. *ReCALL*, *34*(2), 1–16. https://doi.org/10.1017/s0958344021000252

Liontas, J. I. (2015). Developing idiomatic competence in the ESOL classroom: A pragmatic account. *TESOL Journal*, *6*(4), 621–658. https://doi.org/10.1002/tesj.230

Little, D. (2007). Language learner autonomy: Some fundamental considerations revisited. *Innovation in Language Learning and Teaching*, *1*(1), 14–29. https://doi.org/10.2167/illt040.0

Long, M. (1996). The role of the linguistic environment in second language acquisition. In W. Ritchie & T. Bhatia (Eds.), *Handbook of second language acquisition* (pp. 413–468). Academic Press.

Macaro, E., Curle, S., Pun, J., An, J., & Dearden, J. (2018). A systematic review of English medium instruction in higher education. *Language Teaching*, *51*(1), 36–76. https://doi.org/10.1017/s0261444817000350

MacIntyre, P. D., & Gardner, R. C. (1994). The subtle effects of language anxiety on cognitive processing in the second language. *Language Learning*, *44*(2), 283–305. https://doi.org/10.1111/j.1467-1770.1994.tb01103.x

Montero Ferez, M., Peters, E., & Desmet, P. (2015). Enhancing vocabulary learning through captioned video: An eye-tracking study. *The Modern Language Journal*, *99*(2), 308–328. https://doi.org/10.1111/modl.12215

Nation, I. S. P. (2007). The four strands. *Innovation in Language Learning and Teaching*, *1*(1), 2–13. https://doi.org/10.2167/illt039.0

Nation, I. S. P. (2013). *What should every EFL teacher know?* Compass Publishing.

Nation, I. S. P., & Newton, J. (2009). *Teaching ESL/EFL listening and speaking*. Routledge.

Nation, I. S. P., & Yamamoto, A. (2012). Applying the four strands to language learning. *International Journal of Innovation in English Language Teaching and Research*, *1*(2), 167–181.

Paivio, A. (1979). *Imagery and verbal processes*. Psychology Press. https://doi.org/10.4324/9781315798868

Pellicer-Sánchez, A. (2015). Incidental L2 vocabulary acquisition from and while reading: An eye-tracking study. *Studies in Second Language Acquisition*, *38*(1), 97–130. https://doi.org/10.1017/S0272263115000224

Rebuschat, P., & Williams, J. N. (2011). Implicit and explicit knowledge in second language acquisition. *Applied Psycholinguistics*, *33*(4), 829–856. https://doi.org/10.1017/s0142716411000580

Reynolds, B. L., Cui, Y., Kao, C.-W., & Thomas, N. (2022). Vocabulary acquisition through viewing captioned and subtitled video: A scoping review and meta-analysis. *Systems*, *10*(5), 1–20. https://doi.org/10.3390/systems10050133

Reynolds, B. L., & Yu, M. H. (2016). Using web-based video technologies to increase Taiwanese university Staff's willingness to use English as a lingua Franca. In E. Grazzi (Ed.), *Intercultural communication: New perspectives from ELF* (pp. 131–144). Roma Tre Press.

Reynolds, B. L., & Yu, M. H. (2020). Using English as an international language for fluency development in the internationalised Asian university context. *The Asia-Pacific Education Researcher*, *31*(1), 11–21. https://doi.org/10.1007/s40299-020-00534-w

Rogers, J. M. (2018). Teaching collocations. In J. I. Liontas (Ed.), *The TESOL encyclopedia of English language teaching* (pp. 1–7). John Wiley & Sons, Inc. https://doi.org/10.1002/9781118784235.eelt0782

Schmidt, R. (1994). Deconstructing consciousness in search of useful definitions for applied linguistics. *Consciousness in Second Language Learning*, *11*, 237–326.

Schmitt, N. (2010). *Researching vocabulary: A vocabulary research manual*. Palgrave Macmillan.

Schmitt, N., & Schmitt, D. (2014). A reassessment of frequency and vocabulary size in L2 vocabulary teaching. *Language Teaching*, *47*(4), 484–503. https://doi.org/10.1017/s0261444812000018

Skehan, P. (1998). *A cognitive approach to language learning*. Oxford University Press.

Skehan, P. (2009). Modelling second language performance: Integrating complexity, accuracy, fluency, and lexis. *Applied Linguistics*, *30*(4), 510–532. https://doi.org/10.1093/applin/amp047

Stockwell, G. (2010). Using mobile phones for vocabulary activities: Examining the effect of the platform. *Language Learning and Teaching*, *14*(2), 95–110. http://dx.doi.org/10125/44216

Sun, C. (2015). The cultivation of cross-cultural communication competence in oral English teaching practice. *English Language Teaching*, *8*(12), 7–10. https://doi.org/10.5539/elt.v8n12p7

Swain, M. (2005). The output hypothesis, theory and research. In E. Hinkel (Ed.), *Handbook of research in second language teaching and learning* (pp. 471–483). Routledge. https://doi.org/10.4324/9781410612700

Tam, I. A., & Reynolds, B. L. (2022). The relationship between extramural English engagement and the vocabulary size of L1 Cantonese speakers in Macau. *ITL – International Journal of Applied Linguistics.* https://doi.org/10.1075/itl.21003.tam

Vohs, K. D., Baumeister, R. F., Schmeichel, B. J., Twenge, J. M., Nelson, N. M., & Tice, D. M. (2008). Making choices impairs subsequent self-control: A limited-resource account of decision making, self-regulation, and active initiative. *Journal of Personality and Social Psychology, 94*(5), 883–898. https://doi.org/10.1037/0022-3514.94.5.883

Webb, S. (2007). The effects of repetition on vocabulary knowledge. *Applied Linguistics, 28*(1), 46–65. https://doi.org/10.1093/applin/aml048

Winke, P., Gass, S., & Sydorenko, T. (2013). Factors influencing the use of captions by foreign language learners: An eye-tracking study. *The Modern Language Journal, 97*(1), 254–275. https://doi.org/10.1111/j.1540-4781.2013.01432.x

Wong, L. (2012). Student attitudes towards e-learning: The first year accounting experience. *Issues in Informing Science and Information Technology, 9*(1), 195–207. https://doi.org/10.28945/1616

Wray, A. (2005). *Formulaic language and the lexicon.* Cambridge University Press.

Yashima, T. (2002). Willingness to communicate in a second language: The Japanese EFL context. *The Modern Language Journal, 86*(1), 54–66. https://doi.org/10.1111/1540-4781.00136

SECTION IV

The contribution of technology to ELT in new circumstances

13
LANGUAGE TEACHERS AND TEACHING TECHNOLOGIES

Valuing the teacher and teacher values in online learning

Jane Spiro

Introduction

The COVID-critical years accelerated and transformed our knowledge of the impact of technology on our learning lives as both learners and teachers pivoted almost overnight from physical to virtual classrooms. These changes, however, simply gave urgency to the parallel online classroom that has been evolving over two decades. The conversation became a chorus as to what was needed and expected of teachers to support their learners in a time of crisis. These included, for example, transforming the online space into a supportive and nurturing community to relieve learner isolation, recognising a shorter attention span online and thus breaking learning into smaller chunks, giving learners resources to study both in real-time and asynchronously, and recognising the need to support learners both between and in taught sessions. As both needs and strategies for meeting these needs rapidly emerged, there was no time to support the supporters or recognise the toll on their energies and self-esteem. This chapter attempts to address that gap by tracking a group of teachers as their responses to and mastery of online teaching evolved over a year. Their voices are framed by the studies emerging from the covid years, into both learner and teacher experiences. Section 1 reviews our recent past, asking how learners and teachers experienced the covid years 2020 and 2021. It reviews the online study experience from the perspective of students, sharing surveys and research studies about lockdown learning when school children and university students moved from classrooms to screens at home. Section 2 explores where we are now in terms of the impact of 'distance' teaching on teachers' self-esteem and skills. It refers both to the literature that emerged during and since the pandemic years and the voices of 22 language teachers across sectors and age levels as they reflect online about their evolving experiences. What emerges is a timeline of responses to the challenges of online learning, from first encounter to developing expertise. Section 3 asks what we have learnt during the pandemic years to take us forward into the future. It offers directions for the teacher to reflect on the 'human' teacher's contribution and value as an antidote to 'machine learning'.

Learning about learners online: Where we were

As learning in the pandemic year 2020–2021 moved from physical to virtual classrooms, every teacher was propelled to ask new questions about themselves and their learners: how could learning best be supported at a distance and on screen? What did learners need to sustain their learning, support their wellbeing, and encourage their participation from their laptops at home? Were these needs the same, or different from those learners have in physical classrooms? Surveys in multiple settings such as India (Hebebci et al. (2020); Nambiar, 2020), South Korea (Baber, 2020), Thailand (Kornpitack & Sawmong, 2022), and UK (Jackson, 2020, 2021) suggest that learners, as they moved online, valued even more urgently the qualities that were important in physical classrooms. Ginting et al. (2022), for example, surveyed the pandemic online learning experience of 90 university students in four different study programmes. They found, firstly, that learners had the same expectations of best practice irrespective of subject discipline or phase of study. Some of these best practice qualities reflected exactly those articulated in campus/physical settings, such as the need for mutual respect between teachers and learners, and for motivating and well-organised teaching input. Baber's research (2020) with undergraduates in South Korea and India also teased out values in online learning which exactly match those preferred in physical classrooms; for example, learning that included interaction, clear course structure, a teacher who commanded respect and trust, and a course with clear learning outcomes are a few instances of such values. None of these findings are surprising or controversial, and nor is it surprising that interaction, clarity, trust, and organisation are equally valued in either physical or virtual classrooms.

However, some of the insights from learner studies are accented specifically to take account of both technology and distance. For example, whilst interactive classrooms are amongst a list of valued qualities in physical classrooms, the online classroom appears to acquire additional and nuanced importance. To anatomise what interactive learning might look like, it is helpful to refer to the three tiers of interaction suggested by Moore (1989):

learner interaction with one another; learner interaction with the teacher; and learner interaction with content. In the online setting, the management of learning needs to actively build in these layers of interaction to compensate for the physical separation of learner from learner and learner from teacher. Recent surveys into student experience during the pandemic gave clear information about the fear of being demotivated and derailed without dynamic interactions with the teacher (Jackson, 2020, 2021).

> When presented with a scenario of limited face to face teaching, 71% said that in such a scenario they would struggle with motivation to learn and keeping up interest, 65% said they would struggle to stay connected with peers and the university, and 63% said they would feel less prepared to undertake course assignments and activities. Half said they would have difficulty managing their time and keeping track of everything.
>
> *Jackson, 2020, Great Expectations section*

One year later, when surveyed, the student responses highlighted even more clearly the importance of the teacher as a mentor or guide. A year of online learning had made them not less, but more conscious of the need for human support and intervention, synchronously and face-to-face online. Students cited the need for more personal attention, the opportunity to ask questions in real time, one to one video meetings, active discussion fora, and synchronous interactive lectures rather than pre-recorded ones (Jackson, 2021). Kornpitack and Sawmong's study (2022) of 270 high school students in Thailand found similar results, with teacher presence and visibility cited as a critical incentive to learn and essential to staying engaged with online study.

These findings build on what was known practice that has from the start focused on community-building and appreciation of the peculiar nature of online dynamics. Salmon (2013) identifies tendencies specific to the online setting, such as the 'lurker', who stays on the edges of learning interactions and can do so more inconspicuously in the virtual than in the physical classroom. Her learning activities are designed to scaffold the transition into virtual spaces as co-operative, interactive, and collective opportunities for learning, giving all kinds of learners the confidence and incentive to participate. The organisation of learning activities acquires an urgency in the online setting. Students in Ginting's study (2022) found it important that there be consistency in the way online platforms were used, so time is not lost learning and reinventing systems with each programme. Whilst students seemed to value asynchronous material, and the uploading of talks and clips, this too requires support in a distanced setting. Waite (2021) describes the impact of already prepared online videos on a cohort of student nurses. Although this, at surface value, is best practice, videos are not in themselves an indicator of helpful activity. Waite suggests that the educator needs to manage already prepared online clips so the listener is able to pause and reflect. An over-long video can do the reverse of offering asynchronous support when it overwhelms and deskills the learner.

Thus, the pandemic year was merely a reminder that online pedagogies need to be adopted critically, with mindfulness as to how they are received and experienced by learners. Educators may provide the resource but learners need 'inner work' in order to make sense of it (Waite, 2021).

We have learnt too during the pandemic learning period what its specific downfalls and dangers are. The first of these, emerging in many studies of the 2020–2022 period, is learner mental health. The experience of studying alone at a physical distance from both peers and teachers impacted heavily on learners and represented a divide between those learners who had space and support at home for study and those who did not. Frampton (2021) reports on the survey of 1100 higher education students, citing issues of loneliness and isolation which impacted significantly their learning during the pandemic year (Frampton, 2021).

A further risk in online learning is the presence or lack of technical preparedness. Hebebci et al. (2020) identify this as one of the most overarching negatives of online learning, since without a basic shared technology, there is no starting point. The frustrations of erratic internet blocks to login, and patchy video were described by Nambiar (2020) as affecting more than 50% of the students in his study in India. These are significant blocks, not only for the learner to learn but also for the teacher to positively support and intervene. The frustrations of an uncertain technology are not those a teacher can single-handedly overcome. Crucially, the pandemic era of online learning highlighted divides amongst learners: between those in technology-rich environments and those who were not and between learners with quiet and supportive home spaces for learning and those without.

On the one hand, the new online environment has been an equaliser: its newness means everyone is equally learning new technological skills, both teachers and students, both first culture and second culture. It also minimises the difference between students who have travelled to their classrooms, across streets, cities, country borders, and oceans. Many students returned home and continued studies from sitting rooms, kitchens, bedrooms, and spaces shared with homeschooling children, partners, families, and pets. Some students who had felt overwhelmed by the space, noise, and hecticness of campus life felt in some ways safer and more connected in the online setting.

On the other hand, the online learning world has been a great divider, splitting participants between those able to access the technologies economically, socially, and intellectually and those not able to. Although backgrounds in 'zoom rooms' can be manipulated, participants may be embarrassed about the personal space around them, fail to have that personal space, and are subject to the interruptions and disruptions of home life. The experience starkly separates those who have good learning conditions and those who do not.

However, in 2022 when classrooms returned to physical spaces, was it the case that something had been subtly changed? Learners were not always so enthusiastic about returning to real-world classrooms, and teachers report a change in the etiquette of learning with one another. The survey Imagined Universities (Pollard & Aldred, 2022) found, after pandemic conditions had changed, that face to face was no longer the default expectation.

> Had students learnt that asynchronous learning to suit their timetables (and busy lives) was more convenient? Or that some face-to-face sessions were not that satisfying after all? Or that you could save on the journey into town and still learn new concepts? Or were the students coming into campus, just not into the classroom? Or maybe the conception of campus is actually an imagined one.
>
> *Pollard & Aldred, 2022, paragraph 4*

We might raise doubts again as tendencies blow in different directions, in answer to the question: has something changed forever in the expectations of learners and the demands on teachers?

Learning about teachers online: Where we are now

In our urgency to understand learners, much less attention has been given to the teacher whose learning-teaching world also shifted overnight. This section shares responses from teachers regarding the covid-driven imperative to translate their teaching into fully online learning. We ask whether the adaptations were surface ones to do with enhanced technologies or did they challenge the very core of what language teachers believe about their role and their value in the classroom? It confronts teacher concerns that learners are now making new demands on them which may exceed their skills or that challenge the value of the 'human' touch. It aims to throw light on how the 'human' teacher's contribution continues to have value alongside emerging and changing technologies.

Studies into teacher responses during the lockdown year suggest that teachers were very open and able to adopt pedagogies which helped their learners, even where these were new to them. Todd (2020) surveyed 52 English language teachers in a well-regarded Thai university at the start, and several weeks into online teaching, adopted overnight and in the middle of the semester. At the start, the teachers identified multiple problems with online learning, including the management of group work, and the fatigue factor of learning online. After several weeks, however, they had arrived at solutions to these problems, such as using breakout rooms to form groups and reconfiguring content so it could be taught in smaller chunks. They also noted problems which had not at first been evident: the difficulty of giving feedback and marking one to one, the uncertainty as to whether or not their language goals had been met, and the problem of reading learner response when learners are physically distanced and isolated. This limited capacity to 'take the temperature' of the class, to read learners through body language, was frequently reported as a negative to teacher satisfaction in the online setting.

A study of 1060 teachers in India (Kumar et al., 2022) found there were three main factors which helped teachers to feel positive about online learning: if they considered the learning to be valuable and worthwhile; if they felt supported by their institution; and if the technology itself was easy to use and facilitated their needs. We might ask what support from the institution might look like and would be welcomed: whether this is training, equipment, or the presence of technicians to problem-solve. Yang's survey (2020) asked primary and secondary school teachers whether they had received, and availed themselves, of training during the pandemic year, to support the pivot to online learning. 55.31% of the teachers reported that they had received helpful training, but only once the pandemic had made online learning imperative. It accelerated their learning and made them adopt and apply training where they had formerly been reluctant. 36.07% of the teachers had not yet taken up training opportunities in 2021, but planned to do so within weeks of the survey, and a small percentage (8.62%) had availed themselves of training but found it unhelpful.

It is interesting to consider what makes a teacher avail themselves of training or choose not to do so. Childs' study (2021) of 250 university teachers at Durham University (UK) suggests a 'spectrum of responses' as the teachers reflected on the move from physical to virtual teaching. On the extreme ends of this spectrum, Childs notes two kinds of teachers: the first embraced online learning as an opportunity to refresh thinking about pedagogy. This kind of teacher experienced the change as radical and exciting, a chance to rethink 'old techniques', reject the lecture, and reimagine their role as a higher education teacher. This group even saw the move online as heralding an 'educational revolution'. They were excited by the potential for building communities outside the borders of a classroom and to consider ways of creating community online. On the extreme other end of the spectrum were those teachers who felt stretched beyond endurance, were reluctant to change, and vowed to return as soon as they could to their former habits. This kind of teacher also expressed scepticism as to whether meaningful interactions could ever take place online. Thus it becomes critical to ask, not only what does a teacher do as they move from physical to online learning, but also what do they think about that move? The next section asks that question and tracks answers over the course of the academic year 2020–2021 when learning moved online.

Teacher voices in virtual spaces

In this section, we summarise the responses of 22 teachers engaged in a development programme during the academic year 2020–2021. The teachers were all English language educators, teaching concurrent to their own studies in the following settings that had moved online: state primary school; higher education; private language school; 'cram' school; in-company language teaching; one to one tutoring. The forum was an adjunct to their own development sessions on an MA in TESOL, designed to provide them with the opportunity to share concerns and solutions as they evolved. The trigger for the forum, throughout the year, was the question: *how are you feeling as your teaching moves fully online?* Participants were asked if they would like to opt into these reflections contributing to an anonymised report once the year was over. Those who did not opt into this formed a separate group that is not included in the findings reported here. What emerged was a pattern of concerns that can be mapped along a timeline: from the first days to the first weeks and months. Through these voices, we have a dynamic snapshot of how teachers responded to the transition from concrete learning spaces to virtual spaces as this evolved over the course of a year. In reviewing their voices, we might note that the teachers who opted into these reflections were likely to be the more positive and radical teachers on the positive side of the opinion spectrum suggested by Childs et al. (2021). Even so, their journey is not smooth and reveals the same bumps and false starts as Todd recounts (2020). However, the reflections illustrate what it really feels and looks like for a group of teachers to be accelerated into an 'educational revolution', and what is left of who they were at the end of the first year.

The journey through the online learning year can be tracked in five stages labelled as follows: scramble for resources, disarmed by mistranslation, reclaiming pedagogies, beyond pedagogies, and the personal toll. These stages are based on patterns found in the teacher reflections and echoed in the literature described above. Teachers tracked their way through these stages at different paces; some moved very quickly beyond the first stage (scramble for resources) whilst others struggled with this the whole year; some never reached stage four (beyond pedagogies), finding stage three (reclaiming pedagogies) consumed all their time and energies; many reached stage five (the personal toll) very early on, experiencing 'burnout' within weeks of the new teaching load.

Stage one: Scramble for resources

In the first few days as learning made the sudden cut into virtual classrooms, the predominant worry was *how I keep up with the technology*. The teachers worried whether they had the equipment at home that would permit them to do their job well online. Some were asked to physically move their school/college computers back home, only to find that broadband conditions at home still made their connections unreliable. Others felt the burden of finding, buying, or borrowing new equipment. One teacher writes:

> Challenges included competing for a device with the students, low bandwidth internet connection and the six-hour time lapse (with some learners).

The first few days were described as a *scramble for resources*. Several expressed feelings akin to panic, as attention heavily focused on learner satisfaction and neglected the teachers' basic requirements for delivering content.

Even once the teachers felt more settled with the equipment they needed, there was the challenge of finding dedicated spaces at home. This was not just an issue of space and privacy, but of creating boundaries too, between the personal and professional:

> At home I am a mother, housewife, I have all those demanding personal roles, that's what my family expect of me. It was so difficult for me to put a boundary around that and for the family to accept the person I need to be at work: focused on my students and not on them.

For the first time many teachers felt self-conscious or inhibited by their home spaces: with unplanned backdrops such as kitchens, bedrooms, cats and dogs, and background noise of rumbling trains or traffic.

These issues did not so much resolve, as become more familiar and acceptable. The participants realised they were not alone in finding these boundaries difficult: their own learners too had the same challenges and limits to their concentration and time. Some of the participants found the presence of a personal world in the background humanised teaching and made them closer to their learners; others found the situation did not easily resolve. They felt permission was given to learners, but not to teachers:

> It's OK for my own learners to be distracted, pulled in all those different directions – it's my job to understand that and give them good reasons to participate. But it's just not as much OK for me to be distracted – even though the conditions are just as awkward for me.

For some, these issues persisted throughout the year; for others, arrangements were quickly made to borrow or buy suitable equipment, work in a dedicated space that gave them privacy, and find childcare. These teachers, however, were the lucky ones: these solutions were simply not available to everyone. Whether the teachers were able to progress to the more facilitative stages described below depended on whether they were able to travel beyond this 'first post'.

Stage two: Disarmed by mistranslation

The translation of interaction onto screen required a shift in what teachers expected of learners and vice versa. Co-operative principles were flouted and reconstituted in the following specific ways: teachers were disarmed, even alarmed, by the fact that learners could visibly absent themselves by turning off their cameras. Talking to black squares on screen entailed a new kind of dynamic none were trained or prepared for. Struggling with what was mutually respectful, some made the decision to insist on learners appearing on screen; others made the opposite decision, thinking it more respectful to allow learners to be off camera if that was their choice. These decisions did not come without struggle, however, as to what was valued and what was fair.

A second discovery for the teachers was that the natural flow of dialogue significantly changed online. Learners were much more reluctant to respond to verbal elicitations. The screen not only tended to induce a kind of passivity, but it also inhibited speakers from taking the initiative. Teachers described the hovering yellow square that sought out speakers and inhibited learners contributing. During this period of gathering mastery, teachers exchanged and adopted solutions: to use the chat facility, and to formally allocate speakers so every learner was given dedicated time on screen. Yet some teachers did not cease to mourn the loss of spontaneity and informality that resulted.

Stage three: Reclaiming pedagogies

This stage was characterised by gradual mastery of on-screen pedagogies: using breakout rooms more skilfully, using the screen share in a more agile way to include learner presentations, editing on screen, and using emoticons and chat room to engage learners in less daunting kinds of interaction. Some teachers began to feel excited by the opportunities. They describe screen share as a way of directing deep attention to texts which would not be achievable in physical classrooms. The period of experimentation and discovery was also seen as a way of learning from and with learners, who were also meeting these technologies for the first time. One teacher learnt about clipart from her primary school pupil, who had in turn learnt this from a friend.

However, various ways in which teachers had come to expect they might interact with learners needed reconfiguring in the online setting. The most frequently mentioned at this stage was the capacity to *monitor overall progress of small group discussions.* Teachers recognised they could not move freely between groups or discreetly hover at the edge of them. In breakout rooms, they were very visibly beamed into the group and found this changed or even froze the interactions that might have been taking place there. Gradually, some chose to be absent from breakout rooms or to schedule and prepare for their arrival. This too was a source of regret for some, whilst for others, they noted it made them consider more precisely their role when they did join breakout rooms.

Several of the teachers, too, became aware within weeks of the move online that content they might plan for a one-hour session in a physical classroom simply did not translate into screen learning. They noted the fact there are more background distractions online, the skills of holding the group together are much more onerous, and the attention span seems to be shorter. The planning of content thus changed, rapidly for some and gradually for others. More material was prepared in advance, including mini lecture clips, tasks, and readings; more material was uploaded to be accessed asynchronously, and more follow-up was planned.

Stage four: Beyond pedagogies

While teachers came to terms with online pedagogies, or even became energised and refreshed by them, at the same time they reflected on the potential missing links. The first, and most frequently mentioned, was support for the struggling or reluctant learner. *It's like teaching blindfolded and with my arms tied behind my back* one says of her struggle to reach out to the learners who did not attend, muted, or were regularly off screen. The key realisation was that the sessions alone were not enough. The informal conversations around the edges of formal teaching were missing, not just between learner and teacher, but between learner and learner. Frampton's survey (2021) showed the impact on learners' mental health as they studied in isolation from one another; and the teachers, in turn, struggled with the need and wish to support learners, recognising this often had to be done outside formal timetabled sessions.

However, the online exchange enabled teachers to share solutions. These included: encouraging students to run their own social networking groups via WhatsApp or other social platforms; using taught time to meet learners one to one while others are engaged in breakout activities; and leaving ten minutes at the end of each taught session for open discussion about wellbeing – if necessary, stepping out of the meeting so learners could run this for themselves.

Stage five: The personal toll

Throughout the year, teachers reflected on the personal toll these changes were taking. The most frequent comment was that teaching and preparation time were more than doubled. A typical one-hour taught session cascaded into three or four stages. These included preparing more materials in advance of the session, systematically breaking up, and scaffolding content to be accessible to learners independently. After the session, teachers felt the urgency to follow up tasks more systematically and to 'chase up' learners who did not attend or make themselves visible. Alongside these before and after stages, they also felt the need to be continually mindful of learners' mental health and available for one to one meetings. Many teachers felt a continuous sense of failing learners if they could not deliver this extra time. To fulfil online all the levels of interaction required for healthy learning and teaching seemed unachievable: revision and reconfiguring of content; nurturing interaction between learner and teacher; encouragement of learner-learner support inside and outside taught sessions (Moore, 1989).

In addition to these before and after stages, teachers report that the online sessions themselves were much more tiring than sessions taught in physical classrooms. They describe the energy needed to keep an on-screen group lively, interactive, and engaged as more profoundly draining than a similar interaction in physical space. So what is left of the human being, once translated into an online teacher, with all its challenges, changes, and pressures? In addition, what is left of the teacher when the chorus of concern has missed them out in the urgency to pay attention to learners?

The crisis of being human: Where we are going

At the end of the year, the teachers were asked one further question: *what are you most proud of in your handling of online learning this year?* In spite of the challenges discussed in Section 2 above, the list of what makes us human as a teacher, and why technology can never replace the teacher, is a long one. Five significant points emerge from the teacher reflections, corroborated in other studies before and since the pandemic.

Firstly, the teachers describe the importance of providing a role model to learners. Through crisis conditions, as the pandemic learning year was, they felt it important to be a presence for their learners, loyal, consistent, and resourceful in a year of closing down and narrowing. Learners before the pandemic had cited the importance of teacher support, for example, in Hong Kong (Morrison & Evans, 2018) and in Italy (Cavallone et al., 2020). However, student surveys during and after the pandemic (Jackson, 2020, 2021) suggest this teacher presence became even more important and was for many unequivocally the difference between success and failure.

Secondly, the teachers describe their role in 'setting the environment', creating an atmosphere of learning, permission to experiment and make mistakes, and the possibility of learning as enjoyment. We know learners perceive the best classrooms to be those which build a sense of community (see Byrd, 2016 as an example). Even though the translation from physical to virtual settings entailed struggles, the teachers were proud they were able to turn their screens into vibrant learning communities.

Thirdly, the teachers felt the learning journey shared with their students in the pandemic year meant they met as peers and human beings, beamed into one another's homes, and learnt new technologies with one another. One teacher describes the kindness of her learners as she struggled with breakout rooms for the first time; another was taught how to screen share by one of her learners. Human qualities became important: patience, kindness, and empathy. We know these are qualities learners had always deemed important to them (e.g., Kember & Wong, 2000). Yet they became a matter of survival in the online learning year.

Fourthly, the teachers felt proud of their intuitive capacities to appreciate what might be happening outside and around the edges of formal learning: the 'in between' conversations which learners were not able to have in a fully online setting. Many felt they had managed situations just in time, recognising where learners were lapsing in motivation, interpreting absences, or blanked screens in a non-judging and empathetic way and finding strategies to bring learners back into the community of learning. Frampton's survey (2021) suggests just this kind of awareness as critical in the support of learners' mental health during periods of isolation.

Finally, the teachers valued their capacity to adapt content for new learning conditions, revise, reconfigure, and chunk content in new ways to help learners. They describe themselves as guides, curators, and managers of learning. The online learning year made these roles more, rather than less, apparent. Whilst pre-pandemic studies such as Cundell and Sheepy (2018) suggested ways of developing online activities, the year of deepening experience gave every teacher the chance to test out, evaluate, and acquire ownership of these activities.

These accounts are starting points in a rapidly changing relationship between physical and virtual learning worlds. We have learnt that there are many qualities the teacher brings which learners value even more in the virtual setting: their capacity to notice, care, curate, adapt, and support. Qualities such as patience, compassion, kindness, and mindfulness were all noted and are not qualities yet manifested by machines, however clever. Yet teacher adaptation to the online setting is not entirely seamless. We have seen there are changes that need to be made, to expectations, even to notions of best practice: how informal settings are constructed, how groups are managed, how much personal support is needed, and how much content is achievable. Some of these changes entail personal struggle: whether the off-camera and muted learner is or is not acceptable and whether in-between sessions can or cannot be viable in the teacher's working life. However, what can clearly be seen as a result of the pandemic year is that technology might enhance and expand what human teachers are capable of, but it cannot provide the 'human touch'. There are indeed direct threats to the integrity of learning, with ever more sophisticated translation and essay writing tools, but these play to a performance-oriented notion of learning, and not one of learning as supported personal development. As technologies acquire dangerous powers to 'do' the learning for learners, the teacher is needed more than ever to support learning as a process. Whilst technology can deliver and mimic human outcomes, it cannot *be* the learner who develops a language slowly over time, or the teacher who nurtures this process from a position of empathy and shared experience. It is ever more imperative to remember what machines can and *cannot* do, and the interactions human beings need with one another in order to remain human.

References

Baber, H. (2020). Determinants of students' perceived learning outcome and satisfaction in online learning during the pandemic of COVID-19. *Journal of Education and e-Learning Research*, 7(3), 285–292. https://ssrn.com/abstract=3679489

Byrd, J. C. (2016). Understanding the online doctoral learning experience: Factors that contribute to students' sense of community. *Journal of Educators Online*, *13*(2), 102–135.

Cavallone, M., Manna, R., & Palumbo, R. (2020). Filling in the gaps in higher education quality: An analysis of Italian students' value expectations and perceptions. *International Journal of Educational Management*, *34*(1), 203–216. https://www.researchgate.net/publication/335957848

Childs, M., O'Brien, R., & Nolan-Grant, C. (2021). Practical theorising and the new teaching experience: understanding the different responses to online teaching. Presented at *Theorising the Virtual* conference, Oxford Brookes University, May 26, 2021.

Cotton, D. R., Cotton, P. A., & Shipway, J. R. (2023). Chatting and cheating: Ensuring academic integrity in the era of ChatGPT. *Innovations in Education and Teaching International*, 1–12. 10.1080/14703297.2023.2190148

Cundell, A., & Sheepy, E. (2018). Student perceptions of the most effective and engaging online learning activities in a blended graduate seminar. *Online Learning*, *22*(3), 87–102. https://olj.onlinelearningconsortium.org/index.php/olj/article/view/1467/413

Frampton, N. (2021). Listening to higher education communities about mental health. Higher Education Policy Institute. https://www.hepi.ac.uk/2021/08/06/listening-to-higher-education-communities-about-mental-health/

Ginting, D., Fahmi, F., Barella, Y., Rojabi, A. R., & Zumrudiana, A. (2022). Students' perception on TPACK practices on online language classes in the midst of pandemic. *International Journal of Evaluation and Research in Education*, *11*(4), 1995–2009. 10.11591/ijere.v11i4.23014

Hardisty, D., & Windeatt, S. (1989). *CALL computer assisted language learning*. Oxford University Press.

Hebebci, M., Bertiz, Y., & Alan, S. (2020). Investigation of views of students and teachers on distance education practices during the Coronavirus (COVID-19) pandemic. *International Journal of Technology in Education*, *4*(4), 267–282. https://doi.org/10.46328/ijtes.v4i4.113

Hinton, G. (2023). The Godfather of AI Quits Google and Warns of Danger. *New York Times*. Retrieved January 5, 2022, from https://www.nytimes.com

Jackson, A. (2020). The expectation gap: Students' experience of learning during covid 19 and their expectations for next year. Retrieved October 20, 2022, from https://wonkhe.com/blogs/the-expectation-gap-students-experience-of-learning-during-covid-19-and-their-expectations-for-next-year/

Jackson, A. (2021). The expectation gap II: Students' hopes and expectations for learning and teaching in the new normal. Retrieved May 10, 2022, from https://wonkhe.com/blogs/the-expectation-gap-ii-students-hopes-for-learning-and-teaching-in-the-next-normal/

Kember, D., & Wong, A. (2000). Implications for evaluation from a study of students' perceptions of good and poor teaching. *Higher Education*, *40*(1), 69–97. https://doi.org/10.1023/A:1004068500314

Kornpitack, P., & Sawmong, S. (2022). Empirical analysis of factors influencing student satisfaction with online learning systems during the COVID-19 pandemic in Thailand. *Heliyon*, *8*(3), e09183. https://doi.org/10.1016/j.heliyon.2022.e09183

Kumar, P., Kumar, P., Garg, R. K., Panwar, M., & Aggarwal, V. (2022). A study on teachers' perception towards E-learning adoption in higher educational institutions in India during the COVID-19 pandemic. *Higher Education, Skills and Work-Based Learning*. https://www.emerald.com/insight/content/doi/10.1108/HESWBL-03-2022-0052/full/html

Moore, M. G. (1989). Three types of interaction. *American Journal of Distance Education*, *3*(2), 1–7. https://doi.org/10.1080/08923648909526659

Morrison, B., & Evans, S. (2018). University students' conceptions of the good teacher: A Hong Kong perspective. *Journal of Further & Higher Education*, *42*(3), 352–365. https://doi.org/10.1080/0309877X.2016.1261096

Nambiar, D. (2020). The impact of online learning during COVID-19: students' and teachers' perspective. *The International Journal of Indian Psychology*, *8*(2), 783–793. 10.25215/0802.094

Pollard, E., & Aldred, S. (2022). Imagined universities and blank spaces for dreams. Retrieved May 10, 2022, from https://wonkhe.com/blogs/imagined-universities/

Salmon, G. (2013). *E-tivities: The key to active online learning*. Routledge.

Todd, R. W. (2020). Teachers' perceptions of the shift from the classroom to online teaching. *International Journal of TESOL Studies*, *2*(2), 4–16.

Waite, M. (2021). Learning through a crisis, the experiences of involuntary online learning for undergraduate nursing students. Presented at *Theorising the Virtual* conference, Oxford Brookes University, May 2021

Yang, X. (2020). Teachers' perceptions of large-scale online teaching as an epidemic prevention and control strategy in China. *ECNU Review of Education*, *3*(4), 739–744. https://doi.org/10.1177/2096531120922244

14
COMPUTER-ASSISTED LANGUAGE LEARNING AND TEACHING

Emerging trends, challenges, and solutions in ELT

Matt Kessler, Francesca Marino, and Sean Farrell

Background (past trends)

Prior to 2019, issues pertaining to second language (L2) teaching and learning beyond the classroom were already of great importance. At that time, a movement was taking place within applied linguistics, which involved a blossoming interest in investigating learning in online spaces (e.g., Lim & Aryadoust, 2021; Reinders & Benson, 2017). However, following the rise of the global pandemic, such issues took on even more primacy, as teachers and their students were forced to go online in a majority of instructional contexts (Moser et al., 2021). While some educators were prepared for the transition to online teaching, unfortunately, many were not. As such, a sizable body of research emerged, which attempted to explore numerous topics pertaining to teachers' and students' experiences with online and hybrid learning. For instance, studies investigated topics such as how teachers dealt with stress and negative emotions (e.g., MacIntyre et al., 2020), how instructors attempted to manage their online courses (e.g., Taghizadeh & Amirkhani, 2022), how teachers implemented creative tasks in hopes of facilitating interaction (e.g., Loewen et al., 2022), and the extent to which students experienced emotions such as boredom online (e.g., Derakhshan et al., 2021).

Undeniably, this research has provided many valuable insights into the nature of computer-assisted language learning (CALL). Notably, however, most studies have tended to focus on affective individual differences such as emotions and motivation, while fewer pieces have explored some of the more practical applications of CALL technologies for L2 teaching and

DOI: 10.4324/9781003361701-19

learning. Therefore, this chapter addresses these issues by examining recent pedagogical trends in CALL. In this chapter, we highlight three emerging trends, which include the use of (1) multimodal activities, (2) synchronous video computer-mediated communication (SVCMC), and (3) mobile-assisted language learning (MALL). As we will show, these trends have experienced exponential growth in terms of importance, not only among research circles but also in terms of their general use within academic contexts and beyond the classroom more broadly.

In the next section (i.e., section "Current Trends"), there are three parts devoted to each of the aforementioned topics of multimodal activities, SVCMC, and MALL, respectively. For each topic, we briefly define it, we discuss the theoretical rationales and research supporting it, and we also discuss why it is particularly relevant for English language teaching (ELT). After outlining the topic, we highlight examples of multimodal activities or different tools and platforms for SVCMC and MALL. We also suggest how these activities and tools might be implemented in one's classroom. Lastly, in the section "Future Adaptations", we discuss how practitioners and researchers may further respond to new CALL-related challenges if/when they face them in the future.

Current trends

Multimodal activities

Definition, support, and relevance

Multimodal activities, also sometimes referred to as digital multimodal composing (DMC), are defined as any digital text involving the interweaving of multiple modes of communication in the target language (TL). Modes refer to linguistic (i.e., written or spoken language) as well as nonlinguistic (e.g., visual, aural, gestural) resources (Jewitt, 2008). With the advancement of technology and its subsequent integration into education, various multimodal genres have been increasingly implemented by ELT practitioners (Kessler, 2022). Examples of digital multimodal genres include academic posters, slideshow presentations, storyboards, blogs, websites, portfolios, and video projects, among others (see Lim & Polio, 2020).

Importantly, the growing popularity of DMC can be attributed not only to the so-called "digital" turn in education but also to the adoption of a new and widely recognized approach to L2 literacy on the part of language educators. This approach goes under the name of *multiliteracies* and is driven by two decades of research in applied linguistics (Early et al., 2015), especially in social semiotics. The theoretical rationale underpinning this shift in literacy education is that all communication is seen as intrinsically multimodal (e.g., Jewitt, 2008). In fact, coined by the New London Group (1996), multiliteracies expand the traditional and purely linguistic conceptualization of literacy practice to a more dynamic and inclusive construct, conceiving of language learning as a complex and multilayered process that incorporates nonlinguistic forms of communication. In terms of pedagogical applications in second language acquisition (SLA), multiliteracy skills development entails learners' ability to produce multimodal texts in the TL by simultaneously orchestrating multiple meaning-making resources, all of which are complementary to L2 learning (Yi et al., 2020).

Empirical studies have illustrated that having learners engage in multimodal activities has beneficial effects on numerous aspects of SLA. In particular, research has shown that the implementation of multimodal activities can facilitate L2 writing development (e.g., Shin et al., 2020). Additionally, studies like Vandommele et al. (2017) suggest that interventions involving multimodal writing tasks may positively impact L2 learners' writing skills in terms of aspects such as syntactic and lexical complexity, content quality, and communicative effectiveness, among others. Relatedly, researchers have demonstrated that DMC has the capacity to enhance learner autonomy and, as a result, plays a role in developing learners' identities as writers (e.g., Cimasko & Shin, 2017). If implemented properly, compared to traditional monomodal writing tasks, DMC opens up a broader range of options for learners to craft their voices.

Beyond developing learners' writing, previous research has also illustrated that engaging in multimodal activities may increase learners' motivation (e.g., Jiang, 2018), participation in the classroom (e.g., Jiang et al., 2020), and cognitive skills (e.g., Hung, 2019). Notably, as studies on students' attitudes towards DMC-oriented tasks have demonstrated (e.g., Tanrıkulu, 2020), these benefits are mainly attributable to the opportunities offered by DMC for creative writing with the integration of an array of digital tools which not only enable learners to combine modes but also make the learning process more enjoyable. As such, DMC has an obvious appeal that ELT practitioners might want to consider (see Kessler & Marino, 2023 for more).

Example tools and platforms

As referenced, a plethora of multimodal activities can be integrated into the classroom. In this section, we showcase three multimodal activities whose implementation has been largely supported by previous research:

poster-creation tasks, digital storytelling, and video projects. When discussing these DMC activities, we also briefly suggest platforms that can be used to complete them.

The first multimodal activity that ELT practitioners might wish to adopt is poster-creation tasks. Posters are DMC tasks integrating different modes (e.g., text, images, and diagrams) that typically involve the creation of promotional texts/brochures or informative texts (e.g., timelines and scientific sketch notes). For instance, instructors may have their students compose digital posters aimed at advertising a place, or at summarizing and graphically presenting information about a specific phenomenon. Among a wide range of options that can be used to create posters, we suggest two free-to-use graphic design platforms: Canva (canva.com) and Adobe Express (adobe.com). These online tools provide users with an array of free content and templates for different uses. Lastly, an additional benefit is that both platforms are valuable resources for collaborative work since they enable groups of users to work simultaneously on the same project and share comments.

The second multimodal activity that practitioners might consider adopting is digital storytelling tasks. As the term suggests, digital storytelling can be defined as an integrated process involving the creation of storylines carried out through the use of technology. Arguably, the types of stories that students may be assigned vary depending on the prompts that are given. For instance, instructors may have learners work individually or collaboratively to create storylines on specific topics of interest (e.g., historical events and socio-political themes) or personal narratives (e.g., learners' career planning and out-of-class experiences). For completing digital storytelling projects, some free tools that we suggest are Microsoft PowerPoint (microsoft.com), Prezi (prezi.com), and Storybird (storybird.com). When using these tools, learners can combine multiple modes, including text, images, music, voiceovers, and video. Notably, a crucial aspect of digital storytelling which makes it appealing to ELT practitioners is that its compositional process entails numerous steps, ranging from content development to presenting (see Oskoz & Elola, 2016), all of which can promote aspects of SLA.

The third and final activity we highlight is video projects, which have largely been advocated to promote L2 learners' voices and collaborative writing (e.g., Hafner, 2015). With video projects, guided by their instructors, learners may be asked to complete various types of video genres. Examples include research-oriented projects, documentaries, and commercial-style videos. In a nutshell, students are required to shoot their videos and subsequently edit them by using an editing platform indicated by their instructor. This process undoubtedly requires preliminary steps, such as narrowing down the project topic and writing a script. Additionally, students may be asked to upload their final projects to a shared platform (e.g., a course management system) or website (e.g., YouTube) for peer-review activities. To complete video projects, we suggest two free platforms: Movie Maker Online (moviemakeronline.com) and Wondershare Filmora (filmora.wondershare.net). These tools enable learners to creatively craft their projects by adding effects (e.g., merging or cutting video clips) and combining their videos with various other semiotic resources (e.g., captions, stock images, footage, and music). Apart from these platforms, an alternative option is TikTok (tiktok.com), which is an increasingly popular video-sharing platform that allows users to produce videos up to 10 minutes in length.

Implementing multimodal activities in ELT

In this section, we turn to a discussion of two relevant considerations that ELT practitioners should be aware of as they attempt to implement multimodal activities. These relate to (1) time commitment and (2) assessing DMC projects.

First, we recommend that instructors consider and determine the amount of time that may go into each phase of the DMC activity they intend to implement. As illustrated, this is particularly important because students are required to pass through several steps according to the task type. For instance, these phases may include choosing a topic, designing the project, writing and revising a script, rehearsing, shooting and editing videos, selecting external resources to integrate into their projects, and combining modes in order to create coherent meanings. Importantly, since multimodal tasks may require some technical skills, instructors should also consider allocating time to provide students with instructions on what modes they are expected to integrate in their projects. Additionally, instructors should provide students with the necessary training in order to use the tool or platform.

Second, ELT practitioners must acknowledge that assessing DMC projects poses new challenges due to the complex nature of the tasks. Therefore, we recommend that instructors decide whether to concentrate on the final product, the process, or both. For instance, if opting for the adoption of product-based assessment, instructors should develop rubrics for assessing both learners' linguistic competence, such as vocabulary, pronunciation, and accuracy, and multimodal competence, such as semiotic awareness and organization (e.g., Towndrow et al., 2013). Conversely, instructors adopting a process-based model of assessment may measure learners' progress and performance at different stages, including pre-design, design, sharing, and reflecting phases (see Hafner & Ho, 2020, for further discussion). This model implies providing students with forms of ongoing assessments.

Synchronous video computer-mediated communication (SVCMC)

Definition, support, and relevance

SVCMC refers to any video-based communication that happens in real time (i.e., synchronously). This technology itself is likely very familiar to most ELT professionals since SVCMC tools are now ubiquitous in many people's everyday lives (Kessler et al., 2021). For instance, readers may have used multiple commercial SVCMC platforms created by major technology companies, including FaceTime, Microsoft Teams, Skype, and Zoom. Importantly, although such platforms are routinely used for personal and/or business purposes, their use for L2 teaching and learning has also garnered considerable support.

In terms of theoretical support, there are multiple theories of education and SLA that speak to the potential benefits of adopting SVCMC for promoting aspects of L2 development. Most notably, Interactionist Approaches (e.g., Gass, 1997; Long, 1996; Swain, 1993) have frequently been invoked when discussing SVCMC. These approaches stress the importance of learners receiving comprehensible input, producing output, negotiating for meaning, and testing hypotheses when engaging with the TL. Apart from Interactionist Approaches, Sociocultural Theory (Vygotsky, 1978) has also regularly been cited among SVCMC studies. This theory stresses the importance of verbalizing one's knowledge, and how interaction and collaboration with experts have the capacity to mediate or influence one's psychological development. Together, Interactionist Approaches and Sociocultural Theory account for a major portion of SLA-based studies involving SVCMC. Specifically, they have often been used as a rationale for teachers expanding the walls of the classroom to increase the number of chances students have to engage in meaningful communication (e.g., Yang et al., 2012).

In terms of empirical studies, there is a sizable body of research that has shown that if properly integrated into one's curriculum, SVCMC-based activities have the capacity to be beneficial (e.g., Ziegler, 2015). This is particularly the case in contexts where learners may have limited access to speakers of the TL (e.g., EFL contexts). Additionally, as predicted by Interactionist Approaches, researchers have shown that SVCMC can increase students' chances to receive input, produce output, and engage with different aspects of the L2. For instance, studies like Kessler et al. (2020) suggest that when teachers adopt SVCMC for having their learners engage with TL speakers, these interactions may promote students' noticing of new vocabulary. Apart from vocabulary, Levak and Son (2016) have shown that SVCMC can positively influence the development of L2 learners' listening capabilities. By the very nature of increasing the amount of engagement learners have, this, in turn, can also expand students' level of intercultural understanding (e.g., Tian & Wang, 2010). Lastly, an added benefit is that several of the aforementioned studies have reported that learners typically enjoy participating in SVCMC activities. Thus, enjoyment and increased experience can lead to a rise in students' confidence when speaking. Based on such studies, the use of SVCMC holds particular relevance for ELT practitioners.

Example tools and platforms

Because many readers are likely familiar with those popular SVCMC platforms mentioned earlier, in this section, we highlight three platforms that have received less attention. These platforms are HelloTalk, Speaky, and italki. These platforms may be of interest to teachers because, unlike Microsoft Teams, Skype, and Zoom, they have built-in capabilities to connect learners with speakers of the TL.

The first platform, HelloTalk (hellotalk.com), is a free platform that is comparable to some social media in its design and functionality (e.g., Instagram, Facebook). Where it differs, however, is that the goal is to promote tandem learning. This refers to when an L2 learner connects with an L1 speaker of the TL. However, the L1 speaker is also learning the L2 learner's native language. Thus, a tandem is formed in the hopes that both learners will assist one another. In order to use the HelloTalk platform, users must first create an account in which they provide information about the TL they want to study, their approximate proficiency, their L1, and more. After completing a profile, users can navigate and view other HelloTalk users from around the world. Users are able to apply different filters when searching (e.g., to seek a TL partner who speaks a specific variety or is from a particular geographic region). Then, users can contact that person for an informal SVCMC conversation. Apart from SVCMC conversations, learners can communicate in the TL via other modes, such as text-chat, speech-to-text, or by recording asynchronous audio messages (see Rivera, 2017 for more).

The second SVCMC platform, Speaky (speaky.com), is similar to HelloTalk in that it is a free platform that encourages tandem learning. Users again must create a free profile prior to using it. Afterwards, they can search for conversation partners by viewing others' profiles in the Speaky community, which contains information about the user's name, age, languages spoken, and a short bio. Learners then have the option to add them as a friend or send them a message. Like HelloTalk, Speaky users can engage in SVCMC conversations with friends in their community. Additionally, Speaky users may communicate via text-chat, which allows for interactive grammar correction (i.e., the interlocutor can correct the learner's text and highlight errors). Interestingly, Speaky also gamifies aspects of the user experience, for example, by awarding digital badges when users start a new conversation. Although not specifically studied within Speaky, research has shown that gamification in other language apps may enhance learners' motivation (e.g., Hung, 2018; Kessler, 2021b).

The third and final platform we highlight is italki (italki.com). While HelloTalk and Speaky resemble social media in which learners must initiate their own conversations, italki is a more formalized user experience. In particular, after creating an account, italki users search for freelance tutors or teachers to participate in individualized sessions. When using the platform, users can read teachers'/tutors' profiles, watch their self-introduction videos, and also read reviews of their sessions written by previous students. After deciding on a teacher, students then book a private lesson and provide the teacher with specific topics or areas they would like to cover. However, crucial to note is that italki is a paid service, and rates are determined by the teachers (which are shown to students in advance). Therefore, students must pay a fee prior to engaging in an SCVMC session. Unlike HelloTalk and Speaky, italki does not possess some of the more interactive text-chat features (e.g., grammar correction), which have the capacity to promote noticing.

Implementing SVCMC in ELT

In terms of adopting SVCMC, in this section, we highlight two potential considerations for ELT purposes. In particular, these pertain to (1) implementing SVCMC as an out-of-class homework activity and (2) deciding which platform to use (and why).

First, we recommend that teachers consider adopting SVCMC as a homework assignment for students to complete on their own outside of the classroom. We recommend this because, although teachers can provide their students with TL input during class, in many contexts, students may struggle with gaining exposure beyond that of their teacher. Therefore, if implemented for homework, a teacher might assign students a particular week(s) during the semester when they must complete an SVCMC session. For instance, in Kessler et al. (2020), the teachers in the study used SVCMC activities in this manner. Importantly, prior to having students engage in their sessions, during class, students learned about specific topics (e.g., food and music) and related vocabulary and grammar. Then, it was the students' responsibility to engage in one-on-one SVCMC discussions on those topics outside of class. Following their sessions, students completed follow-up activities such as transcribing parts of their conversations and producing oral reports on things they learned. When used in this manner, teachers can use SVCMC to promote meaningful TL interaction.

Second, apart from adopting SVCMC as a homework assignment, ELT professionals must consider which platform they want their students to use. This is important for a number of reasons. For instance, of the three platforms we highlighted, italki is the only one that requires learners to pay a fee for a session. It also does not have the interactive text-chat features that HelloTalk and Speaky possess. That being said, the cost of an SVCMC session is typically minimal, and the experience for L2 learners is more structured. Thus, some teachers may prefer italki. They might even find creative ways to help students afford it (e.g., by removing the textbook requirement for their course and instead requiring students to purchase multiple sessions). Conversely, some teachers may prefer that their learners establish tandem learning connections, in which they simultaneously learn the TL and share their L1 with a partner. If this is the case, then HelloTalk and Speaky may be more appropriate. Regardless, teachers must consider what their goals are when adopting SVCMC and choose a platform accordingly.

Mobile-assisted language learning (MALL)

Definition, support, and relevance

MALL refers to the use of any portable technology by language learners, who are able to use applications (apps) and/or platforms outside of traditional classroom environments at their own convenience (Kukulska-Hulme & Shield, 2007). Despite some early skepticism of MALL, the near-ubiquity of portable devices like smartphones and tablets has led to an explosion of research into mobile learning. As ELT practitioners are likely aware, mobile-learning technologies are increasingly being used by their students, and as such, many teachers have questions about how and/or whether MALL can be integrated into the classroom.

Importantly, there is no one SLA theory that has been used to motivate the use of MALL, as the specific mobile-learning app, platform, or tool itself often dictates the type of theoretical approach taken. That being said, various meta-analyses and synthesis articles have shown that researchers who examine MALL's effectiveness tend to adopt a handful of theories (e.g., Duman et al., 2015). Similar to the SVCMC scholarship described earlier, MALL research has often been supported by Interactionist Approaches (e.g., Gass, 1997; Long, 1996; Swain, 1993) and Sociocultural Theory (Vygotsky, 1978). However, other theories of general learning and awareness have also been cited, such as Flavell's (1979) Metacognition Theory.

Regardless of the theory, the research on MALL to date has shown that it can be beneficial, especially when it comes to using mobile apps for vocabulary acquisition (e.g., Burston, 2015). Other studies have also shown that students oftentimes enjoy learning via apps, and especially those that attempt to gamify different elements, which can motivate learners and encourage continued usage (e.g., Kessler, 2021b). Notably, some studies have found more mixed results for mobile-learning apps, particularly when it comes to comparing L2 learning gains with mobile apps versus learning in a classroom. For instance, Loewen et al. (2019) found improvement for beginning learners of Turkish on the app Duolingo, especially in the areas of reading, writing, and lexicogrammar, with a moderate correlation between the amount of time spent on the app and the gains made by learners. However, even after sustained usage, most learners did not approach the same level of linguistic competence typically achieved by Turkish learners in a university classroom.

Example tools and platforms

In this section, we highlight three MALL apps that instructors may find worthwhile to integrate into their classrooms, but which have received relatively little attention. These apps are Anki, Memrise, and WhatsApp, all of which are free to download using a mobile device.

Anki (apps.ankiweb.net) is an open-source, flashcard-based memorization aid app. Users can navigate to Anki's website to download the app from a browser or find it in the app store on their mobile device. Because it is open source, any Anki user can create their own deck, and many users have generated a huge array of flashcard sets for languages that learners may want to study, including English. A popular deck for English learning is "4000 Essential English Words." Users are presented with the word, a related image, sound files with pronunciation, a dictionary definition, an example sentence, and additional information. In general, Anki decks present words that users do not know well more often, in order to aid memorization. Thus, Anki's spaced-repetition model is particularly useful for learning vocabulary, although it may require some intrinsic motivation on the part of the learner to self-study (Seibert Hanson & Brown, 2020). ELT practitioners should consider making their learners aware of Anki as a resource, and teachers may also consider making their own flashcard sets to share with students via email. Finally, it is worth mentioning that while many existing Anki decks are free, some can be accessed only after paying a fee.

The second MALL app, Memrise (memrise.com), is a language learning app and website that has a wide array of tools. Memrise presents learners with more opportunities to use the TL, such as by engaging in vocabulary learning and testing (e.g., flashcards, multiple choice, and rearranging), listening to dialogues, and answering comprehension questions. Like Anki, Memrise spaces out words and phrases depending on the level of difficulty the learner has with them. The app has a basic (free) version, along with a pro (fee-based) version, which has additional features. For instance, the pro version allows users to engage in text-chat conversations with bots, along with accessing extensive clips of native speakers using the TL. If ELT practitioners are interested in using Memrise's freely available resources, then it is likely best used as a tool for supporting vocabulary learning (Zhang, 2019). Like Anki, Memrise is a resource that is worth making one's learners aware of, especially those students who may be interested in paying a small fee to gain additional TL practice beyond the classroom.

The final MALL app, WhatsApp (whatsapp.com), is unique among the others discussed here because it is not primarily designed for language learning. WhatsApp is a popular instant messaging service that allows users to send end-to-end encrypted messages and make phone/video calls. Users can download WhatsApp on their phones or use a web browser and sign up with their phone number. Although not designed for L2 learning, teachers and researchers have used WhatsApp primarily as a means for engaging their learners beyond the classroom. For instance, in a study that took place in an EFL context, Tragant et al. (2021) sent learners optional language learning tasks via WhatsApp, in addition to having learners practice English for informal communication purposes. Their study demonstrated how WhatsApp could be used as a resource to spur spontaneous interactions among students and also for learners to occasionally negotiate grammatical forms. Because WhatsApp can be used for multiple modes of communication, including text and speech, it affords more possibilities for learners to be creative and to practice different skills. Therefore, teachers might consider how they can integrate such types of text- or speech-based activities into their own pedagogies.

Implementing MALL in ELT

In this section, we highlight two important considerations for implementing MALL in ELT, namely (1) leveraging learner familiarity with mobile technologies and (2) dealing with accessibility issues.

First, in terms of learner familiarity, there is a substantial body of research suggesting that many students have relatively positive perceptions of using mobile devices for L2 learning purposes (e.g., Duman et al., 2015). However, it is important for teachers not to simply rely on mobile technologies to entice their learners. Instead, instructors should integrate MALL into their lessons only when it is relevant, or when doing so has the capacity to enhance their instruction (e.g., by expanding the activity into a real-world context). In general, it can be helpful for instructors to first assess how their students feel about MALL before integrating it into class activities to ensure that learners' attitudes towards technology are positive (García Botero et al., 2018). Instructors may also wish to know how their learners use mobile-learning technologies outside of class so that teachers can understand to what extent their learners already have prior experiences with the target apps/tools. Ultimately, it is important for ELT professionals to leverage learner familiarity with mobile devices by ensuring that they see them not only as entertainment but also as a source of learning.

Second, practitioners should carefully consider accessibility issues for students who may be less familiar with mobile technologies and/or lack access to them. For instance, some students may have difficulties using MALL apps due to self-ascribed technological literacy issues and/or because of an aversion to technology. Therefore, with such students, instructors should attempt to cultivate an appreciation for the affordances of the platforms to be used in class (Puebla et al., 2022). This can be accomplished simply by telling one's students the rationale for using a specific app/tool. Additionally, prior to assigning a MALL-based activity, teachers should confirm that every student has access to a mobile device outside of class for completing the task. Regardless of context, this is critical to consider. Even if some students do lack access, teachers may attempt to troubleshoot such issues by modifying tasks so that they are collaborative in nature.

Future adaptations

In this final section, we expand on our discussion of CALL technologies by providing ELT practitioners with recommendations for how to respond to new technologically related challenges if/when they encounter them in the future. In particular, we discuss two major recommendations, which pertain to (1) leveraging one's students as a resource and (2) forming teacher learning communities.

The first recommendation pertains to leveraging one's students and using them as a resource. Research has suggested that many teachers often feel that their role dictates that they be a figure of authority in their classroom, serving as an arbitrator and distributor of knowledge (e.g., Farrell, 2011; Kessler, 2021a). Unfortunately, these role identities oftentimes result in many practitioners feeling as if they always need to possess the answers, knowing precisely how to guide students through every step of the learning process. Although many instructors are taught in teacher training programs to understand their students' needs and backgrounds (e.g., by implementing needs analyses), many are not taught to explicitly ask their students about the types of tools and technologies that they are using beyond the classroom, along with how/why they are using them. Recently, some scholars have criticized both research and pedagogy, in that students are often portrayed as agency-less individuals who are passively waiting for input and to be corrected. For instance, Papi et al. (2020) have noted that a "fundamental shift in perspective is needed" by which researchers and teachers investigate "learners' pursuit of their goals" (p. 486).

In light of this, we feel that it is important for teachers to set aside time in their classrooms to ask students about the different digital apps, games, and tools they use for L2 learning purposes. This might be accomplished through creating a brief survey (assigned as homework) and asking students how they use technology when reading, writing, etc. Afterwards, teachers can compile this information and target specific tools they are unfamiliar with. In class, collectively, teachers and their students can engage in brief group discussions about how the students use such tools. Importantly, this not only can be an opportunity for teachers to learn more about their students but also an opportunity for teachers to see demonstrations of how different tools are used (and subsequently might be used in future classes).

The second and final recommendation we suggest pertains to forming teacher learning communities, a recommendation which builds on the previous theme of continuing one's learning as a teacher. As referenced, during training programs, pre-service teachers often receive guidance in terms of assessing their students' needs. Many also receive formal instruction on how to integrate CALL technologies into their practice. However, as Kessler and Hubbard (2017) have noted, once teachers enter the workforce, their CALL training and learning typically come to an abrupt halt. Therefore, it is important for in-service teachers to proactively engage in professional development – especially with CALL – since technologies are perpetually evolving.

In addition to typical professional development opportunities (e.g., attending an academic conference), we suggest that instructors try to form their own teacher learning communities. Teacher learning communities are small groups of practitioners, who regularly meet for the purpose of professional development. During the 2021–2022 academic year, the first author of this chapter formed a CALL teacher learning community with several language instructors from his university, and the community met once per month on Fridays during lunchtime to discuss and demonstrate how they used various tools, games, and apps to address different topics in their classrooms (e.g., teaching vocabulary and reading). By the end of the year, each community member walked away from the experience having gained several new ideas about how to approach their own teaching. Importantly, previous research has examined similar communities in TESOL and other L2 learning contexts (e.g., Kulavuz-Onal, 2015), showing that these communities of practice can play a powerful role in fostering teachers' education.

In closing, we recommend that instructors consider forming their own communities. Being an effective teacher necessitates a willingness to be open to new ideas. Additionally, when it comes to CALL and technology, teachers must be willing to engage in continuous learning and professional development.

References

Burston, J. (2015). Twenty years of MALL project implementation: A meta-analysis of learning outcomes. *ReCALL*, *27*(1), 4–20. https://doi.org/10.1017/S0958344014000159

Cimasko, T., & Shin, D. S. (2017). Multimodal resemiotization and authorial agency in an L2 writing classroom. *Written Communication*, *34*(4), 387–413. https://doi.org/10.1177/0741088317727246

Derakhshan, A., Kruk, M., Mehdizadeh, M., & Pawlak, M. (2021). Boredom in online classes in the Iranian EFL context: Sources and solutions. *System*, *101*, 102556. https://doi.org/10.1016/j.system.2021.102556

Duman, G., Orhon, G., & Gedik, N. (2015). Research trends in mobile assisted language learning from 2000 to 2012. *ReCALL*, *27*(2), 197–216. https://doi.org/10.1017/S0958344014000287

Early, M., Kendrick, M., & Potts, D. (2015). Multimodality: Out from the margins of English language teaching. *TESOL Quarterly*, 447–460. https://www.jstor.org/stable/43893767

Farrell, T. S. C. (2011). Exploring the professional role identities of experienced ESL teachers through reflective practice. *System*, *39*(1), 54–62. https://doi.org/10.1016/j.system.2011.01.012

Flavell, J. H. (1979). Metacognition and cognitive monitoring: A new area of cognitive–developmental inquiry. *American Psychologist*, *34*(10), 906–911. https://doi.org/10.1037/0003-066X.34.10.906

García Botero, G., Questier, F., Cincinnato, S., He, T., & Zhu, C. (2018). Acceptance and usage of mobile assisted language learning by higher education students. *Journal of Computing in Higher Education*, *30*(3), 426–451. https://doi.org/10.1007/s12528-018-9177-1

Gass, S. (1997). *Input, interaction, and the second language learner*. Erlbaum.

Hafner, C. A. (2015). Remix culture and English language teaching: The expression of learner voice in digital multimodal compositions. *TESOL Quarterly*, *49*(3), 486–509. https://doi.org/10.1002/tesq.238

Hafner, C. A., & Ho, W. Y. J. (2020). Assessing digital multimodal composing in second language writing: Towards a process-based model. *Journal of Second Language Writing*, *47*, 100710. https://doi.org/10.1016/j.jslw.2020.100710

Hung, H.-T. (2018). Gamifying the flipped classroom using game-based learning materials. *ELT Journal*, *72*(3), 296–308. https://doi.org/10.1093/elt/ccx055

Hung, S.-T. A. (2019). Creating digital stories: EFL learners' engagement, cognitive and metacognitive skills. *Journal of Educational Technology & Society*, *22*(2), 26–37. https://www.jstor.org/stable/26819615

Jewitt, C. (2008). Multimodality and literacy in school classrooms. *Review of Research in Education*, *32*, 241–267. https://doi.org/10.3102/0091732X07310586

Jiang, L. (2018). Digital multimodal composing and investment change in learners' writing in English as a foreign language. *Journal of Second Language Writing*, *40*, 60–72. https://doi.org/10.1016/j.jslw.2018.03.002

Jiang, L., Yang, M., & Yu, S. (2020). Chinese ethnic minority students' investment in English learning empowered by digital multimodal composing. *TESOL Quarterly*, *54*(4), 954–979. https://doi.org/10.1002/tesq.566

Kessler, M. (2021a). Investigating connections between teacher identity and pedagogy in a content-based classroom. *System*, *100*, 102551. https://doi.org/10.1016/j.system.2021.102551

Kessler, M. (2021b). Supplementing mobile-assisted language learning with reflective journal writing: A case study of Duolingo users' metacognitive awareness. *Computer Assisted Language Learning*. https://doi.org/10.1080/09588221.2021.1968914

Kessler, M. (2022). Multimodality. *ELT Journal*, *76*(4), 551–554. https://doi.org/10.1093/elt/ccac028

Kessler, G., & Hubbard, P. (2017). Language teacher education and technology. In C. A. Chapelle & S. Sauro (Eds.), *The handbook of technology and second language teaching and learning* (pp. 278–292). Wiley.

Kessler, M., Loewen, S., & Trego, D. (2020). Synchronous VCMC with TalkAbroad: Exploring noticing, transcription, and learner perceptions in Spanish foreign-language pedagogy. *Language Teaching Research*. https://doi.org/10.1177/1362168820954456

Kessler, M., Loewen, S., & Trego, D. (2021). Synchronous video computer-mediated communication in English language teaching. *ELT Journal*, *75*(3), 371–376. https://doi.org/10.1093/elt/ccab007

Kessler, M., & Marino, F. (2023). Digital multimodal composing in English language teaching. *ELT Journal*. https://doi.org/10.1093/elt/ccac047

Kukulska-Hulme, A., & Shield, L. (2007). An overview of mobile assisted language learning: Can mobile devices support collaborative practice in speaking and listening? *ReCALL*, *20*(3), 1–20.

Kulavuz-Onal, D. (2015). Using netnography to explore the culture of online language teaching communities. *CALICO Journal*, *32*, 426–448. https://www.jstor.org/stable/10.2307/calicojournal.32.3.426

Levak, N., & Son, J. B. (2016). Facilitating second language learners' listening comprehension with Second Life and Skype. *ReCALL*, *29*, 200–218. DOI:10.1017/S0958344016000215

Lim, M. H., & Aryadoust, V. (2021). A scientometric review of research trends in computer-assisted language learning (1997-2020). *Computer Assisted Language Learning*. https://doi.org/10.1080/09588221.2021.1892768

Lim, J., & Polio, C. (2020). Multimodal assignments in higher education: Implications for multimodal writing tasks for L2 writers. *Journal of Second Language Writing*, *47*, 100713. https://doi.org/10.1016/j.jslw.2020.10071

Loewen, S., Buttiler, M., Kessler, M., & Trego, D. (2022). Conversation and transcription activities with synchronous video computer-mediated communication: A classroom investigation. *System*, *106*, 102760. https://doi.org/10.1016/j.system.2022.102760

Loewen, S., Crowther, D., Isbell, D. R., Kim, K. M., Maloney, J., Miller, Z. F., & Rawal, H. (2019). Mobile-Assisted language learning: A Duolingo case study. *ReCALL*, *31*(3), 293–311. https://doi.org/10.1017/S0958344019000065

Long, M. (1996). The role of the linguistic environment in second language acquisition. In W. Ritchie & T. Bhatia (Eds.), *Handbook of second language acquisition* (pp. 413–468). Academic Press.

MacIntyre, P. D., Gregersen, T., & Mercer, S. (2020). Language teachers' coping strategies during the covid-19 conversion to online teaching: Correlations with stress, wellbeing and negative emotions. *System*, *94*, 102352. https://doi.org/10.1016/j.system.2020.102352

Moser, K. M., Wei, T., & Brenner, D. (2021). Remote teaching during COVID-19: Implications from a national survey of language educators. *System*, *97*, 102431. https://doi.org/10.1016/j.system.2020.102431

New London Group (1996). A pedagogy of multiliteracies: Designing social futures. *Harvard Educational Review*, *66*(1), 60–92.

Oskoz, A., & Elola, I. (2016). Digital stories: Overview. *CALICO Journal*, *33*(2), 157–173. https://www.jstor.org/stable/10.2307/calicojournal.33.2.157

Papi, M., Bondarenko, A. V., Wawire, B., Jiang, C., & Zhou, S. (2020). Feedback-seeking behavior in second language writing: Motivational mechanisms. *Reading and Writing*, *33*, 485–505. https://doi.org/10.1007/s11145-019-09971-6

Puebla, Fievet, T., Tsopanidi, M., & Clahsen, H. (2022). Mobile-assisted language learning in older adults: Chances and challenges. *ReCALL*, *34*(2), 169–184. https://doi.org/10.1017/S0958344021000276

Reinders, H., & Benson, P. (2017). Research agenda: Learning beyond the classroom. *Language Teaching*, *50*(4), 561–578. https://doi.org/10.1017/S0261444817000192

Rivera, A. V. (2017). HelloTalk. *CALICO Journal*, *34*(3), 384–392. https://www.jstor.org/stable/10.2307/90014703

Seibert Hanson, A. E., & Brown, C. M. (2020). Enhancing L2 learning through a mobile assisted spaced-repetition tool: An effective but bitter pill? *Computer Assisted Language Learning*, *33*(1-2), 133–155. https://doi.org/10.1080/09588221.2018.1552975

Shin, D., Cimasko, T., & Yi, Y. (2020). Development of metalanguage for multimodal composing: A case study of an L2 writer's design of multimedia texts. *Journal of Second Language Writing*, *47*, 100714. https://doi.org/10.1016/j.jslw.2020.100714

Swain, M. (1993). The output hypothesis: Just speaking and writing aren't enough. *Canadian Modern Language Review*, *50*, 158–164.

Taghizadeh, M., & Amirkhani, S. (2022). Pre-service EFL teachers' conceptions and strategy use in managing online classes. *System*, *104*, 102671. https://doi.org/10.1016/j.system.2021.102671

Tanrıkulu, F. (2020). Students' perceptions about the effects of collaborative digital storytelling on writing skills. *Computer Assisted Language Learning*, 1–16. https://doi.org/10.1080/09588221.2020.1774611

Tian, J., & Wang, Y. (2010). Taking language learning outside the classroom: Learners' perspectives of eTandem learning via Skype. *Innovation in Language Learning and Teaching*, *4*, 181–197. https://doi.org/10.1080/09588221.2015.1061020

Towndrow, P. A., Nelson, M. E., & Yusuf, W. F. B. M. (2013). Squaring literacy assessment with multimodal design: An analytic case for semiotic awareness. *Journal of Literacy Research*, *45*(4), 327–355. https://doi.org/10.1177/1086296X13504155

Tragant, E., Pinyana, A., Mackay, J., & Andria, M. (2021). Extending language learning beyond the EFL classroom through WhatsApp. *Computer Assisted Language Learning*. https://doi.org/10.1080/09588221.2020.1854310

Vandommele, G., van den Branden, K., van Gorp, K., & de Maeyer, S. (2017). In-school and out-of-school multimodal writing as an L2 writing resource for beginner learners of Dutch. *Journal of Second Language Writing*, *36*, 23–36. https://doi.org/10.1016/j.jslw.2017.05.010

Vygotsky, L. S. (1978). *Mind in society: The development of higher psychological processes*. Harvard University Press.

Yang, Y. C., Gamble, J., & Tang, S. S. (2012). Voice-over instant messaging as a tool for enhancing the oral proficiency and motivation of English-as-a-foreign-language learners. *British Journal of Educational Technology, 43*, 448–464. https://doi.org/10.1111/j.1467-8535.2011.01204.x

Yi, Y., Shin, D. S., & Cimasko, T. (2020). Special issue: Multimodal composing in multilingual learning and teaching contexts. *Journal of Second Language Writing, 47*, 100717. https://doi.org/10.1016/j.jslw.2020.100717

Zhang, X. (2019). Learning technology review: Memrise. *CALICO Journal, 36*(2), 152–161.

Ziegler, N. (2015). Synchronous computer-mediated communication and interaction: A meta-analysis. *Studies in Second Language Acquisition, 38*, 553–586. 10.1017/S027226311500025X

15

A MULTIMODAL ANALYSIS OF ROLEPLAYS BETWEEN UPPER INTERMEDIATE LEVEL LEARNERS

Lessons for teaching oral language competency in online contexts

Gerard O'Hanlon and Anne O'Keeffe

Introduction: Pivot to the virtual classroom

During the COVID-19 pandemic, the classroom pivoted for teachers and students to a virtual space. This sudden shift brought both challenges and opportunities. For researchers interested in exploring the multimodal dimension of communication in online educational contexts, the abundance of situations in which this pivot happened has generated new research opportunities and questions which can be addressed using data from this new classroom space. Such questions hitherto may not have seemed so relevant but now, as we move into an era where virtual language teaching is ever more mainstream, understanding all modes of communication in online discourse has gained more importance (McKenzie et al., 2020)

This chapter shall focus on requests in virtual ELT roleplay contexts. As we discuss, requests, as a speech act, have received much attention over the years in the context of pragmatics. However, the prevailing approach to transcribing spoken interactions orthographically means coverage of non-verbal features (e.g. gesture and gaze) is lacking. Multimodal corpora therefore offer a principled and balanced collection of audiovisual recordings which can be used to represent (a) a variety of speech and written genres and (b) a variety of modes, such as images or sounds (Bateman, 2013). While any such annotation process can be time-consuming, it does offer a contextual richness to the systems and behaviours of language learners. In the context of language pedagogy, looking at how learners speak in multimodal contexts (in online and face-to-face contexts) will advance our understanding of L2 pragmatics. By extension, this can better inform us about spoken language competence across the Common European Framework of Reference (CEFR, 2001).

Past – Backgrounds to multimodal teaching, learning, and research

Here we provide a background on multimodal research, pragmatics and non-verbal expression. In the past two decades, research and frameworks have evolved that are rife for application to the context of the virtual learning environment within the context of English language learning. In this section, we draw together the antecedent areas of research that are important for us to build on. We start by looking at how the definition of the concept of modes has evolved and then we trace the impact of multimodal research on language pedagogy and explore the related challenges.

What is a mode?

Simply put, modes are the resources we use to communicate meaning. Linguistic research has traditionally focused on speech and writing systems as the main modes of human communication. Kress (2010, p. 79) further defines mode as 'a socially shaped and culturally given semiotic resource for making meaning', citing examples such as image, writing, layout, music, gesture, speech and moving image. Modes are always combined in various as we communicate meaning. Language learning and teaching are multimodal activities. They employ a variety of meaning-making resources, involving the use of speech, gesture or gaze, amongst others. There is a growing awareness that to better understand multimodal communication within English language learning and teaching contexts, it is important to investigate the utility of meaning-making resources beyond speech and writing (Urbanski & Stam, 2022). Central to the concept of multimodality is that of *mode*.

Adami (2016) emphasises the power of modes to make meanings and express and shape values, ideologies, and power relations. Modes are not a mere accompaniment to verbal language. When combined with speech or writing, modes add a functional load to the overall meaning. From a pedagogical perspective, there has long been an awareness that teachers and students group gesture, gaze and facial expression to augment spoken interaction (Kress et al., 2005). It is also accepted that factors such as layout, colour, text, music and image are key components of educational texts and digital resources (O'Halloran et al., 2016).

Interactional modes may be embodied or disembodied (Norris, 2004). Embodied modes include gaze, gesture, facial expression, head and body movements and posture. The actions and positions of the body, head and limbs play a kinesic role in communication (Harrigan, 2005). Salient in teaching situations, embodied modes aid comprehension and input (Brown, 2022), both virtually and in-person. Disembodied modes encompass a wider range of meaning-making resources, including image, layout, sound and music, all of which play key roles in classroom resources and spaces (Kress et al., 2005). We return to embodied modes in our Case Study.

Multimodality and language pedagogy

The strong multimodal character in language pedagogy has grown more evident over the last two decades (O'Halloran et al., 2016). In that time, a broad range of modalities has confronted and challenged students' communicative competence in learning environments. Hyland noted that students must negotiate an increasingly complex web of text types, tasks and modes in classroom contexts, in order to graduate and adapt to workplace environments (2006). For example, Stein (2000) made the case for language teachers focusing on tasks and projects for students that require multiple modes of representation, with language being only one part. A multimodal pedagogy that goes beyond language has the potential to promote alternative ways of reading, interpreting and composing semiotic texts for language learners (Ruiz-Madrid & Valeiras-Jurado, 2020). Such methods were most notably introduced via a 'multiliteracies' approach, a form of pedagogy which promotes the idea that students develop a broader set of literacies to better engage with multiple modes in meaning making. This sought to cater to the increasing multiplicity and integration of modes in society, where the textual is related to the visual, the audio, the spatial, the behavioural and so on (New London Group, 1996). Incorporating this multimodal literacy into curricula would empower students to meet 'the challenges and affordances offered by technology ... and new media where language combines with image and sound resources in complex and changing ways' (O'Halloran et al., 2015, p. 1). Multiliteracies introduced creativity, innovation, dynamism and divergence as normal semiotic states at the centre of learning. Cope and Kalantzis (2009) later outlined four major dimensions of multiliteracies: Experiencing (e.g. out-of-school learning), Conceptualising (pushing beyond the textbook), Analysing (e.g. inferring and deducing using multimodal texts) and Applying (e.g. testing multimodal inferences in real-world settings).

Multimodality in EAP/ESP, teacher training and assessment

There has been a growing awareness over the last decade of the utility of a multimodal approach by language practitioners engaging with electronically mediated interaction in areas such as English for Academic Purposes (EAP) (e.g. lectures), English for Specific Purposes (ESP) (e.g. Medical English) as well as those working in teacher training. Awareness has involved developing an explicit multimodal pedagogy in academic literacy which provides students with a working knowledge of how semiotic resources can be combined in meaning making. A critical analysis of multimodal resources (e.g. how speech combines with body language, or written texts with graphs and charts) is central to this approach (O'Halloran et al., 2016).

How gaze, facial expression, posture and body movement are combined alongside spoken language as multimodal strategies during Plenary Addresses was examined by Zhang (2015). Smiling and facial expressions proved highly functional for the speaker during disagreement phases in post-plenary questioning with Zhang recommending the integration of these strategies into EAP teaching (2015). Querol-Julián (2010) analysed a corpus of interpersonal meaning during a post-presentation discussion at chemistry and linguistics conferences. This research examined gesture, facial expression, gaze and head movement alongside paralinguistic elements. The aforementioned features, when annotated in a multimodal corpus, have the potential to make for teaching and learning materials which can help learners and researchers explore, discover and better understand academic genres.

Verbal and non-verbal strategies interplay during communication. Crawford Camiciottoli (2015) examined this interplay during explanation phases in Humanities lectures. Lecturers tended to accompany verbal explanations with gestures and outward gazes, signifying the central role of these features during delivery. Multimodal instruction in educational training programmes was recommended to help teachers recognise the utility of non-verbal signals. Crawford Camiciottoli proposed that audiovisual resources be employed in listening skills courses for language learners, with evidence suggesting that non-verbal signals improve listening comprehension in language learners (see also Campoy-Cubillo & Querol-Julián, 2022). A pedagogical approach based on the analysis of business and academic pitches was devised by Ruiz-Madrid and Valeiras-Jurado (2020) with the purpose of analysing how presenters used gesture and annotation alongside their words. The aim of this project was to raise learner awareness of these modes and how to use them coherently. Activities were created as part of their study, which included rating pitches according to their persuasiveness and noting which modes were employed, and to what extent, by the presenters.

ESP studies have advocated a multimodal approach to help learners understand and create texts in the target language more effectively. In terms of Medical English, Franceschi (2018) found that facial expressions, hand gestures, and body movements play a key role in establishing rapport and trust in physician-patient relationships. In the context of Legal English, film clips, with different genres characterising samples of English in specialised domains, were used by Bonsignori (2018) to examine visual, gestural and spatial elements alongside spoken rhetorical devices, with the further aim of promoting intercultural awareness.

In the area of teacher training, there have been examples of modules being designed for undergraduates (Busà, 2010) and postgraduates (Sindoni, 2021) to raise awareness of the construction of social meaning through multimodal resources. Firstly, Busà (2010) examined intonation, body language, photographs, audio files and video clips from authentic resources to provide audiovisual feedback to learners while Sindoni (2021) encouraged student teachers to record and annotate online exchanges via *Skype* to encourage reflection on how modes such as speech, body actions and space are transferred to online media. Here, Sindoni sees a place for these projects on teacher training programmes as a gateway to realising the potential of multimodal resources in language education. In addition, the employment of classroom space, gaze and gesture – together with spoken and written language – proved vital to instructors in setting up pairwork activities, supervising students and eliciting information during lecturing (Morell, 2018). This study demonstrated that effective pedagogy involves multimodal competence with Morell recommending better awareness among trainee teachers of the potential of combining modes for making and eliciting meaning.

Finally, in terms of assessment, the development of a multimodal metalanguage is vital to enhancing the interpretation of semiotic texts and improving methods of assessment for multimodal pedagogy in language learning contexts (Diamantoppulou & Ørevik, 2022). The Common Framework of Reference for Intercultural Digital Literacies (CFRIDiL) (Sindoni et al., 2019) provides one notable example of multimodal metalanguage for assessment. Through a series of descriptors, CFRIDiL sets out to promote change in teaching, learning and assessment in the area of intercultural digital literacies. This includes four interrelated strands: Multimodal Orchestration (e.g. learning to combine multiple meaning-making resources, rather than only language); Digital Skills (e.g. knowledge of media affordances and meaning potential), Intercultural Communication (learning to interact with and understand perceived others) and Transversal Skills (soft skills, e.g. managing collaboration, information and context).

Researching multimodality

Multimodal research has demonstrated how people combine meaning-making resources in communication. When engaging in such research, Jewitt et al. (2016) distinguish two approaches. The first is *Doing Multimodality*, in which multimodal theory is central to the aims of the research questions. The second is *Adopting Multimodal Concepts*, designing a study in which multimodal concepts (e.g. modes) are used selectively. Additionally, the mode or modes a teacher or researcher chooses to investigate is very much dependent on the research question. Within ELT, gesture, for example, plays an important role in the input learners receive, facilitating language comprehension (Inceoglu & Loewen, 2022). Researchers have also looked at the role of gaze in turn-taking or next speaker selection (e.g. Bavelas et al., 2002). Kress et al. (2005, p. 23) used a wider approach to examine a range of conditions in which 'English gets actualized, realised, produced in all the variability that one encounters across classrooms'. These conditions include observing the teachers' use of speech, gaze, gesture, facial expression, quality of voice and embodiment as well as the physical layout of the classroom and the recourses used in it (e.g. texts, posters and visual displays).

Looking across the body of work that has been established, it can be observed that research approaches to multimodality are diverse but all share important features (Jewitt et al., 2016). Firstly, they frequently draw on disciplines concerned with what people do with language in their everyday lives. Secondly, they collect and analyse video recordings of natural social interaction. The aim is to describe, transcribe, annotate and analyse the form and meaning of the modes in the collected materials. This analysis is often carried out in fine detail (e.g. through a taxonomy of gesture types). This might be termed a *narrow approach*. A less-detailed transcription and annotation system may also be employed, depending on the aims of the research project (e.g. charting only when gestures occur). This might be termed a *broad approach*. Realistically, a combination of both narrow and broad approaches is often applied (Urbanski & Stam, 2022). Such research can be carried out using specialised (and open access) video software such as ELAN (2022). The collected results help garner further insights into social interaction and it is common for multimodal research to take an interdisciplinary approach, as is detailed in our Case Study.

Challenges

Researching multimodality in pedagogical contexts poses a series of challenges. Here we outline three aspects for consideration: transcription, annotation and the dilemma of capturing natural conversation or eliciting spoken responses from participants. Firstly, transcription is a time-consuming pursuit. O'Keeffe et al. (2007) estimate that it can take up to two working days to broadly transcribe the audio file of one hour of conversation. Layer into this the transcription of any visual mode (e.g. when someone nods, uses a hand gesture, changes their gaze, etc.) and the task becomes more challenging. It is for this reason that multimodal corpora are usually small compared to other corpora. For example, the Nottingham Multimodal Corpus comprises 250,000 words, alongside headtalk and handtalk (Adolphs & Carter, 2013; Knight, 2011).

Secondly, multimodal data needs to be annotated to make it searchable. This process may be done manually or with partial automatic assistance. Annotation in ELAN is done in tiers or layers, with each layer representing an embodied mode (e.g. speech, gaze, gesture, etc.) in addition to the spoken orthographic layer. Figure 15.1 shows a screenshot from ELAN. In the top left we can see the video player function while the top right shows the transcribed turns of the conversation in a grid format (in this case, Participant A). Across the centre, we can see the acoustic waveforms of the audio (these are useful for identifying stress, pitch and silences, for example). The bottom segment contains tiers for the representation of speech, gaze and gesture, all belonging to Participant A. The gaze and gestures are time-aligned and correspond with Participant A's speech. Note how the requests, broader gaze patterns and gestures may be annotated in this sample using basic xml coding (e.g. <g> Gaze Right </g>) in the lower panel (Figure 15.1).

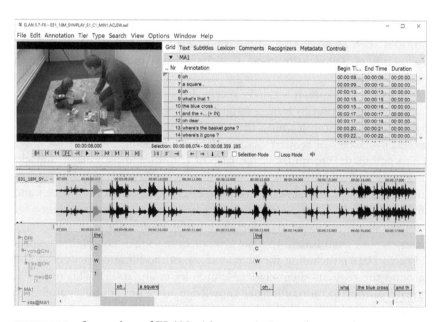

FIGURE 15.1 Screenshot of ELAN with transcription and annotations

ELAN allows the user to search through these annotations and the transcription, making for rapid indexing in the dataset. Due to the complexities of annotation, any such process needs a clear and logical system in place before starting (Jewitt et al., 2016). Within the ELT context, a community of practice, sharing experiences and practical knowledge would provide a boost to multimodal research.

Multimodal data can often be experimental, that is to say elicited in controlled conditions rather than garnered from natural settings (Lin & Chen, 2020). Experimental approaches can augment the frequency of occurrences of the modes under investigation, be they spoken or embodied. Open role-plays, for example, can provide naturalistic data as is evident from the study we now discuss.

Multimodal corpus pragmatics and non-verbal expression – Methodological background to a case study

Our multimodal case study (see section 'The Present') requires an interdisciplinary approach. These are outlined below as *pragmatics, multimodal corpus linguistics* and *non-verbal expression*, each highlighting aspects pertinent to the study. We feel these disciplines have commonalities, thus permitting the employment of the broader perspective required for this project. *Pragmatics* in this case study looks at two core areas of the field: Speech Acts and Politeness. Searle (1976) defines Speech Acts as a range of categories which can be further broken down into linguistic notions such as predicting, suggesting, promising and thanking, among many others. These correspond with the notions and functions, common to ELT syllabi.

Requests, as a speech act, have received considerable attention from researchers in relation to learner language. Developmental trajectories have been charted in the learning of requests. Kasper and Rose (2002) proposed five stages of request development, these being the pre-basic stage (non-pragmatic), formulaic stage (use of chunks and formulae), unpacking stage (use of indirectness; awareness of social context variables), pragmatic expansion (syntactically complex utterances; use of mitigation) and fine tuning (target-like use of forms; utterances more recipient-designed for various situational contexts). Developmental studies show that language learners shift from brief formulaic utterances to longer, complex structures (Leech, 2014), including the increased use of modification devices in and around the requests themselves (Alcón Soler et al., 2005). This results in greater automatization of learner knowledge and a better understanding of the social relationships and cultural norms in the target language (Taguchi & Roever, 2017).

Linguistic politeness theory (Brown & Levinson, 1987) is closely associated with speech act theory. Politeness is central to understanding requests in spoken interaction as it influences how we modify our interactions (through positive or negative face – e.g. being acknowledged and accepted vs avoiding imposition and being independent). The dynamics of a relationship during spoken discourse are also important to Politeness, with these relating to the social distance, power and/or imposition between interlocutors. Requests prove an imposition to both speaker and listener – according to the context – and interlocutors will modify the forms of their requests in adapting to politeness dynamics. The use of direct, indirect and non-conventional request forms are some well-known examples.

Multimodal corpus linguistics refers to corpora (collections of spoken or written texts, electronically stored, and searchable through the use of specialist software) that have been annotated for modes and are thus available for research into many more variables than an orthographically transcribed spoken corpus. Knight and Adolphs (2020, p. 354) describe multimodal corpora as physical repositories where records of modes 'are represented through multiple forms of media, typically ... aligned video, audio and textual representations, within a single digital interface'. This mixing of modes is captured as digitized data and includes orthographic transactions of acoustic data and annotated video data. Annotations may be inserted using xml coding, for example, to allow the researcher to jump to these pre-annotated segments for further exploration via search functionalities (Bateman, 2013). In this case study, requests sequences, gesture and gaze were annotated in the video data.

Non-verbal expression describes the ways in which human communication operates alongside and beyond the verbal message. Of importance to this case study is how we use gesture and gaze. McNeill (2012) defines gesture as an expressive action that enacts imagery, generated as part of the process of speaking, most often using the hands. Gestures perform a range of functions, from those interconnected with accompanying speech to gesture acts which substitute utterances. Gesture may be literal or metaphoric in meaning and is often used to point to temporal or spatial notions or mark stress in speech (McNeill, 1992). Gestures are of immense use to language teachers and language learners. Pedagogical gestures help teachers inform, manage and assess in classroom contexts (Urbanski & Stam, 2022). Gestures help learners solve lexical problems, overcome grammatical difficulties and generally help with non-fluency (Gullberg, 2008). Gaze for its part involves 'the organisation, direction and intensity or looking' (Norris, 2004, p. 9) and plays a key role in face-to-face interaction. Gaze functions, for example, to regulate turn-taking, facilitate task goals (e.g. encourage student participation in class) and demonstrate attentiveness (Kleinke, 1986).

Digital technologies, such as videoconferencing, enable people to combine means of communication in new and ever-evolving ways (Kress, 2010). Such technology also facilitates the recording or capture of large multimodal datasets. Yet digital technologies produce a paradox of proximity by creating interconnectedness without embodied co-presence (Cekaite & Mondada, 2021). This means that interactions via webcam have an impact on spoken communication (e.g. faulty connections) and embodied interaction (e.g. full visualisation of gesture; lack of clarity on gaze direction). Videoconferencing has created a realignment of verbal and non-verbal resources, including changing patterns of embodied resources and spoken interaction, which have ramifications for online English language pedagogy.

The present – Insights from a multimodal analysis of roleplays in requests on *Zoom*

Multimodal pedagogy: Affordances and opportunities in ELT

We contend that ELT multimodal research has the potential to help us understand communication, language learning and acquisition in online educational contexts. To this end, we intend to illustrate multimodal affordances through a case study involving a roleplay between English language learners. This roleplay has been analysed multimodally with the aim of investigating how B2 language learners use requests during spoken online interactions and how they employ embodied resources during these interactions.

Data

This case study involved the elicitation of requests from four adults at the B2 level through roleplays. Three female participants (two French L1; one Spanish L1) and one male participant (French L1) took part. The excerpts in our Case Study involve a French female L1 speaker and a Spanish female L1 speaker. Open roleplays were used for this study (Félix-Brasdefer, 2018) (see Figure 15.2). Open roleplays are beneficial in that they result in complete conversational interactions (e.g. openings, closing, turn-taking), impose less researcher control on interactions and approximate authentic discourse (Kasper & Dahl, 1991). The data were elicited and recorded via *Zoom*. This resulted in approximately 15 minutes of video-mediated interaction, a spoken dataset consisting of 2681 words, including 16 request sequences. The spoken mode was transcribed (Diemer et al., 2016) in ELAN and the requests, gestures and gaze were manually annotated as separate layers using xml annotation (Kirk, 2016).

A multimodal analysis of roleplays between upper intermediate level learners **255**

Open roleplay (Student A)

You need to get a specific book for your studies – *The Exam Guide*. It is expensive and you can't find a digital copy online.

You've seen a person in your class with a copy. You often say 'Hi' or 'goodbye' but don't know them very well.

You want to ask for a loan of the book for a few days to scan some chapters.

You see this person alone after class. Say hi and ask for the book!

Open roleplay (Student B)

You have just finished English class and a friendly classmate you don't really know comes over to say 'hello'. You are in a little bit of a rush because you want to go home and get studying with your new book (*The Exam Guide*) for an exam you have soon.

Continue the conversation.

FIGURE 15.2 Open roleplay elicitation task used in this study

Methodology

The multimodal methodology here involves four steps, including an iteration between software and formats of data.

1 Transcription of the open roleplays directly into ELAN.
2 Exportation of the orthographic transcription from ELAN as a .txt file.
3 Analysis of these texts with corpus software, in this case *AntConc* (Anthony, 2022a).
4 Returning to ELAN to view segments of the dataset that have been identified for closer analysis through *AntConc* (i.e. where the recurring patterns in *AntConc* need to be reviewed in their audiovisual context).

Here we list the corpus functions as used in *AntConc* (for a fuller explanation of these functions, see Anthony, 2022b). These allow us to focus on aspects and patterns within the request sequences in our dataset:

- The keyword in context (*KWIC*) tool shows the immediate contexts of the annotated requests, allowing us to see with which words the requests begin (e.g. a modal verb) or what forms they take (e.g. declarative or interrogative).

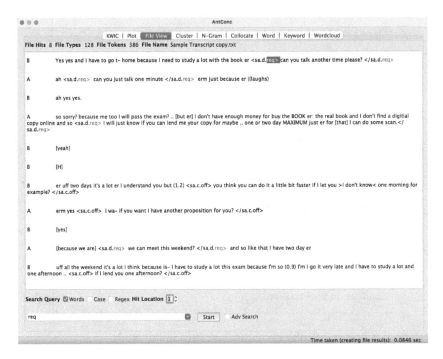

FIGURE 15.3 The AntConc *file* function – A request in context

- The *Plot* function allows us to visualise the dispersion of the speech act across the dataset. When we click on one of these *Plot* lines, AntConc jumps to the *File* option, allowing us to view the Request within the full context of the original transcribed conversation (Figure 15.3).

ELAN, the other key tool in this case study, is an audiovisual programme that adds a multimodal dimension to this research. The ELAN Search Function allows the user to search the video dataset and explore any features from the transcriptions and annotations (i.e. request, gesture, gaze) (see Figure 15.4). By clicking on any of the results, ELAN will jump directly to that selected transcribed/annotated utterance in the video dataset. This audiovisual segment can then be looped, slowed down and paused as needed for closer analysis. Most importantly, the researcher can hear and see the extract, as well as read the transcription and observe the annotations. This allows a deeper, qualitative exploration of any gestures and gazes that accompany the request segments. We will now demonstrate this method with one example of a request from the dataset.

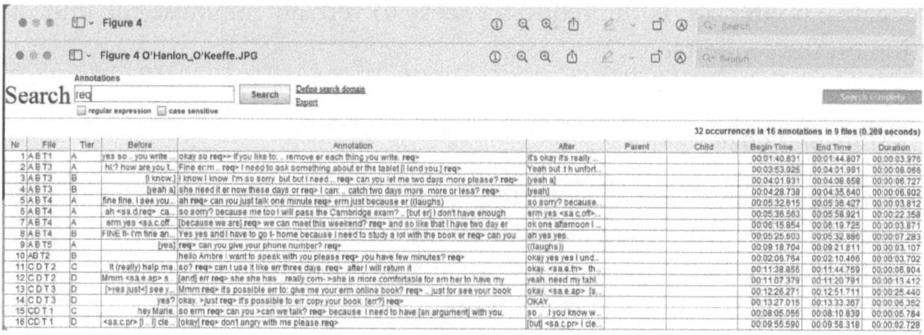

A multimodal analysis of roleplays between upper intermediate level learners **257**

FIGURE 15.4 The search function in ELAN (*Annotated Requests <req>*)

A sample request

This example of a request in Figure 15.5 was extracted after exploration in *AntConc* and *ELAN*. In this case, the roleplay portrayed the participants as classmates, requiring Participant One to borrow a textbook from Participant Two. Closer inspection reveals that Participant One uses a range of lexical devices to modify what is an indirect request. These devices extend backwards from the core (*lend me your copy*), employing two modal verbs. *Will* is frequently used with requests. Note *just* is added to soften this aspect of the request. *Can* is another common feature of requests and permission. Note the use of an if-clause (*if you can*) with this modal, downtoning the request even further. Moving forward from the request, Participant One hedges her utterance (using *Maybe*) by asking for the book *for maybe one or two days maximum*. The combined use of all these devices points to

> <One>: [but er] I don't have enough money for buy the BOOK er: the real book and I don't find a digital copy online and so **I will just know if you can lend me your copy** for maybe … one or two day MAXIMUM just er for [that] I can do some scan.
>
> **Transcription Key**
> <ONE> Participant One
> Core features of the request marked in Bold
> Er: colon indicates elongated sound
> CAPITALS – Stress/Loudness

FIGURE 15.5 An example request from the case study

negative politeness, as the requester seeks to verbally minimise the imposition on the requestee.

Gesture and gaze

We can now align this particular request and its pragmatic features with the visual evidence from the video dataset in *ELAN*, thus permitting a multimodal perspective. Gaze and gesture are the features which play the most prominent roles in this stretch of discourse. Gaze aversion (see Figure 15.6) is common among speakers when they are holding the floor (as Participant A is doing in this example). It is noticeable in this extract that Participant A averts her gaze (or holds a longer blink) during most of the request, only returning her gaze to the screen/camera at points where she is potentially allowing her interlocutor to take the floor. These gaze windows allow Participant B a range of options, from interrupting to denying or acceding to the request (none of which Participant B chooses to do).

In terms of gesture, Participant A uses gesture as an accompaniment to her request (see Figure 15.7). Gesture is most frequently used during aspects of important or focused conversation. Participant A brushes her hand towards herself alongside the verb *lend* in a literal manner, then points to herself alongside the pronoun *me*. When she indicates that she wants to borrow the book *for ... one or two days*, she holds her hands in parallel, palms facing each other, and beats them in an up-and-down movement, demonstrating a gesture which often accompanies quantity or manner in speech. Finally, when she states that she wants the book for *maybe .. one or two day MAXIMUM*, she holds her hands up and palms out, this being a less literal, more metaphoric gesture, signalling acceptance of – or an apology for – the imposition of her request.

When viewed from a multimodal perspective, the above request highlights the range of verbal and embodied devices that learners produce when communicating speech acts during online, embodied social interactions. This is just one small example but it brings into focus the affordances of the research tools and the insight that are possible from more data of this type. It supports the case made by Bonsignori (2018), Busà (2010) and Sindoni (2021), among others, for the examination of visual, gestural and spatial elements alongside the spoken message and rhetorical devices so as to better understand and promote intercultural awareness.

Looking to the future

When we interact through videoconferencing technology, meaning making takes place. Hampel (2015) sees language learning as a social phenomenon

A multimodal analysis of roleplays between upper intermediate level learners 259

Speech	Gaze	Visual Unit
and so I will just know if you can lend me your	Avert Gaze (her) right	
copy	Fix gaze interlocutor/camera	
(Potential for turn transition here)		
For maybe	Averts gaze (her) right	
One or	Eyes closed (longer than blink)	
Two day	Fix gaze interlocutor/camera	
(Potential for turn transition here)		
MAXIMUM	Averts gaze (her) right	

FIGURE 15.6 Gaze aversion and request

Speech	Gesture	Visual Unit
because me too I will pass the exam	Points to self Both hands (**Deictic**)	
but er: I don't have enough money for buy the BOOK	Both hands out, Palms up (**Metaphoric**)	
er: the real book and I don't find a digital copy online and so I will just know	---	---
if you can lend me your copy	Brushes hands to herself on 'lend' – (**Iconic**) Point to self 'me' (**Deictic**)	
for maybe .. one or two day	Parallel hands, move up and down vertically (**Beat**)	
MAXIMUM	Hands up, open palms out (**Metaphoric**)	

FIGURE 15.7 Gesture and request

mediated by a number of tools, including digital environments. In this chapter, we have shown from a pedagogical perspective that videoconferencing platforms, such as *Zoom*, are also multimodal spaces which present potentialities as well as limitations to English language teachers and learners. Our devices, webcams and microphones can complement spoken learner communication through the use of facial expressions, gesture, paralanguage, head nods and gaze, among other features. Online communication permits socialisation among participants, stimulating active participation and collaboration (Stickler & Hampel, 2015) and such exchanges allow knowledge to be socially constructed.

The multimodal lens that we have discussed in this chapter has much to offer online language learning and we are only beginning to tap into its potential. For example, Virtual Reality (VR) extends pedagogical benefits through platforms that help facilitate video collaboration as well as increase engagement and motivation. VR employs 3D environments, headsets, cameras and tracking sensors which combine to permit immersive learning experiences. Further developments such as Augmented Reality and Mixed Reality, both of which overlay interactive content on live video, are becoming ever more common on social media. These offer great potential for new language learning experiences in terms of Mobile Assisted Language Learning. Ultimately, VR has the power to make online learning a richer, active experience, one which allows the user to use multiple senses during interaction with fully immersive environments. This strengthens the process of knowledge construction through interaction alongside digital others. Mowbray (2020) cites an example of students learning through digital interaction, using VR and gamification (i.e. working up levels through trial and error) to gain knowledge and experience.

Advances in Machine Learning and Artificial Intelligence (AI) can also drive multimodal pedagogy in new directions. These range from the collection of data for multimodal pedagogical applications (e.g. to generate tasks or gather texts, audio and video for bespoke pedagogical materials) to the creation of avatars for enhanced embodied exchanges (e.g. the avatar responding to spoken interaction with nods, facial expressions, etc.). While tools such as Chatbots (interactive AI-powered messengers which enable users to interact via chat interfaces), particularly AI-generated large language models (such as ChatGPT), are generating much debate, Studente and Ellis (2020) see potential for online learning through their use, for example, helping to improve student engagement, or through the encouragement of collaborative online learning. AI applications like ChatGPT can be used to translate, help with writing tasks, generate visualisations and respond to sound and image, making it a valuable addition to the multimodal classroom toolkit.

References

Adami, E. (2016). Multimodality. In O. Garcia, N. Flores, & M. Spotti (Eds.), *Oxford handbook of language and society* (pp. 451–472). Oxford University Press.

Adolphs, S., & Carter, R. (2013). *Spoken corpus linguistics: From monomodal to multimodal*. Routledge.

Alcón Soler, E., Safont Jordà, P., & Flor, A. (2005). Towards a typology of modifiers for the speech act of requesting: A socio-pragmatic approach. *RAEL: Revista Electrónica De Lingüística Aplicada, 4*, 1–35.

Anthony, L. (2022a). AntConc (Version 4.2.0) [Computer Software]. Tokyo, Japan: Waseda University. Retrieved September 2023, from https://www.laurenceanthony.net/software

Anthony, L. (2022b). What can corpus software do? In A. O'Keeffe & M. J. McCarthy (Eds.), *The Routledge handbook of corpus linguistics* (2nd ed.) (pp. 103–125). Routledge.

Bateman, J. A. (2013). Multimodal corpus-based approaches. In C. A. Chapelle (Ed.), *The encyclopedia of applied linguistics* (pp. 3983–3991). Wiley Blackwell.

Bavelas, J. B., Coates, L., & Johnson, T. (2002). Listener responses as a collaborative process: The role of gaze. *Journal of Communication, 52*, 566–580. https://doi.org/10.1111/j.1460-2466.2002.tb02562.x

Bonsignori, V. (2018). Using films and TV series for ESP teaching: A multimodal perspective. *System, 77*, 58–69. https://doi.org/10.1016/j.system.2018.01.00

Brown, A. (2022). Investigating gesture in non-naturalistic, scripted contexts. In G. Stam & K. Urbanski (Eds.), *Gesture and multimodality in second language acquisition: A research guide* (pp. 124–146). Routledge.

Brown, P., & Levinson, S. (1987). *Politeness: Some universals in language usage*. Cambridge University Press.

Busà, M. G. (2010). Sounding natural: Improving oral presentation skills. *Language Value, 2*(1), 51–67.

Campoy-Cubillo, M. C., & Querol-Julián, M. (2022). Assessing multimodal listening comprehension through online informative videos: The operationalisation of a new listening framework for ESP in higher education. In S. Diamantoppulou & S. Ørevik (Eds.), *Multimodality in English language learning* (pp. 238–256). Routledge.

Cekaite, A., & Mondada, L. (2021). Towards an interactional approach to touch in social encounters. In A. Cekaite & L. Mondada (Eds.), *Touch in social interaction – Touch, language, and body* (pp. 1–26). Routledge.

Cope, B., & Kalantzis, M. (2009). Multiliteracies: New literacies, new learning. *Pedagogies: An International Journal, 4*(3), 164–195. https://doi.org/10.1080/15544800903076044

Council of Europe (2001). *Common European framework of reference for languages: Learning, teaching, assessment*. Cambridge University Press.

Crawford Camiciottoli, B. (2015). Elaborating explanations during opencourseware humanities lectures: The interplay of verbal and nonverbal strategies. In B. C. Camiciottoli & I. Fortanet-Gómez (Eds.), *Multimodal analysis in academic settings: From research to teaching* (pp. 144–170). Routledge.

Diamantoppulou, S., & Ørevik, S. (2022). Introduction: Multimodality in English language learning: The case of EAL. In S. Diamantoppulou & S. Ørevik (Eds.), *Multimodality in English language learning* (pp. 3–15). Routledge.

Diemer, S., Brunner, L., & Schmidt, S. (2016). Compiling computer-mediated spoken language corpora: Key issues and recommendations. *International Journal of Corpus Linguistics, 21*(3), 349–371. https://doi.org/10.1075/ijcl.21.3.03die

ELAN (Version 6.4) [Computer software] (2022). Nijmegen: Max Planck Institute for Psycholinguistics, The Language Archive. Retrieved May 2023, from https://archive.mpi.nl/tla/elan

Félix-Brasdefer, J. C. (2018). Role plays. In A. H. Jucker, K. P. Schneider, & W. Bublitz (Eds.), *Methods in pragmatics* (pp. 305–331). Mouton de Gruyter.

Franceschi, D. (2018). Physician-patient communication: An integrated multimodal approach for teaching medical English. *System, 77*, 91–102. https://doi.org/10.1016/j.system.2018.02.011

Gullberg, M. (2008). Gestures and second language acquisition. In P. Robinson & N. C. Ellis (Eds.), *Handbook of cognitive linguistics and second language acquisition* (pp. 286–315). Routledge.

Hampel, R. (2015). Theoretical approaches and research-based pedagogies for online teaching. In R. Hampel & U. Stickler (Eds.), *Developing online language teaching: Research-based pedagogies and reflective practices* (pp. 134–149). Palgrave Macmillan.

Harrigan, J. (2005). Proxemics, kinesics, and gaze. In J. Harrigan, R. Rosenthal, & K. R. Scherer (Eds.), *The new handbook of methods in nonverbal behavior research* (pp. 137–198). Oxford University Press.

Hyland, K. (2006). *English for academic purposes: An advanced resource book*. Routledge.

Inceoglu, S., & Loewen, S. (2022). Analyzing nonverbal corrective feedback. In G. Stam & K. Urbanski (Eds.), *Gesture and multimodality in second language acquisition: A research guide* (pp. 48–72). Routledge.

Jewitt, C., Bezemer, J., & O'Halloran, K. (2016). *Introducing multimodality*. Routledge.

Kasper, G., & Dahl, M. (1991). *Research methods in interlanguage pragmatics*. University of Hawaii Press.

Kasper, G., & Rose, K. (2002). *Pragmatic development in a second language*. Blackwell.

Kirk, J. M. (2016). The pragmatic annotation scheme of the SPICE-Ireland corpus. *International Journal of Pragmatics, 21*(3), 299–322. https://doi.org/10.1075/ijcl.21.3.01kir

Kleinke, C. L. (1986). Gaze and eye contact: A research review. *Psychological Bulletin, 100*(1), 78–100. https://doi.org/10.1037/0033-2909.100.1.78

Knight, D. (2011). *Multimodality and active listenership: A corpus approach*. Continuum.

Knight, D., & Adolphs, S. (2020). Multimodal corpora. In M. Paquot & S. T. Gries (Eds.), *A practical handbook of corpus linguistics* (pp. 353–371). Springer.

Kress, G. (2010). *Multimodality: A social semiotic approach to contemporary communication*. Routledge.

Kress, G., Jewitt, C., Bourne, J., Franks, A., Hardcastle, J., Jones, K., & Reid, E. (2005). *English in urban classrooms: A multimodal perspective on teaching and learning*. Routledge.

Leech, G. (2014). *The pragmatics of politeness*. Oxford University Press.

Lin, P., & Chen, Y. (2020). Multimodality I, speech, prosody, and gestures. In S. Adolphs & D. Knight (Eds.), *The Routledge handbook of English language and digital humanities* (pp. 66–84). Routledge.

McKenzie, S., Garivaldis, F., & Dyer, K. R. (2020). Preface: Opportunities and challenges for a brave new education world. In S. McKenzie, F. Garivaldis, & K. R. Dyer (Eds.), *Tertiary online teaching and learning: TOTAL perspectives and resources for digital education* (pp. vii–x). Springer.

McNeill, D. (1992). *Hand and mind: What gestures reveal about thought*. University of Chicago Press.

McNeill, D. (2012). *How language began: Gesture and speech in human evolution*. Cambridge University Press.

Morell, T. (2018). Multimodal competence and effective interactive lecturing. *System, 77*, 70–79. https://doi.org/10.1016/j.system.2017.12.006

Mowbray, T. (2020). From virtual to reality – A practical guide to creating educational virtual reality content. In S. McKenzie, F. Garivaldis, & K. R. Dyer (Eds.), *Tertiary online teaching and learning: TOTAL perspectives and resources for digital education* (pp. 87–106). Springer.

New London Group (1996). A pedagogy of multiliteracies: Designing social futures. *Harvard Educational Review, 66*, 60–92.

Norris, S. (2004). *Analysing multimodal interaction: A methodological framework*. Routledge.

O'Halloran, K. L., Tan, S., & Marissa, K. L. E. (2015). Multimodal analysis for critical thinking. *Learning, Media and Technology, 42*(2), 147–170. https://doi.org/10.1080/17439884.2016.1101003

O'Halloran, K. L., Tan, S., & Smith, B. A. (2016). Multimodal approaches to English for academic purposes. In K. Hyland & P. Shaw (Eds.), *The Routledge handbook of English for academic purposes* (pp. 256–269). Routledge.

O'Keeffe, A., McCarthy, M. J., & Carter, R. A. (2007). *From corpus to classroom: Language use and language teaching*. Cambridge University Press.

Querol-Julián, M. (2010). Multimodality in discussion sessions: Corpus compilation and pedagogical use. *Language Value, 2*(1), 1–26. http://www.e-revistes.uji.es/languagevalue

Ruiz-Madrid, N., & Valeiras-Jurado, J. (2020). Developing multimodal communicative competence in emerging academic and professional genres. *International Journal of English Studies, 20*(1), 27–50. https://doi.org/10.6018/ijes.401481

Searle, J. R. (1976). A classification of illocutionary acts. *Language in Society, 5*, 1–23. https://doi.org/10.1017/S0047404500006837

Sindoni, M. G. (2021). Mode-switching in video-mediated interaction: Integrating linguistic phenomena into multimodal transcription tasks. *Linguistics and Education, 62*, 1–11. https://doi.org/10.1016/j.linged.2019.05.004

Sindoni, M. G., Adami, E., Karatza, S., Marenzi, I., Moschini, I., Petroni, S., & Rocca, M. (2019). *The common framework of reference for intercultural digital literacies*. Retrieved May 2023, from https://www.eumade4ll.eu/common-framework-of-reference-for-intercultural-digital-literacy/

Stein, P. (2000). Rethinking resources in the ESL classroom: Multimodal pedagogies in the ESL classroom. *TESOL Quarterly, 34*(2), 333–336. https://doi.org/10.2307/3587958

Stickler, U., & Hampel, R. (2015). Transforming teaching: New skills for online language learning spaces. In R. Hampel & U. Stickler (Eds.), *Developing online language teaching: Research-based pedagogies and reflective practices* (pp. 63–77). Palgrave Macmillan.

Studente, S., & Ellis, S. (2020). Enhancing the online student experience through creating learning communities—the benefits of chatbots in higher education. In S. McKenzie, F. Garivaldi, & K. R. Dyer (Eds.), *Tertiary online teaching and learning: TOTAL perspectives and resources for digital education* (pp. 25–33). Springer.

Taguchi, N., & Roever, C. (2017). *Second language pragmatics.* Oxford University Press.

Urbanski, K., & Stam, G. (2022). Overview of multimodality and gesture in second language acquisition. In G. Stam & K. Urbanski (Eds.), *Gesture and multimodality in second language acquisition: A research guide* (pp. 1–25). Routledge.

Zhang, Z. C. (2015). Disagreements in plenary addresses as multimodal action. In B. C. Camiciottoli & I. Fortanet-Gómez (Eds.), *Multimodal analysis in academic settings: From research to teaching* (pp. 17–38). Routledge.

CONCLUSION

Nima A. Nazari and A. Mehdi Riazi

Introduction

The breakout of COVID-19 and other unexpected turmoil like the Russian invasion of Ukraine, as well as rapid advances in technology and Artificial Intelligence (AI), have impacted various facets of our lives, including education and higher education. Among these, English language learning and teaching have been influenced in that well-established and conventional approaches to learning, teaching, materials design, assessment, and feedback succumbed to the inevitable changes caused by the above events and developments. For instance, the rather orthodox face-to-face in-class teaching could not cope with health and safety considerations such as social distancing in periods like COVID-19. These instances, which will inevitably occur in the future as well, culminated in revising and initiating heretical and innovative approaches to English language learning and teaching. A great deal has been learnt, and still left to learn, from what happened and how that would shape the future of ELT and ELT research. Given this necessity, looking at the past, present, and future trends in ELT and ELT research will help with filling gaps in our knowledge, practice, and research. It will also equip us with what we need to tap into and utilize what is looming on the horizon. The chapter contributors in this volume have delved into the past and current trends and elaborately described and explained the advances and frameworks for responding to new circumstances. This chapter synthesizes the gist of the chapters and draws concluding remarks from them so we gain a better outlook for adapting to novel situations.

DOI: 10.4324/9781003361701-21

Synergies and future directions

At the outset of the first section of the volume, to empower English language teachers, Macalister expounded a comprehensive, dynamic, and improvement-oriented language curriculum design conceptual map and exemplified how the model could work in new and unforeseen circumstances. He also advocated raising language teachers' awareness of such dynamic models during teacher education. To this end, Reed, Kharchenko, and Bodis argued for sustainability in teacher education. They pointed out that language teacher education should equip teachers to think critically and proactively about unforeseen changes in their teaching context. To train teachers to be adaptable, the authors offered and exemplified a number of strategies to integrate an awareness of the past, present, and potential future into language teacher education, rather than preparing teachers for a relatively stable working condition, which is an unlikely scenario.

Part of Macalister's dynamic model also highlighted the role of needs assessment (NA) in language curriculum development. Elaborating on NA as an ongoing and dynamic process, Light, Lo, and Guardado described the interface between NA and English for Academic Purposes (EAP). They also argued for the necessity of incorporating learner digital needs in EAP course design (also see O'Hanlon & O'Keeffe's chapter in this volume) and applying digital tools to gauge and analyze learner needs. Moving forward, the authors expressed their avant-garde views on digital agility, inclusion, and equity in NA and EAP. As for inclusion and equity in L2 education, Bao looked into the issue of learner silence and silent learning and conceptualized it as an autonomous, proactive learning behavior. He argued that silence is part of autonomous learning and that considering silence and speech as unequal learning tools would cause inequity within educational contexts. Within an inclusive and forward-looking agenda, silence training needs to be incorporated into language teacher education and Continuous Professional Developments (CPDs) so language teachers can tap into and utilize learner silence in a productive and creative fashion, as and when they come across classes and teaching within cultures where less (silence) is sometimes more.

In the second section of the volume, Seed, Salamoura, and Saville followed suit in regard to equity, inclusion, and diversity and maintained that future L2 assessments will make further attempts to factor the above in. They also pointed out that due to rapid advancements in AI, Automatic Speech Recognition (ASR), and educational technology and their use in new circumstances, future L2 tests and language assessment research will endeavour to capture the plurilingual repertoires of language learners, mediation activities, and multimodality in communication (also see O'Hanlon & O'Keeffe's chapter in this volume). According to the authors, future language assessments aim to provide comprehensive insights into learners' language proficiency, learning progress, and feedback. Taras followed up on the issue of feedback, situated it within assessment theories, and pointed out that feedback results from explicit and/or implicit assessment and assessment processes should be made explicit to 'all' stakeholders (also see Graham's chapter in this volume). The author also elaborated on the process of Student Self-Assessment (SSA) and, in line with Bao (see Chapter 4 in this volume), linked it to autonomy in learning and learner empowerment. Taras argued that we have made considerable progress in L2 assessment and feedback research, and the future direction is to put the findings into practice. She pointed out that empowering L2 learners without disempowering L2 teachers necessitates SSA and the implementation of ethical, transparent, and collaborative assessment and feedback procedures throughout every phase of L2 education.

Drawing on the issues discussed in the previous chapters of the book, Graham discussed that classroom management is influenced by factors like teacher beliefs, learner needs, teaching mode, and other factors and argued that the future of classroom management will involve considerations like translanguaging, learner and teacher well-being, and further integration of justice and 21st-century skills into education. Graham emphasized that enhancing collaboration among 'all' stakeholders (also see Taras' chapter in this volume), promoting the exchange of ideas pertaining to English language classroom management, language teacher training, and discussing the challenges encountered by English language teachers in managing their classes will play a pivotal role in advancing the ELT profession and ELT classroom management in times of change.

The third section of the volume addressed teaching and learning English language skills and sub-skills in new circumstances. In accordance with O'Hanlon and O'Keeffe's line of research, Siegel elaborated on the influence of multimodality on L2 listening skills and discussed the change of the role of the L2 listener from a passive participant to an active co-constructor of meaning (also see Watkins' chapter in this volume). To teach L2 listening in new circumstances, Siegal recommended a holistic approach, including recognizing the substantial impact of multimodal channels on the listening experience, the increasing enormity of listening materials, the diversity of listening goals, the availability of various listening strategies, the appreciation of the new role of the listener as a co-constructor of knowledge, and the importance of the use of the Internet and various digital tools and platforms in teaching and learning L2 listening. Looking into another receptive skill, i.e., reading, and comparing it with listening, Watkins stated that reading, unlike listening, does not happen naturally. In a similar vein to Siegel, Watkins pointed out that due to the changes occurring since the beginning of the 21st century, reading requires the reader to be a co-constructor of knowledge and information. In keeping with Taras, Watkins argued for empowering the L2 learner by developing their online reading skills, including the ability to choose the most suitable responses for a search based on their objectives, to determine which hyperlinks to click on and assess their usefulness, to discern the tone in messages with limited context, and to implement specific metacognitive techniques to monitor their reading performance.

In terms of productive skills, Trent elaborated on what L2 speaking entails and how online teaching and learning has added to the complexity of this interactive and spontaneous skill. As for future directions of teaching speaking, to empower learners (also see chapters by Taras, Siegel, and Watkins) and have further learner-centred speaking classes, Trent suggested allowing learners to select their own speaking materials and activities and promoting group and individual project-based speaking activities based on the materials selected by learners. Trent also suggested exploring additional speaking opportunities outside the classroom and gradual shifting of the responsibility for designing L2 speaking activities from the teacher to learners so they (co)construct and implement their own learning opportunities. Fazel presented an overview of the other productive skill, i.e., writing, and showed that more recently a number of pedagogic approaches including genre-based approaches, translanguaging, technology-enhanced L2 writing, collaborative L2 writing, and multimodal composition (also see O'Hanlon & O'Keeffe's chapter in this volume) have influenced the teaching and learning of L2 writing. Concerning future directions and responding to new circumstances, against the backdrop of the past and present research and practice in L2 writing, Fazel pointed out that areas such as multimodal writing, automated written feedback and assessment (also see Seed, Salamoura, and Saville's chapter in this volume), L2 writing teacher training, and the use of AI and ChatGPT in learning and teaching L2 writing will receive more attention in the field.

Regarding learning and teaching the English language sub-skills, He and Reynolds, in line with Trent, pointed out that classroom time is not enough for improving L2 learners' sub-skills and L2 learners should be encouraged to engage with L2 outside the classroom too. To this end, the authors suggested the use of digital platforms and resources, i.e., informal digital learning of English, where L2 teachers' roles include fostering engagement among learners by creating a collaborative learning environment that would cultivate a sense of community (also see chapters by Spiro, Kessler, Marino, and Farrell).

The final section of the volume centred on technology and its contribution to ELT in new circumstances. Kessler, Marino, and Farrell shed new light on how English language teachers can respond to new technology-related challenges as and when they encounter them. These include leveraging one's L2 learners as a resource and forming L2 teacher learning communities. They also recommended that L2 teachers consider establishing their own teacher learning communities. As for the use of technology in L2 learning and teaching, O'Hanlon and O'Keeffe pointed out that to understand language learning, we must investigate (digital) multimodality. They also argued that integrating (digital) multimodal literacies into the curriculum would empower students (also see chapters by Trent, Taras, Siegel, and Watkins). They pointed out that digital multimodal spaces, e.g., Augmented Reality and AI applications, offer great potential for multimodal L2 learning, teaching, and research. On the interface between technology, learners, and teachers, Spiro showed that the teacher's support is paramount to organize online teaching and learning activities to ensure quality, cooperation, and interaction. Spiro argued that technology can amplify and broaden the capabilities of human teachers, yet it cannot replicate the essential 'human touch' provided by teachers. To be adaptive and responsive to new circumstances, it is increasingly vital to bear in mind what machines can and cannot do, as well as the crucial input of the teacher who nurtures the process of learning from a position of empathy, shared experience, and human interaction.

Concluding remarks

This book has not only revolved around the recent advances in ELT but also laid the foundation for envisioning future trends. It has centered on adapting recent frameworks to future trends and delved into a variety of topics to respond to the ELT community's emerging needs. The recommendations made have aimed at striking a balance among teacher agency, learner agency, and the role of technology (in its broad sense). To enable English language teachers to respond effectively when faced with new challenges, English language educators should embrace AI, integrate technology-enhanced ELT, include multimodal literacies, foster learner communities, and scaffold learners' self-regulation. They should also empower both teachers and learners, promote teacher learning communities, offer reflective teacher training, engage teachers in CPDs, encourage teacher-learner collaboration, and involve all stakeholders in the process of responding to evolving situations. In a nutshell, the book has reconsidered established practices and frameworks, brought to light advances and the latest trends in ELT, and presented adaptable ways to respond to new circumstances. We hope that this volume contributes to bringing to light research trends and outcomes to deal with novel situations in ELT and enlightens the research and practice requirements of the ELT community.

INDEX

Note: Pages in *italics* represent figures.

Adami, E. 246
Adams, T. E. 46
adaptability 2, 31, 33–35, 187
adaptive expertise 28, 31, 34, 187
Adolphs, S. 253
Ali, A. M. 44
Allahyar, N. 166
Allwright, D. 151
Amirian, Z. 42
Anki 237
AntConc 255–257, *256*
artificial intelligence (AI) 25, 87–88, 91, 188–189, 261, 266; ethical use of 90
Assessment Reform Group (ARG) 97
Audio-Lingual method 134
authentic materials (AM) 137–138
autoethnography 46–47
automarking 83–84
automated speech recognition (ASR) system 83–84
autonomy 28–31, 33–34, 36, 57, 66, 71, 170–171, 198

Baber, H. 214
Bailey, K. 164–167
Bamford, J. 158
Banda machine 11
Bao, D. 4, 56–71, 267–268

Bean, J. C. 59
Belletti Figueira Mulling, A. 159
bibliographic information 182–183
Bodis, A. 3, 25–37, 267
Bonsignori, V. 249
bottom-up listening process 136
broad approach 250
Brumfit, C. 165
Bryman, A. 63
Busà, M. G. 249

ChatGPT 1, 88, 188–189
chat rooms 167–168
Clark, E. 136
Clark, H. 136
classroom management: Covid-related issues 116–117; definitions 114–115
Clinton, V. 152
collaborative reflection 32–33, 35–36
Common European Framework of Reference for Languages (CEFR) 84–85, 136–137
Common Framework of Reference for Intercultural Digital Literacies (CFRIDiL) 249
communication modes 84–85
Communicative Language Teaching 134, 151
Complexity Theory 25–26, 32

comprehension approach 135, 143
Computer-assisted Language Learning (CALL) 12, 228–229, 239–241
computer-based (CB) testing 80–81
confidence building 32, 206
Content and Language Integrated Learning (CLIL) 86, 121
Convention on the Rights of the Child 110–111
co-occurrence analysis 183–185, *184*
Cope, B. 247
Cope, M. 62
corrective feedback (CF) 97, 101–102
COVID-19 pandemic 1, 5–6, 16, 25, 27, 29–31, 42, 45, 47, 82–84, 88, 115–117, 122, 128–129, 168, 182, 213, 245, 266
Cowie, N. 169
Crawford Camiciottoli, B. 248
critical reflection 26, 30, 32–33, 35–36
Cundell, A. 225

data triangulation 43–45, 51
Day, R. 158
digital divide 88, 117–118
digital equity 52–53, 118
digital inclusion 50, 52–53
digital literacy 52, 181
digital multimodal composing (DMC) 229–232
digital storytelling 231
digital technology 42, 79–81, 88, 180–181, 202, 254
digital turn 180–181, 229
disembodied modes 247
Dolya, G. 68
Dörnyei, Z. 140
Duddley-Evans, T. 43

ELAN Search Function 250–252, *251*, 256, *257*
Ellis, R. 203
Ellis, S. 261
embodied modes 246–247
emergency remote teaching (ERT) 27, 29, 42, 45, 47–48, 122
English as a second/foreign language (ESL/EFL) 195–196, 198
English Central 204
English for Academic Purposes (EAP) 3–4, 41–53, 248, 267

English for Specific Purposes (ESP) 41, 180, 248–249
English language teaching (ELT) 1–2, 4–7, 97, 101, 107, 115–116, 118–122, 124–125, 128, 231, 266, 268, 270–271; MALL in 238–239; multimodal activities in 232; multimodality 254–258; SVCMC in 235–236; 21st century skills into 125–127
environment analysis circle 15, *15*
eye-tracking 89

fairness 90–91
Farrell, S. 6, 16, 228–241
Farrell, T. S. C. 22, 26, 32, 138
Fazel, I. 6, 44, 176–189, 269
Ferris, D. 159
Field, J. 143
'fighting fires' 26–28
first language (L1) learners 119–120, 133, 135, 137–138, 150–152, 178, 234
fluency 165–166, 199, 201–205
formative assessment (FA) 98–100
formulaic expressions (FEs) 203–204
four strands principle 199–201
Frampton, N. 216, 223–224
Franceschi, D. 248

gamification 89
General Service List of English Words 196
generative artificial intelligence (Gen AI) 1
genre-based instruction 179–180
gesture and gaze 251, 253, 258, *259–260*
Ginting, D. 214–215
Goldilocks syndrome 12, 23
GPS 18, 20
Grabe, W. 201
Graham, C. 4–5, 114–129, 136, 141–142, 268
Guardado, M. 3–4, 41–53, 267

Hall, L. A. 61
Hampel, R. 258
Hebebci, M. 216
Hedgcock, J. 159
Hedge, T. 140
HelloTalk 234

He, X. 6, 195–207
higher-level processing skills 149
high-frequency vocabulary 196, 199–200
Hubbard, P. 12, 16–17, 240
Hyland, K. 247

IdiomsTube 203–204
IELTS teachers in Australia 32
incidental learning 202
informal digital learning of English (IDLE) 205
informal language learning 205–207
Institute for Ethical AI in Education 90
integrated learning and assessment 86–87
intentional learning 202
italki 235–236
item response theory (IRT) 81

Jewitt, C. 249–250
John, M. S. 43

Kalantzis, M. 247
Kasper, G. 252
Kessler, G. 240
Kessler, M. 6, 228–241, 270
keyword co-occurrence analysis 183–185, *184*
keyword in context (KWIC) 255
Kharchenko, Y. 3, 25–37, 267
Knigge, L. 62
Knight, D. 253
Kohnke, L. 168–169
Kornpitack, P. 215
Kress, G. 246, 250

Lan, G. 182, 185, 187
language assessment 81, 84–87, 91–92
language curriculum design 13–18, *14*, 21, 23, 267
language-focused learning 199–200
language learning, cost-benefit principle of 196
language teacher education (LTE) 26, 28–34
learner-centred classroom 127–128
learning-oriented assessment (LOA) 86–87
learning styles 166–167
Lee, J. S. 205
lifelong learning 26–27

Light, J. 3–4, 41–53, 267
linguistic politeness theory 253
Lo, D. 3–4, 41–53, 267
Loewen, S. 237
Long, M. 198
Long, M. H. 44
lower-level processing skills 149

Macalister, J. 3, 11–23, 267
Macaro, E. 151
machine learning 84, 214, 261
Mandarin Chinese 197
Marino, F. 6, 228–241, 270
Markee, N. 12
Mavridi, S. 29
McNeill, D. 253
meaning-focused input and output 199
mediation 85
Memrise 237–238
Mercedes model 14, 18, 21
Mercer, S. 30, 122
microteaching 33–35
Mihai, F. M. 21
mobile-assisted language learning (MALL) 236–237; definition 236; in ELT 238–239; tools and platforms 237–238
Moore, M. G. 214–215
Moorhouse, B. 168–169
Morgan, S. 87
Movie Maker Online 232
Mowbray, T. 261
multilingual turn 85–86
multiliteracies 229–230
multimodal activities 229–230; definition 229; in ELT 232; tools and platforms 230–232
multimodal corpus linguistics 253
multimodality 85, 139–140; *AntConc* 255–257, *256*; challenges 250–252; in EAP/ESP 247–249; ELAN Search Function 250–252, *251*, 256, *257*; gesture and gaze 251, 253, 258, *259–260*; and language pedagogy 247; mode 246–247; research 249–250; roleplays in Zoom 254–258, *255*
Musgrave, J. 22

Nambiar, D. 216
narrow approach 250
Nation, I. S. P. 196, 199, 202–204

Nazari, N. A. 1–7, 43, 166, 266–271
needs analysis (NA) 41–45, 267; bias on 50–51; cyclical process 51–52; data triangulation 43–45, 51; digital inclusion and equity 52–53; digital literacy 52; to emergency remote teaching 45, 47–48
New London Group 230
New Zealand 16–17
non-verbal expression 253
Nottingham Multimodal Corpus 251

O'Hanlon, G. 7, 245–262, 267–270
O'Keeffe, A. 7, 245–262, 267–270
online applications 6, 203–205; accuracy and quality 206–207
online learning 214–220; beyond pedagogies 222–223; mistranslation 221; personal toll 223; reclaiming pedagogies 222; scramble for resources 220–221; teachers value 224–225
online reading 156–157
open-minded pedagogy 70
Optical Mark Readers (OMR) 83

Papi, M. 240
Peterson, D. 59
Petress, K. 59
Plot function 256
power hierarchy 58–59
pragmatics 252
problematic sounds 197
process approach 178–179, 187
process feedback 100–102
product feedback 100–102
product-oriented approach 177–178
professional development 17, 21–22, 27–30, 34, 123, 195, 240
Purmensky, K. 21

Querol-Julián, M. 248

readers, 21st-century 156–157
reading 148; comprehension 149–150; criticisms 154–156; extensive 159; first language and second language 150–151; fluency 157–160; lessons 153–154; online 156–157; skills 152–153
Rebuschat, P. 202
Reed, M. 3, 25–37, 267

reflective students 60–61
Reinders, H. 170
Remedios, L. 57
remotely-delivered assessment 82–83
requests 252
resource management 121–122
Reynolds, B. L. 6, 106, 195–207, 269
Riazi, A. M. 1–7, 43, 181–182, 187, 266–271
Richards, J. 164, 167
Richards, J. C. 137
Ridgway, A. J. 68–69
Rogers, C. R. 65
Rose, K. 252
Ruiz-Madrid, N. 248
Ryan, S. 140

Salaberry, M. R. 13, 17, 23
Salamoura, A. 4, 79–92, 267
Salmon, G. 215
Saville, N. 4, 79–92, 267
Sawmong, S. 215
Schmidt, R. 198
Schmitt, D. 196
Schmitt, N. 196
scripted *vs.* authentic material 151
Scriven, M. 98, 100–101
Searle, J. R. 252
second language acquisition (SLA) 230–231, 233
second language (L2) listening 133–135, 137–139; classroom activities for 143–144; cognitive strategy 142; metacognitive strategy 142; models for 140–143; multimodality and 139–140; socio-affective strategy 142
second language (L2) reading 150–151
second language (L2) writing 176–189, 269
Seed, G. 4, 79–92, 267
self-marking 107–108
self-motivation 207
Sheepy, E. 225
Siegel, J. 5, 133–145, 268–270
silence (silent learning) 56–57; autonomous choice 65–67; defined 57; disruption to learning 59; intensive cognitive work 63–64; natural part of learning 64–65; reflective students 60–61; and speech 58–60, 68–69

Simulated Oral Proficiency Tests (SOPIs) 82
Sindoni, M. G. 249
social justice 90–91
social media 117–119, 128, 235, 261
social orientation theory 59
Sound Standard 106–108
speaking 164–165; *see also* teaching speaking
Speaky 234–235
Speech Acts 252
speed-reading 201
Spiro, J. 6, 213–225, 270
Stein, P. 247
Stoller, F. L. 201
Studente, S. 261
student self-assessment (SSA) 96–97, 99–102, 104–109, 111, 268; standard 106–107; Taras' three versions of 108–110
subjectively-marked language tests 83
summative assessment (SA) 98–100
Sun, Y. 182, 185, 187
survival mode 27, 47
sustainability 3, 26, 30–34
synchronous video computer-mediated communication (SVCMC) 233–234; definition 233; in ELT 235–236; tools and platforms 234–235
Systemic-Functional Linguistics (SFL) 180

Taras, M. 96–111, 268–269; three versions 108–110
target language (TL) 229–230, 233–238
target language use (TLU) 79, 81, 84
Tavakoli, M. 42
teachers: agents of change 22–23; classroom changes 19–21; control and change 18–19; empowerment 21–22; value 224–225
Teaching English to Speakers of Other Languages (TESOL) research 26, 33, 219
teaching speaking 170–172; beyond the classroom 167–168; challenges 172–173; communication lost 165; errors 167; fluency 165–166; goal of 165; learning styles 166–167; student reticence 166; trends of 168–169
technological innovation 12–13, 80
TikTok 232
Todd, R. W. 218–219
top-down listening process 136
Tragant, E. 238
translanguaging 120–122, 125, 128, 180
translingualism 180
Trent, J. 5, 163–173, 269–270

Ur, P. 165–166
user experience (UX) principles 89

Valeiras-Jurado, J. 248
validity argument 79
Vandommele, G. 230
videoconferencing 254
virtual classroom management 116–117
Virtual Reality (VR) 261
vocabulary learning 200, 202
VoiceThread 34
VOS viewer software 183

Waite, M. 215–216
Watkins, P. 5, 148–160, 268–270
Web 2.0 201–202, 205
Webb, S. 202
Web of Science (WOS) Core Collection 182
wellbeing 28, 122–123, 128–129
Wellington, J. 62–63
West, M. 196
WhatsApp 238
Williams, J. N. 202
Wisdom of Practice 32
Wondershare Filmora 232

Yang, K. S. 59
Yang, X. 218
YouTube 203
Yu, M. H. 200, 204

Zoom 254–258, *255*